T0315100

Surveillance Capitalism in America

HAGLEY PERSPECTIVES ON BUSINESS AND CULTURE
Roger Horowitz, Series Editor

A complete list of books in the series is available from the publisher.

Surveillance Capitalism in America

Edited by
Josh Lauer and Kenneth Lipartito

PENN

UNIVERSITY OF PENNSYLVANIA PRESS

PHILADELPHIA

Published by
University of Pennsylvania Press
Philadelphia, Pennsylvania 19104-4112
www.upenn.edu/pennpress

Printed in the United States of America
on acid-free paper
10 9 8 7 6 5 4 3 2 1

A catalogue record for this book is available from the Library of Congress.
ISBN 978-0-8122-5335-1

CONTENTS

Surveillance Under Capitalism

JOSH LAUER AND KENNETH LIPARTITO

Surveillance capitalism, according to recent scholarship, is a new and distinct form of capitalism—and perhaps its most malevolent form ever.[1] Since the 1990s, digital technologies and mobile devices have enabled unprecedented accumulations of personal information, raising startling privacy concerns. Harvesting the data detritus of our lives, a new breed of corporate media giants—Facebook, Google, Amazon, and others—now seek to manipulate our wants and desires with a level of precision that earlier media companies and advertisers could only dream of. At the same time, political partisans, including shadowy private interests and foreign governments, promise to swing voters and elections with microtargeted social media campaigns. Over the past twenty years it has become clear that the powerful tools developed for interactivity and instant connection, so useful, delightful, and ostensibly free, also pose serious risks to democracy, social justice, and personal autonomy.

Surveillance capitalists, this new literature argues, have an insatiable need for our data, which in turn compels them to colonize more of human life and experience.[2] The "data exhaust" we spew while browsing and communicating online is the cheap raw material and outsourced labor they depend on. Information that rightly belongs to us, or formerly existed as a shared public resource, is now privatized in the interests of profit and power. Surveillance capitalists deploy our data in profit-seeking programs, including advertising, market analysis, risk management, and predictive scoring algorithms. "Once we searched Google, but now Google searches us," Shoshana Zuboff, author of *The Age of Surveillance Capitalism*, has quipped.[3] The future promises more of the same. With access to vast stores of human data, artificial intelligence systems are able to perform increasingly complex tasks and, in the process, to replace human actors and dispense with human subjectivity. Machine learning systems can pursue open-ended objectives, setting algorithms free to discover associations and strategies as they go, whether winning chess matches, planning a course of medical treatment, paying (or denying) insurance bills, or identifying would-be criminals.

The scholarship of surveillance capitalism is closely aligned with the academic field of surveillance studies. Since the 1970s, when this interdisciplinary field emerged, its leading figures have drawn attention to the social, political, and ethical consequences of automation and the growing range of monitoring technologies and techniques. Largely dominated by scholars working in sociology, cultural theory, and communication, surveillance studies has produced a vast body of groundbreaking critique.[4] A parallel corpus of legal writings emerged at nearly the same time to address privacy threats posed by computerization and information-sharing systems.[5] In both cases, authors have focused on new and emerging technologies, from database computers in the 1970s to algorithmic systems, biometrics, and internet-enabled devices in the early twenty-first century, often writing with regulatory solutions in mind. The alarming implications of contemporary technologies certainly warrant such scrutiny and policy recommendations. Yet, a preoccupation with the here and now has left the study of modern surveillance strangely detached from history.

The same constraint of presentism appears in works about surveillance capitalism. Zuboff's widely discussed *cri de coeur*, for example, puts a premium on newness rather than surveillance's long development and entanglement with the state, the market, and technology. Without historical context, however, each new technology appears unprecedented and anomalous, an artifact of shifting political winds and Silicon Valley whims. An obsession with the present, anchored in the politics of fear and given over to a simplistic technological determinism, fails to account for the deep historical relationships between surveillance and capitalism.

This volume offers a crucial and long overdue historical intervention in the study of modern surveillance and capitalism in the United States. At a basic level, it historicizes what has been taken as unprecedented, revealing a deep logic to surveillance as a mode of rationalization, bureaucratization, and social control traceable to the late eighteenth century forward. The chapters in this book highlight a variety of surveillance practices that predate computers and miniaturized electronics—from the disciplinary control of enslaved labor, to the management of customer service staff, to the solicitous scrutiny of hotel guests before 1950. Many of the chapters illustrate the power of written records—account books, lists, and reports—as technologies of control, monitoring, and investigation. By historicizing modern surveillance, this volume shows how post-9/11 surveillant practices and contemporary digital platforms are elaborations, rather than breaks, from the past. In doing so it also provides examples of how influential surveillance theories, such as those of Michel Foucault, Gilles Deleuze, and sociologists Kevin Haggerty and Richard Ericson, can be operationalized in historical scholarship.[6] Though surveillance themes are often implicit in historical studies, as in the fields of labor history and the history of civil rights, the chapters in this collection make such themes explicit and central to the story of American capitalism.

The volume's second and equally significant purpose is to focus on the role of *business* in the historical development of modern surveillance. While studies of surveillance capitalism today certainly recognize the role of business, they lack historical scope and depth. At the same time, historically oriented works on surveillance are almost wholly focused on the role of the state to the exclusion of business. In much of this writing the origins of surveillance are traced to government recordkeeping practices for taxation, conscription, policing, demography, and public welfare that emerged in early modern Europe and elsewhere.[7] This perspective is anchored in the historical sociology of Max Weber and Anthony Giddens and is central to Foucault's seminal studies of state-sponsored total institutions: prisons, barracks, hospitals, and schools.[8] *Surveillance Capitalism in America*, however, draws attention to the commercial sector as a generative site of the technologies, practices, and values that constitute modern surveillance. Recent historical works on the insurance and credit reporting industries, for instance, illustrate the foundational role of the private sector in information gathering on the health, finances, and morality of individuals.[9]

By amplifying the significance of business, rather than the state, as a source of modern surveillance techniques and institutions, we show how twenty-first-century forms of information expropriation are part of capitalism's heritage, not a deviation from it. Managers monitored workers, merchants observed consumers, and businesses investigated each other throughout earlier periods of history. In each case they developed elaborate practices for recording and storing information and using that information to control behaviors. Just as it is a mistake to look only at the surveillance practices of the central state, so, too, we argue, is it a distortion to give all attention to today's tech giants. Google and its contemporaries did not invent the monetization of surveillance and personal information. Their innovations, we argue, are an elaboration of earlier commercial efforts to convert observation into systems of control and profit.

By excavating the unexamined role of business in the history of surveillance, this volume has a third purpose: to bridge the overly sharp divide between politics and the marketplace in the development of modern surveillance. Studies of the American economy have asked how much the expansion and operation of capitalism depended on the state, and how public and private power interacted. The chapters here offer a new perspective on this debate on American state capacity. While scholars have questioned the trope of a weak American state, they have not deeply examined the ways in which the American state gathered information and kept track of people.[10] Following the insight that the American state involved a deep intermixing of private and public power, the studies in this volume show how private surveillance at times provided the informational resources needed for the state to carry out its legal, juridical, economic, and social welfare functions. They also make clear that the growth of private sector surveillance relied on informational resources and infrastructures that the state supplied. Whatever the capacity of the American state in making war, regulating the economy, or meeting social needs, it is clear that the private sector provided a key part of the surveillance apparatus that allowed for the operation of a public bureaucracy that was able to regulate, study, order, and control its citizens.

Capitalism's Surveillant Origins

Collectively, then, the chapters in this volume argue that modern surveillance and modern capitalism should be viewed as coeval developments.[11] In fact, the word "surveillance" emerged almost at the same moment that modern capitalism itself came into being. It was coined during the French Revolution as Europe transitioned from the *ancien régime* of subjects under a king in a seigneurial economy to citizens of a state in an economy of private property. Its etymology is similar to other, older words such as "survey" or "supervise," both of which derived from Latin combining *videre* (to see) with the prefix *sur* (over). But whereas "survey" moved from Latin into French through the word *viere*, "surveillance" originated from a slightly different word, *veiller*, meaning "to watch." It seems there was a need for a new word, one with a different connotation than to survey in the sense of looking over or managing (supervise) lands, buildings, or estates; "surveillance" was applied directly to people.[12]

"Surveillance capitalism," as we use the term, refers to broad range of strategies and techniques, both formal and informal, that commercial actors—including lenders, merchants, employers, managers, service providers, and others—deploy to observe, record, predict, and control human behavior and relationships. The targets of such commercial surveillance typically include clients and customers, borrowers and buyers, staff and laborers (free and unfree), markets and competitors. This private sector surveillance connects to but is also distinct from the purposes of state surveillance. While states count, tax, police, and conscript citizens in the name (if not always the reality) of collective prosperity and security, commercial actors seek prosperity and security for themselves. The market, according to traditional economics, works by means of the invisible hand. Our attention to the imbrication of surveillance and capitalism, by contrast, shows how surveillance provides the market's ubiquitous eyes and ears. Information gathering is clearly an important aspect of capitalism, but attention to the role of surveillance adds another dimension to the story. The market's eyes and ears are not neutral information-gathering devices. They are invasive and strategic, designed to gain an informational advantage over workers, clients, and customers. Those with greater information have power, whereas those in information deficit, perhaps unaware of how much is known about them, are at a disadvantage.

Though the term "surveillance" seldom appears in early writings on capitalism, it is implicit in foundational texts beginning with Karl Marx. The supervision of labor—"the work of directing, superintending, and adjusting"—became a central task for capitalists as soon as laborers were brought into their factories and driven toward a common aim. "The directing motive," Marx observed, was essential to "exploit labor-power to the greatest possible extent."[13] Industrial capitalism would build upon surveillance to maximize productivity and profitability. It was conducted by watchful shop managers and involved account books to document outputs and wages, codes and fines to discipline behavior, and clocks to mark time. In his classic essay on time discipline, British historian E. P. Thompson describes the effects of industrial clock time on the separation of "life" and "work," a distinction that became crucial for capitalists who purchased alienated labor.[14]

For the enslaved, the same supervisory imperatives described by Marx were intensified. Historians now recognize that the slave plantation was part of, not distinct from, capitalism. Combining the overseer's lash with accountant's pen, plantation owners and their managers tracked the productivity of slaves and used this data, recorded in account books, to coerce more effort and calibrate discipline.[15] Such careful calibration became routine for free labor after the end of slavery. At the turn of the twentieth century Frederick W. Taylor explained how managers could seize control from workers by closely studying their "traditional knowledge" and discovering inefficiencies that permitted idleness. In his book *The Principles of Scientific Management*, Taylor argued that managers must commit themselves to "classifying, tabulating, and reducing this knowledge to rules, laws, and formulae," and then forcing their workers to abide by them.[16] Taylor's managerial innovation, in short, was to squeeze more labor—and profit—out of a recalcitrant workforce through systematic surveillance.

Throughout the twentieth century, scholars occasionally noted techniques of capitalist surveillance. In the 1950s, for example, William H. Whyte drew attention to the carefully regulated and monitored life of the middle-class manager, a group that earlier had been the surveillers rather than the surveilled. "Organization men" (and women) were subjected to more strict and regulated work lives in office settings, and their employment depended on invasive tests of intelligence and personality.[17] In the 1960s, the power of information gathering entered popular consciousness, spurring new privacy debates in the United States. Best-selling exposés such as Vance Packard's *The Naked Society* (1964) and Myron Brenton's *The Privacy Invaders* (1964) revealed the intelligence-gathering techniques of employers and commercial interests, contributing to a burgeoning "literature of alarm."[18] Congressional hearings and investigative journalists would eventually drag private-sector surveillance into the open, leading to a number of landmark privacy and information-handling regulations, from the Fair Credit Reporting Act (1970) to the Health Insurance Portability and Accountability Act (1996). To date, however, privacy law has struggled to keep pace with commercial data gathering, which accelerated during the 1990s as millions of Americans connected to the internet.[19]

Infrastructures of Surveillance

From Marx on, studies have tended to highlight surveillance's individual instantiations more than its pervasive presence as a fundamental structure of capitalism. In this volume, we redirect attention to the structures of surveillance, or more precisely the infrastructures. Infrastructure conventionally refers to large-scale sociotechnical artifacts that societies depend on for basic functioning, such as roads and water systems, electrical power grids, and communication networks.[20] For surveillance, the infrastructure consists of interconnected systems and administrative processes of control, observation, supervision, and information extraction. Infrastructures of surveillance involve more than just "hardware." They extend beyond roads, power plants, pipes, wires, routers, and computers to encompass knowledge, norms, and systems of thinking. They embody representational and discursive practices, including classification schemes, standards, maps, and rules that shape society's mental architecture just as physical hardware shapes the built environment.[21] In fact, the mental and material domains are inseparable, so infrastructure is seen as the materialization of knowledge and social values.[22] For us, the concept of infrastructure is useful for analyzing the array of intersecting structures, agents, and categories that make surveillance capitalism "work."

One of the defining characteristics of infrastructures is their invisibility. They sit in the background, taken for granted because they develop gradually, often as accretions of hardware, social relationships, laws, and routines that evolve so slowly we hardly notice them. That is, until they break down. Not surprisingly, the impetus for recent scholarship on surveillance capitalism is the system's failure. In this case, failure is not broken equipment or interrupted service. Indeed, surveillance capitalism's infrastructure works *too* well. Rather, it is the failure of the social compact. Critics of contemporary surveillance capitalism direct their animus at the infrastructures that prey upon our data, automate content and social relationships, and colonize human experience, all without much public oversight. This critique began in the 1960s and 1970s, as scholars struggled to penetrate the mysteries of computerization, and it continues today in efforts to pry open the black-boxed algorithms that govern contemporary life.[23] Here historical study of surveillance infrastructure can be extremely useful, peeling back the layers of construction that arose through time, following process, agency, and contestation.

Viewing surveillance capitalism through the lens of infrastructure also offers opportunities for theoretical bridge building. An infrastructural perspective, with its focus on ubiquity, embeddedness, and sociotechnical qualities, aligns with Foucauldian studies of disciplinary surveillance. Foucault's well-worn description of Jeremy Bentham's panopticon is, of course, an analysis of infrastructure. Though the architectural metaphor is often taken too literally, leading to overemphasis on hierarchy and sight, Foucault's broader insights into the role of writing, classification, and examination as technologies of control remain compelling. His project shows how modern power operates invisibly and automatically through more exacting—and ostensibly enlightened—practices of recordkeeping, tabulation, and case files. "This turning of real lives into writing," he proclaims, "is no longer a procedure of heroization; it functions as a procedure of objectification and subjection."[24] The textualization of people and their bodies was a massive infrastructural project through which political order, law, and behavioral norms were built into everyday life.

A similar infrastructural perspective is implicit in James Scott's concept of "legibility," which draws attention to how states impose control over cities, populations, and natural resources through standardization.[25] Scott, like Foucault, devotes most of his attention to the state but, as we argue, state infrastructures often overlap with and contribute to private-sector infrastructures. Beyond roads, schools, legal institutions, and a security apparatus, state infrastructures also include vast administrative systems for documenting identities, relationships, property, housing, travel, and demographics. These government infrastructures—census data, economic reports, tax rolls, driver's licenses, voter registrations, postal addresses, and zip codes—all double as business resources. Likewise, technologies developed in the private sector may be employed by the state for its own purposes, as for example when the Census Bureau procured early Hollerith tabulators, or the Defense Department became a major purchaser of early mainframe computers. The entanglement of state and commercial information infrastructures is strikingly illustrated by contemporary data brokers, private firms that specialize in producing detailed personal profiles based on a fusion of public information, customer records, and online behavioral data.[26] These individual "data doubles," each animated by thousands of data points, help businesses and political organizations target ads.[27] Seen this way, today's surveillance capitalism is the working out and working together of these multiple entities, state and private, gradually tightening criteria and operations, extending the purview.

Technology and Knowledge

The foundations of modern surveillance capitalism were laid during the nineteenth century, when administrative recordkeeping practices and new information-processing technologies were brought to bear on problems of knowledge and control. As populations grew, markets expanded, and an impersonal money economy flourished in the United States, commercial actors struggled to manage their relationships with business partners, laborers and employees, and customers.[28] Their difficulties paralleled those of the state, which sought to exert greater control over its citizens, subject populations, and resources. In both cases these were matters of knowledge, of knowing people and predicting their behavior. They were addressed, first and foremost, by writing things down.[29] In the commercial sphere, the importance of documenting identities, relationships, and transactions formed the basis of systematic management and two of the nation's earliest personal data businesses, life insurance and credit reporting. Likewise, the rise of salaried managers, multiunit corporations, and mass retailers during the second half of the nineteenth century relied upon increasingly standardized policies, procedures, and recordkeeping to oversee daily operations and to anticipate the future.[30]

At the center of these changes sat the lowly bureaucratic file. It is difficult to overstate the significance of filing technologies for the growth of surveillance in general, and surveillance capitalism in particular. The shift from ledger books and bundled papers to filing cabinets and card systems did more than simply change the way information was stored; it changed the way information was used. Filing made information modular, standardized, easy to classify, and simple to retrieve.[31] The "filing revolution," which began in the late nineteenth century and became a hallmark of modern office management during the early twentieth century, also revolutionized surveillance. While states employed filing systems for criminal identification, exemplified by Alphonse Bertillon's biometric rogue's gallery, businesses developed their own systems to identify and investigate customers. Insurance

companies, credit-granting retailers, and mail-order firms were early adopt-
ers of these technologies, as were the hundreds of local credit bureaus that
emerged throughout the United States.[32] New categories of identity, notably
financial identity, arose out of these files and began to circulate as disembod-
ied data doubles. Internally, businesses used filing systems to track transactions, employees, and the performance of individuals and units. More
broadly, filing technologies facilitated new forms of visibility, allowing managers and their minions to quickly identify cases, pull records, and produce
reports. Visibility here was not just metaphorical. It was literally the name
of "visible file" products introduced by several leading manufacturers during the 1920s. Visible files, as one advertisement announced, had ushered in
"the age of vision in business affairs."[33]

Much of this technology was hardware, though more accurately the hardware of physical files plus the software of storage and organizing systems. But
equally important were new forms of knowledge that revealed—and, more
important, helped to predict—the behavior of populations. This knowledge
grew out of earlier developments in statistical science, making the infrastructure a form of technoscience. Statistical science was pioneered in Europe during
the 1820s and 1830s through efforts to reduce problems of demography, public
health, and criminality to quantitative facts. Numbers alone, however, are
not neutral. "Enumeration demands *kinds* of things or people to count,"
as Ian Hacking observed. "Counting is hungry for categories."[34] Statistical
analysis would become a technology of social control because those who
named the variables defined the categories of reality that mattered.

Statisticians, medical experts, and social scientists thus called into being
categories of citizenship, race, intelligence, mental illness, and deviance.
Though many of these efforts, especially in Europe, were conducted under
the banner of the state, commercial actors embraced statistics in the name
of profit. Foremost among these was the American insurance industry,
which compiled its own health and mortality data to calculate risk and
commodify life.[35] During the early twentieth century, advertisers and media
executives also turned to quantitative analysis, probing the public's buying
habits and preferences in a barrage of surveys and polls.[36] Ironically, in their
hunt for the "average" American, consumer analysts carved twentieth-
century mass society into an increasing number of distinct market segments, psychographic profiles, and lifestyle clusters. These "data aggregates,"
as termed by Dan Bouk, represent a group-level counterpart to individual
data doubles.[37] Categories, like the fictions of citizenship and race, would

also become powerful tools of socioeconomic classification and, in some cases, discrimination.

Together, systematic filing and statistical analysis provided a framework for organizing information and a justification for collecting more of it. New technologies, from punch cards to electronic computers, would extend these instrumental capabilities. During the late twentieth century, paper filing systems and statistical analysis were reborn as databases and algorithms. These twin technologies are the driving forces behind contemporary surveillance capitalism. To see these developments as new, however, is to ignore capitalism's long-running effort to know and control markets, employees, and consumers through advances in information-processing technologies and techniques. Today's data doubles and data aggregates were spawned by nineteenth-century customer files and actuarial tables.

Profits, Logics, and Risk

While surveillance has long been bound together with capitalism, it cannot be explained simply by the pursuit of profit. As some of the studies in this collection show, the deployment and expansion of surveillance practices by firms may not have even been profitable. Power over workers, the staving off state regulation, and a reduction or transfer of risk often stood behind the adoption of surveillance technologies. Nonrational motivations also counted, as invidious assumptions about race, gender, and other social identifiers directed surveillance strategies. Commercial surveillance, like state surveillance, is inextricably bound up with ideological investments in the social order and its preservation. By identifying then turning away large swathes of paying customers and skilled workers—women, African Americans, gays and lesbians— profit-seeking businesses deliberately *shrank* markets. This losing strategy only makes sense if business is not just about opportunistic expansion but also about policing the parameters of markets and prosperity through exclusion.

Likewise, commercial surveillance is also tied up with beliefs about the role of technology for the advancement of society. The ideals of administrative efficiency that suffused late-nineteenth-century business culture are reflected in technologies of recordkeeping, office management, and communication developed to serve these goals. Time clocks, cash registers, standardized forms, filing systems, store credit cards, city directories, and telephone books represented technological remedies for informality, idiosyncrasy, and anonymity, all of which were antithetical to "progressive" business methods. During the early twentieth century, purveyors of communication and office technologies, including industry giants like AT&T and Remington Rand, trumpeted the revolutionary significance of their products. This conflation of technological progress and moral progress imbued American industrialization with an aura of the sublime; it also provided an alibi for new technologies of control in the workplace and the marketplace.[38] Today's surveillance capitalists take for granted that the goals of business—efficiency, convenience, the elimination of risk—are agreed upon social ideals. Such assumptions rest on the ideological premise that technology is essentially good, and a further premise that existing problems, including those exacerbated by technology, can be "solved" by new and better technology.[39] The history of commercial surveillance, like state surveillance regimes, are intimately bound up with the history of the idea of technological progress.

The development of commercial surveillance has also followed a logic often seen with other big technical systems and networks. As the great historian of technology Thomas Hughes noted, inventors focus their attention on "reverse salients," or those parts of a complex interconnected system that do not seem to be working well or are not yet complete enough to provide the desired level of service (and possibly business profit as well). It is not just the engineers who seek to iron out rough spots, though their professional training and standards make them extremely attentive to such things. Makers of business technologies, management consultants, and entrepreneurs also throw up new products and solutions aimed at the presumed inadequacy of existing infrastructures. Their interventions are often short term and focused mainly on making the sale, though sometimes what begins as an add-on to an existing system will grow into an adjacent or even whole new system.[40]

On the other side of the market, business users of such technologies often cite risk as the justification for their behavior. But risk calculation is merely a method for quantifying the inherent uncertainty of life—whether in business decisions or in matters of law, criminality, and state security. Risk involves both the statistical likelihood of an event occurring, something that itself may require substantial surveillance to establish, as well as the likely cost of the occurrence, a highly subjective determination when dealing with events that have not yet transpired.[41] At one extreme, risk can be merely a language cloak for surveillant behavior that an actor wants to undertake anyway. At the other extreme, the riskiness may be as much political as financial, as when fear that the state will impose penalties or hold a company responsible if it does not engage in expanded surveillance and information gathering.[42] Risk produces a powerful isomorphism, whereby companies feel compelled to follow practices of competitors and neighboring companies lest they appear out of compliance with risk norms. Such motivations are fed by suppliers of surveillance and risk-mitigation services, from early detective agencies serving business such as the Pinkerton Detective Agency, to latter-day background check and cybersecurity firms.[43] These actors developed business models that both benefit from this conformity but also help to promote to clients the need to conform (and hence buy their services). Risk avoidance is also implicit in statistical modeling aimed at identifying optimal markets and demographics while avoiding—and therefore discriminating against—those that seem to promise subpar yields.[44]

Viewed historically, we also see cases where efforts to enhance profits and control outcomes created new, unforeseen risk possibilities or led to unexpected outcomes that subverted control. The Taylorization of labor and schemes to impose total worker control, for example, may decrease rather than increase productivity.[45] In defiance of its presumed disciplinary effects, increased surveillance breeds resentment and resistance among its targets. Employees find shortcuts to avoid accountability and reclaim their autonomy. Coworkers punch each other's timecards, burdensome reports are fudged, heavy-handed rules are ignored. Similar dynamics play out among consumers. Whenever businesses erect barriers against fraud or free-riding, increasingly elaborate countermeasures become necessity as cheats discover new vulnerabilities. A century ago, new conveniences such as charging bills to credit accounts, ordering by telephone, and self-service exposed businesses to new risks. These in turn required new modes of surveillance—credit verifications, account numbers, and enhanced retail security.[46] The intensification of business surveillance, from this perspective, can be seen as a perpetual battle for control over labor, property, and consumer behavior that continues down to the present.

Surveillance Norms

Infrastructures depend critically on broad social norms; the infrastructure of surveillance is no different. Norms set criteria for what is to be expected in terms of performance, outcomes, dependability, and application. They operate on electric power grids, for example, in terms of expectations of dependable and reliable service. They operate on the internet in terms of accessibility, speed, and free content. Norms can certainly change, and conflict over norms is often a crucial part of the history of infrastructure. Today, norms surrounding internet accessibility and privacy are challenged by threats to net neutrality and compulsory data sharing.[47] Meanwhile, expectations about "always on" electricity and ubiquitous computing, powered by voracious server farms, contribute to global warming that threaten the environmental conditions of life itself.

With surveillance, norms revolving around who is in need of monitoring and who should be shielded are paramount. The first to be subjected to new surveillance practices are almost always the marginalized—recipients of public welfare and charity, people of color and immigrants, women, the working class, conscripts, and criminals. This practice continues today, with drug-testing for recipients of government benefits, immigrant screening, biometric policing, and algorithmic sentencing. Over time, however, surveillant practices tend to expand beyond these initial categories and encompass more of the citizenry. What had been seen as appropriate for only suspect and disenfranchised populations—fingerprinting, lie detectors, drug tests, body scans—becomes normalized as part of everyday life for all but perhaps the most elite, who are usually the last to be surveilled.[48] It is often only when surveillance goes beyond the marginal that it appears as a problem or provokes calls for privacy. Practices that had grown normal, accepted, and even invisible suddenly are thrown into the light of day when more socially privileged groups are threatened with expanded surveillance. Businesses, both as suppliers of the technology and also as users, are a crucial part of this expansion. Unlike state actors, private actors are far less subject to constitutional restrictions in the United States and given far more leeway in how they treat workers or customers.

The ways that surveillance infrastructures grow through a combination of normalized practices, profit-seeking innovation, risk-reducing strategies, and deeply embedded cultural assumptions produces a continued extension and deepening of its apparatus, a probing for opportunity and weakness, reverse salients, and loopholes in privacy laws and norms. Where surveillance is not formally prohibited, it will sneak in. When the law reacts, it will often be too late. Where one law stops one behavior, entrepreneurs will have incentive to find places that the law does not yet apply. Zuboff describes this kind of commercial prospecting and appropriation as a "dispossession cycle," which begins with the "unilateral incursion into undefended space."[49] Her exemplar is Google, whose "declarations" are akin to colonial proclamations. For media scholars Couldry and Mejias, the analogy to colonialism is not metaphorical. The new global imperialists, they argue, follow the historical logic of colonialism, establishing beachheads on digital platforms and claiming all the indigenous resources—our data and networked relationships—for themselves.[50]

Even efforts to slow or stop surveillance can end up having the opposite effect. When conflicts arise over privacy, for example, parties may seek resolution through some sort of objective or scientific procedure that claims to reduce intrusiveness and capricious application. At various times DNA tests, police body cameras, recording of license plates, personality or intelligence testing all promised to overcome objections by making surveillance more complete and thus seemingly less arbitrary. If employees are suspected of using drugs, then all employees must be tested so that no one is unfairly singled out. If some drivers deviate from their scheduled routes or approved travels, then all company vehicles must be equipped with GPS trackers. Of course, the truth claims of these devices and methods will often themselves be contested, so science is invoked to prove the validity and trustworthiness of the very information that surveillance is designed to provide. This recursive problem often motivates still more surveillance or the search for the impossible: absolutely secure epistemologies. The answer to the problems of surveillance, in short, is more surveillance, pushing the infrastructure still deeper into our lives. This is the essence of surveillance "creep."

Momentum and Resistance

Well-articulated infrastructures accumulate extensive power, but we should remember that this process of accumulation is historical. Complex systems develop unevenly, so most infrastructures are not top down, rationalized systems, but palimpsests. They arrive bearing the marks of preceding systems, practices, and technologies. The internet is not a smooth single network but multiple layers of technologies, lines of transmission, standards, and software, all jury-rigged to look as seamless and work as smoothly as possible.[51] Surveillance capitalism has the same aspect. It is composed of different regimes of surveillance and different business functions, organizations, and practices. It often works as a hybrid of older and newer technologies, through trade-offs between people and machines, bureaucratic routines, and automated processes. Infrastructures acquire a direction or momentum, pushed on by the engineering desire to conquer reverse salients and by ideologies of perfected, utopian technology. But their apparent seamlessness is also a carefully crafted illusion. Gaps and points of resistance remain.

These features of the surveillance infrastructure are often missed, in part because there is a parallel tendency in the history of capitalism itself to assume it takes on a single, all-encompassing form. Many histories of capitalism are written this way, looking at a dominant form or mode of production in a particular time period: merchant capitalism, industrial capitalism, networked capitalism, surveillance capitalism. These periodizations call attention to the way practices that might originate in one sector can spread and converge on others—information technology, for example, moves from information industries to entertainment, to manufacturing, finance, and even agriculture, reworking sectors of production far from its origin point.[52] But while this is an important insight, we should not forget that at any moment capitalism is a hybrid of multiple economic systems and practices, some highly technological, some still quite labor intensive. Surveillance capitalism is no different, with multiple technologies, practices, interests, actors, and incentives articulating together but with plenty of gaps as well.[53]

The same powerful architecture of surveillance that seems to command and infiltrate so much of life also breeds alternatives that permit a quite different range of action. Thus, infrastructures of command and control put in service of profit can also encourage voluntary, non-market-mediated interactions found in open-source software projects, blockchain, wikis, and crowdfunding sites. Even market exchange can be rendered more open and democratic, as with eBay and Etsy, profit-motivated web services that allow a far greater variety of economic engagements by ordinary people in their daily lives. Likewise, social media platforms capture our information for profit while allowing for many types of interactions to occur without the heavy hand of corporate media. Those subjected to surveillance are often resourceful enough to find ways to evade or resist the disciplinary effects.[54]

Understanding how surveillance capitalism works thus requires looking at multiple actors. We can look at decisions made at the highest levels of companies, for example, where strategies are formed. We can look outside companies to regulatory or legal authorities or the state, which may impinge on business practices and define acceptable risks. We can consider the financial system, often imposing expectations and discipline that drives outcomes in ways that encourage greater use of surveillance. We can look at the supplier industry that invents, manufactures, and sells the technologies, or the consultants that share information on how competitors are using technology and information. We can also look within the company, where the crucial design and implementation decisions occur that realize broad policies and strategies. These decisions are carried out by experts in the software and information technology field, who have their own distinct professional identities and criteria for how things are to be done. While some decisions about surveillance and privacy are made through public discussion, in many cases infrastructures come about by decisions taken deep in the bowels of private corporations, decisions completely opaque to citizens.[55]

Equally complex are the temporalities that mark an infrastructure's growth and development. They go through life cycles, with early years occupied with putting together parts in a functioning way and later years focused on extending functionality so that the infrastructures generate profits and become sustainable. A third stage occurs once the infrastructure is deeply embedded and routinized in our lives. None of this involves a neat linear sequence, since infrastructures are composed of different parts and components with different temporalities. At critical moments, changes in technology, law, politics, economics, or norms and values may throw open supposedly settled matters once more. Such moments are often seen in controversies over access, equity, and privacy.

Still, at a certain point many infrastructures enter a "black box" phase when they are operating smoothly with few challenges. While not fully autonomous or determinative, they acquire a logic of growth and support from multiple institutions and actors that make it very hard to stop, change, or deflect. At this point, the inner workings of the system become extremely remote and opaque to those on the outside, and the possibility of resisting or opting out goes down substantially. Today, for example, algorithms and artificial intelligence systems that are taking over decision-making from humans in various jobs and functions have this characteristic. It is not even that one needs sophisticated technical skills to understand the workings of software. Connections between technology, economics, and social life have grown so deep that many now uncontestable decisions have already been made in defining categories, setting acceptable norms, and standardizing operational routines and expected outcomes. So algorithms may easily reproduce social prejudices without even intending to, as when marketing or lending decisions are made on the basis of census data (incomes, zip codes, employment) that correlate with racial or other identity categories, even though no explicit criteria of identity is part of the data.[56] The problem is also not due to technology per se, but with how information and knowledge about people are captured and categorized, as we see with the long history of target marketing based on racial or gender assumptions. Whether decisions are made by machines or by human agents, invariably black-boxed surveillance operates by simplifying and categorizing data, allowing little room for individuality or particularities that stand outside the imposed norms of behavior.

To change or challenge an established infrastructure once it has grown deeply embedded is a collective not an individual matter. At the level of individual choice, infrastructures enable action but also restrict and channel it in predetermined ways. Thus, the individual who wants to stop driving to work and ride a bicycle or take public transit in theory is free to do so, but much depends on the affordances of urban design. Once cities are built on the car model, with a substantial percentage of housing (usually less expensive housing) in suburbs, public transit withers. People with cars have less incentive to support public transit. Bike lanes interfere with the smooth flow of car traffic. Individuals who try to buck the car find themselves overmatched by the transportation infrastructure and pay a tremendous price for opposing it—in time, risk, physical inconvenience, and social ostracization. The same is true of the surveillant infrastructure. At the individual level our powers to challenge it are weak for the same reasons that the individual cyclists' ability to challenge car culture is weak. When access to jobs, housing, essential services, and information about one's community and the world require an internet connection, it is not possible to opt out. Theoretically, our online searches, browsing, social media accounts, and transactions are voluntary; practically, there is little choice. This impasse is reflected in an attitude of resignation among Americans when it comes to protecting their digital privacy.[57]

To some degree, a collective solution can be found in traditional political fixes. Significant power is wielded the old-fashioned way in surveillance, by the monopolistic or oligopolistic industry structure. Social media platforms, popular web-based companies, large employers, and credit reporting agencies have enormous market power over customers and workers. Antitrust policies could thus make a difference here, but only to a degree. One reason that individual attacks on well-established infrastructure tends to be weak is the spillover or externality effect. Privacy for any one person requires doing more than protecting the data of that person. Individuals seeking to withhold their data or guard their privacy cannot completely hide their connections to others, short of living as a hermit. Networked surveillance exposes the hidden. Likewise, machine learning systems and algorithms cannot be stopped or slowed because one or a small number of people opt out; there will still be plenty of others feeding the algorithm. Put another way, stopping the proliferation of surveillance requires herd immunity.

This problem of collective versus individual action points to an enduring paradox in the role surveillance has played in capitalism. How, one might ask, did such broad surveillance (and concomitant erosion of privacy) occur over the past two hundred years given the presumed association of capitalism with liberty, freedom, rights, and the free market? The answer reflects the long debate about the construction of the free market. As Karl Polanyi observed of the eighteenth-century market revolution, it took quite a bit of power, state power but private as well, to create the ideal of the "free and autonomous market." Far from being a natural occurrence that sprang forth once restrictions on prices and buying and selling were removed, the great expansion of the market had to be actively cultivated and people had to be "forced to be free," so to speak.[58] Surveillance is a crucial part of this process and has been from the start. People must be enrolled in the market, made into market subjects. That effort requires an enormous amount of detailed information on people, or surveillance. The utopian dream of the free market that Polanyi identified requires information to penetrate down to more and more minute levels of existence so that every subject is perfectly known, every want and desire accounted for. At that point the market can operate with no frictions or restrictions. So, in that way, surveillance and the expansion of the market reinforced each other, often under the umbrella of expanding individual choice and freedom.

While in highly abstract theory markets operate on and benefit from good information and transparency to establish trust between parties, in the actual competitive market the battle for information advantage is ongoing. Capitalism's market is one in which actors continually seek strategic advantage through information, and surveillance is the means to get it. Surveillance—of employees, customers, competitors, and markets—is therefore integral to capitalism and a driving force behind the growth and intensification of modern surveillance society.

While this volume focuses on capitalism and surveillance in the United States, we should note that Zuboff and other scholars look at capitalism as a whole, without much regard for legal, political, cultural, or national context.

Given the ubiquity of information and related technologies and the widespread dominance of capitalism around the world, one might argue that surveillance capitalism is, or is tending to become, everywhere the same, with perhaps only minor differences reflected in privacy laws, regulations, and legal frameworks. Looked at with a more historical lens, however, surveillance shows itself capable of significant variation and adaption to different contexts, much as capitalism does. While beyond the scope of this collection, a true global history of surveillance capitalism would need to take account of such matters as colonialism and the use of surveillance in colonial settings. It would pay attention to the distinctive evolutionary economic processes and patterns that give rise to *varieties* of capitalism even in the industrial world. And it would unpack the place of cultural, racial, gender, and ethnic difference, in terms of how the power of surveillance is deployed, something that we take up here with regard to race and sexuality in America but that clearly has many more dimensions.

Looking at the world now, it is not even clear that surveillance *capitalism* captures the full extent of surveillance, given the recent populist and authoritarian challenges to liberal capitalism and the growth of global disease threats. China especially stands out, either as an extreme confirmation of what surveillance can do and how it operates in the world or as a counterexample that suggests capitalism itself is not necessarily the most important force behind surveillance's growth and deployment. Despite earlier predications, China's economy and political system have not converged to the Western liberal (or neoliberal) model. At the same time, China has made extensive use of surveillance, inching toward an Orwellian nightmare that for now at least goes beyond what any other nation is contemplating. China's most ambitious feature is its social credit system, which tracks all of one's activities and assigns scores according to one's financial, professional, and pro-social behavior.[59] This is a serious intensification of the sort of credit rating that emerged in capitalist America during the nineteenth century and has grown to be extensive and ubiquitous since then. Is China merely extending and making more explicit the sort of disciplinary power over many activities embedded in traditional credit scores and insurance monitoring under Western capitalism, or has it taken surveillance in a new, disturbing direction? A second prominent, and ominous, feature of the Chinese surveillance system is its focus on certain minority groups, notably the Muslim Uighurs. Seen as a threat for their religiosity and cultural separateness, they are relentlessly tracked, their activities monitored and subject to sometimes brutal sanctions, their movements limited and controlled. But then, too, through-out history, states, including the United States, have used such tactics against minority groups, often accusing them of disloyalty or else seeking to separate and segregate them to reduce their economic opportunities in favor of others.

Where China may be different is in fronting state surveillance activities, in contrast to the surveillance capitalism model. But even in capitalist socie-ties, governments have drawn on the private sector to provide significant amounts of surveillance data and the tools of surveillance to use on those whom they want to track. Business supplies the technology and infrastruc-ture of surveillance to the state, as when political or legal authorities access GPS location data, demand inspection of personal cell phones, or monitor social media activity of suspects and immigrants. China's surveillance architecture relies on the ubiquity of information technology and apps as well, notably the universal WeChat "super-app" that combines text, social media, payment, and other features usually provided separately in the West.[60] Surveillance capitalism has yet to produce such an integrated application, but even separate applications and activities can render a single, accessible data stream about people.[61] So perhaps the differences in business and tech-nical structure between China and elsewhere are not that significant. Indeed, depending on how business strategies and the now weakened antitrust policy of the United States play out, it is entirely conceivable that the now separate platforms will be even more interlinked than they have been. Surveillance may have grown up with capitalism, but now it seems adaptable to many different economic and political environments.

How technology, data, politics, and economic systems may converge for surveillant purposes is still not clear, but the recent health crisis caused by the coronavirus offers one possible example. Public health authorities have long used various tracking and surveillance tools to manage health, control contagion, and address outbreaks. Now the coronavirus emergency is prompt-ing them to look to the private sector for faster and more extensive tools to locate the infected. Apple and Google have announced that they are coordi-nating changes to their cell phone operating systems to assist with contact tracing of possible virus infections, using the phones' Bluetooth signals. Life-saving innovations of this sort, produced during a health emergency, raise deep privacy concerns and threaten to further expand the data collection programs that fuel modern surveillance capitalism and extend the surveil-lance infrastructure into new parts of private life.[62]

We know from history that the desire, however laudable, to improve health also has a dark side in what Foucault called "biopower" that can go well beyond narrow medical concerns. In the early twentieth century, for example, economists, business leaders, and public officials connected health and vitality with productivity to justify interventions in individual choice such as prohibiting smoking or consumption of alcohol. More darkly still these same ideas fed into a eugenics movement that sought to categorize and separate out superior and inferior individuals in the name of racial improvement. Refining, targeting, and identifying individuals or groups in the context of preventing disease or improving health provides the informational basis for discriminating against those whose health or whose environment renders them susceptible to disease and infirmity. As with other uses of surveillance, it is quite easy to encode existing prejudices into the policies of protecting health, as when public health authorities in the late nineteenth and early twentieth centuries focused solely on female sex workers as carriers of venereal disease, ignoring their male patrons, or later when AIDS was marginalized as a major health crisis by being categorized as a "gay disease."[63] The biopower of the state and of the private sector, together forming a vast surveillance infrastructure, will continue to raise questions of where people's private lives and their "revealed" selves are available for observation, display, and oversight.

Chapters Overview

The nine chapters in this collection address the historical development and deployment of surveillance infrastructures in America, focusing on the role of business and its interactions with the state. Together, the essays cover two hundred years of history, from the late eighteenth century to the late twentieth century, and address a variety of surveillance practices, contexts, and subjects, from enslaved people to internet users.

In the first chapter, Caitlin Rosenthal and Cameron Black explore the role and position of enslaved watchers on Caribbean plantations. Reflecting the now established connections between slavery and capitalism, the authors show how slave masters used the most vulnerable slaves, often the aged or infirm who could no longer work in the fields, to watch property and people. On one level, this ensnarement of slaves in the plantation information system explains how a handful of whites could control the much

larger black population, a problem of ratio less prevalent on U.S. plantations, where the use of watchmen was less common. Yet the watchmen also
had a degree of agency in how they deployed information, sometimes helping escapees to flee, other times, it was feared by the owners, helping to plan
rebellion. Abolitionists understood this dual role and used the title "The
Watchman" in their antislavery publications.

The second chapter, by Richard Popp, takes us through the ways that
businesses have extracted information about consumers and tailored their
sales, marketing, and advertising to what they learned. This sort of surveillance has a long history that predates modern internet advertising and online commerce. Mail-order companies, for example, bought and sold lists of
names and addresses in bulk, creating databases that could be used in marketing. List brokers had very clear strategies about what they wanted, notably good contacts who might buy mail-order merchandise based on their
past behavior with other merchants. As Popp shows, the level and extent of
this information business ran to tens and hundreds of thousands of names.
Correspondence, one of the oldest information technologies, was successfully adapted to yield rich and valued information about consumer behavior, and a broker market in names and letters soon developed. Interestingly,
rather than trying to sort and reduce this vast quantity of highly variable
and particularized information into registers of names and addresses alone,
brokers and buyers valued the physical letters themselves. These packets of
letters provided deeper information about their authors and served as proof
that the information being sold was true and valid, not merely made-up lists
hawked for profit.

The third chapter, by Jamie Pietruska, reexamines the history of the no-
torious Pinkerton Detective Agency. Founded in the nineteenth century,
Pinkerton profited by supplying business firms with a variety of information-
gathering services, from spying on labor activists to tracking down debtors
to gathering intelligence on competitors. Such practices were controversial
and riven with conflict, particularly between labor and management when
it came to Pinkerton's spying activity. Pietruska focuses on how the agency
established legitimacy for its work by exploring the long-running battle between
the "original" Pinkerton detective agency and its upstart rivals. As Pietruska
shows, Pinkerton relied on meticulous recordkeeping and paperwork—the
same bureaucratic systems it used to serve its clients—to defeat its near-
name rival, the United States Pinkerton Agency, and, in doing so, establish
its credentials as the true, legitimate enterprise.

With the Pinkerton case, surveillance expanded as part of a competitive business strategy, while Daniel Robert's chapter shows how surveillance could be deployed to make workers at large public service companies conform to specific standards of behavior. Here there was no fear of violence or rebellion, as on the slave plantations, or of uncontrolled competition as for the Pinkertons. Instead, workers were watched to ensure they performed sufficient emotional labor for customers in a consumer-oriented society. This was especially important, Robert notes, at public utilities, which were under the threat of public ownership and heavy regulation in the Progressive Era. To mitigate this political risk, astute managers emphasized service and encouraged customers to report on rude or inattentive employees. These companies also pioneered new monitoring techniques, such as mystery shoppers and embedded listening devices, and even rearranged workspaces to give supervisors clear sight lines to their workers. Such surveillance strategies aimed to force employees to self-monitor their affect and internalize solicitous behavior toward the public.

In the leisure and hospitality industry, new and controversial surveillance practices were aimed at a third economic group: the customers themselves. As Megan J. Elias shows, American hotels adopted observational and monitoring practices in the first half of the twentieth century to identify bill skippers, check bouncers, gamblers, and prostitutes. Ironically, in their effort to provide a first-class experience, many hoteliers found themselves defrauded and victimized by the very guests they served. A policy of "the customer is always right" needed a complementary policy of "the customer is carefully watched." Overly accommodating service to guests risked the hotel's pocketbook and its public reputation. No hotel wanted to be known as a den of thieves and sex workers. Hotel employees were trained to spot unwanted guests—a practice that encoded existing prejudices against minorities and unaccompanied women—and hotel operators created information-sharing networks, circulating descriptions of known cheats and frauds.

Similar practices of customer surveillance were deployed in urban bars and cabarets at nearly the same time. As Jennifer Le Zotte shows in her study of New York City nightlife, the targets of exclusion were "sexual deviants"—gays, transgendered people, cross-dressers, and transvestite performers. As in Elias's study of hotels and Robert's study of public service companies, Le Zotte relates how bar employees were trained to surveil the public, and how the public was enlisted to assist businesses toward this end. While in other cases businesses engaged in such sorting and surveillance to fend off state regulation, in this case the state very directly forced drinking establishments to do its bidding. Bars and cabarets that entertained or turned a blind eye to sexual nonconformists risked losing their liquor licenses. Le Zotte clearly illustrates how the state and private business could be deployed in tandem to achieve disciplinary ends via surveillance.

A similar state-business pact emerged for the policing of drug consumption under the Drug-Free Workplace Act, as Jeremy Milloy relates. Under pressure from the Reagan White House, employers began to institute employee drug testing. Politics following the conservative reaction against the growth of personal liberty and individual freedom in the 1960s reinforced the desire by employers to reassert control over their workforces. Drug testing was a practical means of discipline but also a larger project of dominance that reasserted managerial prerogatives while also rendering once truculent unionized workers more docile. As with the inculcation of emotional labor decades before, the question of drug monitoring reflected an evolution of capitalism that went well beyond standard concepts of worker performance and productivity. Increasingly, it embraced the whole body and "soul" of the worker, on and off the job. The control of bodies and minds, once thought to distinguish slavery from free labor, was breaking down in the late twentieth century as the workplace became a site of increasing surveillance.

The use of surveillance to target the individual's vices comes up in a different way in Dan Guadagnolo's study of Uptown cigarettes, a short-lived brand marketed to African Americans by tobacco company R. J. Reynolds (RJR Nabisco), during the 1990s. Uptown became a flashpoint in debates about target marketing and racial discrimination in the United States. Though target marketing could be seen as a means of inclusion, acknowledging previously ignored demographic segments and their particular interests, it could also be used to reinforce harmful stereotypes and exploit underserved neighborhoods. In the case of Uptown, the cigarette elicited outrage from African Americans, who saw the brand and the target marketing program as a cynical attempt to flood their community with vice products and to profit from their suffering. By concentrating on vice products like cigarettes and liquor, target marketing both failed to identify lucrative opportunities to sell a broad range of goods to African Americans and further ghettoized urban consumers.

Information-powered advertising and marketing stand at the center of controversy over surveillance capitalism. But critics often assume that the extraction of consumer information is a straightforward process, built into the logic of accumulation. Meg Jones's history of the internet cookie shows that the trail is much more winding. Early programmers and those who wanted to profit from the commercialization of the internet understood that tracking the movement of users could yield valuable information. But while some quickly sought to monetize such information, others worried about the ethical and legal status of this new form of "property"—that is, information consumers had unintentionally left behind. As we know, gathering left-over information has long been a business strategy for profit-minded companies, whether in the form of letters, past sales records, or consumer credit. But the information on the internet was something new. Cookies began as a tool to negotiate between the commercialization of consumer information and the protection of consumer privacy. The result of these decisions and the failures of self-regulation would have far-reaching implications.

Together these studies map a substantial part of the terrain of surveillance capitalism in America. They show how far back some practices extend and illustrate the process by which the surveillant infrastructure was built, piece by piece, through the actions of private companies and state actors. Though there is still much more ground to excavate, we offer this book as a starting point and hope that more scholars will begin to work on the history of surveillance capitalism.

CHAPTER 1

Enslaved Watchmen

Surveillance and Sousveillance in Jamaica and the British Atlantic World

CAITLIN ROSENTHAL AND CAMERON BLACK

An enduring question about the history of Atlantic slavery is how a very small number of free men maintained power over many more enslaved Africans. As of 1780, free whites composed less than 10 percent of the population across the British Caribbean.[1] The ratio was even more dramatic on individual planta-tions, where the proportion of enslaved to free often reached or exceeded 40:1. Indeed, laws on some islands mandated 40:1 as a minimum ratio as a bul-wark against rebellion. To borrow the terms of business history: plantations had incredibly steep organizational structures. Where workers were arrayed into an organizational pyramid, the bottom was much wider than the top. Field hands dramatically outnumbered managers (both enslaved and free), and enslaved people far outnumbered free men.

From one perspective, that the system functioned smoothly with such dramatic imbalances is unsurprising: we know that free managers enjoyed massive power advantages over enslaved workers, often including a mono-poly on weapons and horses. Planters supplemented this power with the twin threats of violence and sale, and they manipulated access to food and lodging to increase their control. And yet, even considering these strategies, the number of free workmen remained remarkably small, particularly con-sidering the brutal nature of the work and the well-documented resistance of enslaved people.

This chapter argues that the management of large plantations in the British West Indies relied on complex information systems and that these systems deployed networks of enslaved watchmen to gather intelligence. Differently put, plantation security depended on the eyes and ears of enslaved people. Such labor was not given willingly, and the chapter explores the strategies planters used to build systems of surveillance and to extract information from those who did not wish to give it.

Critical to this history is the position of enslaved "watchmen." Watchmen were tasked with keeping watch over plantation grounds, stores, and other enslaved people working alongside them. They were then required to report back to white overseers and bookkeepers. Forced to trade information for subsistence and sometimes for survival, they could sometimes protect the same people they were forced to spy on. They were among the most vulnerable and also the most potentially dangerous individuals laboring on plantations. Though a lack of sources from the perspective of watchmen themselves limits what we can know about their thoughts and desires, reconstructing their position begins to offer a window into the circumstances they faced as planters attempted to extract their obedience. We can also see faint contours of countersurveillance—signs that enslaved people were sometimes able to turn the position of watchmen against enslavers, building information networks of their own.

This countersurveillance emerges most clearly from the pages of an abolitionist Jamaican newspaper called the *Watchman*. This paper, whose title gestured to the figure of the watchman, engaged in a form of what theorist Simone Browne has described as "dark sousveillance." Browne's phrase, which builds on work in surveillance studies, recognizes how discriminated persons have reacted to and resisted racialized surveillance, rendering themselves out of (white) sight. In dark sousveillance, surveilled people of color leverage surveillance techniques against their oppressors, conducting a kind of countersurveillance.[2] Browne describes surveillance on American plantations as "an exercise of both sovereign power and racialized disciplinary power, working simultaneously, discretionarily, and in a prescribed fashion . . . to render slave life expendable."[3] Watchmen on Jamaican plantations likewise became tools that planters used to exercise power. However, these same watchmen could also challenge planters' sovereignty by threatening their information networks. In the *Watchman* newspaper, the broader community of color in Jamaica—both enslaved and free—also turned the symbolic figure of the watchman against the planter class, conducting systematic countersurveillance for their own purposes.

In order to get some sense of the position of watchmen—and to make the most of a thin source base—what follows focuses on Jamaica, but also ranges across the British West Indies and the American South in the late eighteenth and early nineteenth century. Our analysis combines close analysis of one complex of Jamaican plantations with references from printed sources such as plantation manuals, published diaries, and newspapers. In Jamaica and the other sugar islands, the large scale of plantations made watchmen absolutely essential to maintaining control. References to watchmen in the American South are far fewer, likely a reflection of the very different ratio between free and enslaved people and of differences in crop. But planters nonetheless sought to develop information systems that would help them to maintain control. Understanding the role of watchmen offers a starting point for thinking about the surveillance of enslaved people across the Atlantic world.

To lay this foundation for thinking about slavery and surveillance, this chapter moves through four sets of questions. First, who served as watchmen and what were their duties? Second, how did planters come to "trust" these watchmen. Differently put, how did they secure the labor of workers who did not want to give it? Third, what can we learn from planters' fear of rebellion? Here we describe and analyze a Jamaican case where a prominent watchman was put on trial for planning an insurrection. Though it is impossible to determine the watchman's actual role in the event (or even whether there was a conspiracy at all), the sources vividly reflect planters' anxieties: they feared losing control over watchmen because it meant losing control over information systems and thus, potentially, over the slave system itself. Fourth and finally, we consider systems of countersurveillance, in particular a Jamaican abolitionist newspaper called the *Watchman*.

Watching

On Parnassus Plantation in Jamaica in 1779, there were 449 enslaved people and ten free whites. Among the 449 enslaved men, women, and children, eighteen were watchmen, led by Shadwell, the "head watchman." Parnassus was the largest single plantation in a massive complex of properties held by absentee owner Henry Dawkins. Attorney John Shickle managed these properties for Dawkins in Jamaica, and he prepared detailed reports and inventories for review back in England. In Clarendon Parish, where Parnassus was located, Dawkins owned a total of nine plantations and livestock pens, and as of December 1779, some 1,797 men, women, and children lived on these properties. Out of these 1,797 lives, 100 enslaved people were classified as "watchmen."[4] On average, across Henry Dawkins's properties in Clarendon Parish, there was one watchman for every eighteen enslaved people.

The number of watchmen varied widely across different plantations—likely varying based on factors ranging from geography to the availability of labor to plantation sentiment. In 1788, on Hope Estate in St. Andrew Parish, eight enslaved men owned by Anna Eliza Hope-Elletson watched a property where 351 enslaved people lived and worked. In 1784 on Pleasant Hill Plantation, in St. Thomas in the East Parish, seventeen watchmen kept surveillance over 305 people enslaved by Nathaniel Phillips. Across a nonrandom sample comprising these and several other large properties, on average, there was one watchman for every twenty-one enslaved people. Assuming a similar ratio held across the 800,000 people enslaved in the British West Indies at the time of emancipation in 1833, there would have been 38,000 men working as watchmen.[5] The number may well have been higher: in 1790, reflecting on nearly forty years of experience as a resident and absentee planter, Alexander Campbell estimated that "in 180 or 200 negroes" there would be "about 15" watchmen.[6]

Those keeping watch were, as one late eighteenth-century observer explained, "generally made up of the old and infirm."[7] Managers took advantage of the task's comparatively sedentary nature to employ those who could not work productively in the plantations' more punishing tasks. This was true on Parnassus, where the detailed inventory lists their conditions (Figure 1.1). Shadwell, the head, was "with [only] one hand," and he was followed by Robin, "very old," Peter, "Ruptur'd," and Sam, "Distemp'd." From here, the list continued, with every enslaved watchman described as elderly, infirm, or both: conditions include "Old & Sickly," "has lost a leg," "has lost a hand," "Pox'd," and "bad Sore leg." The same was true of the watchmen on Sutton's Estate, also owned by Henry Dawkins. There, every one of the twenty watchmen was described as elderly or ill.[8] On Hope Estate, owned by Anna Eliza Hope-Elletson, six of eight were "old and infirm," while two were "old and weak."[9] On York plantation, owned by William Gale, eighteen watchmen included those described as "Worthless," "Lame," "Indiff't," "Invalid," and "Ruptured." York also employed able men as watchmen, though among these men, four were described as "formerly runaway."[10] These able men might have been recovering from punishment or perhaps have agreed to return on

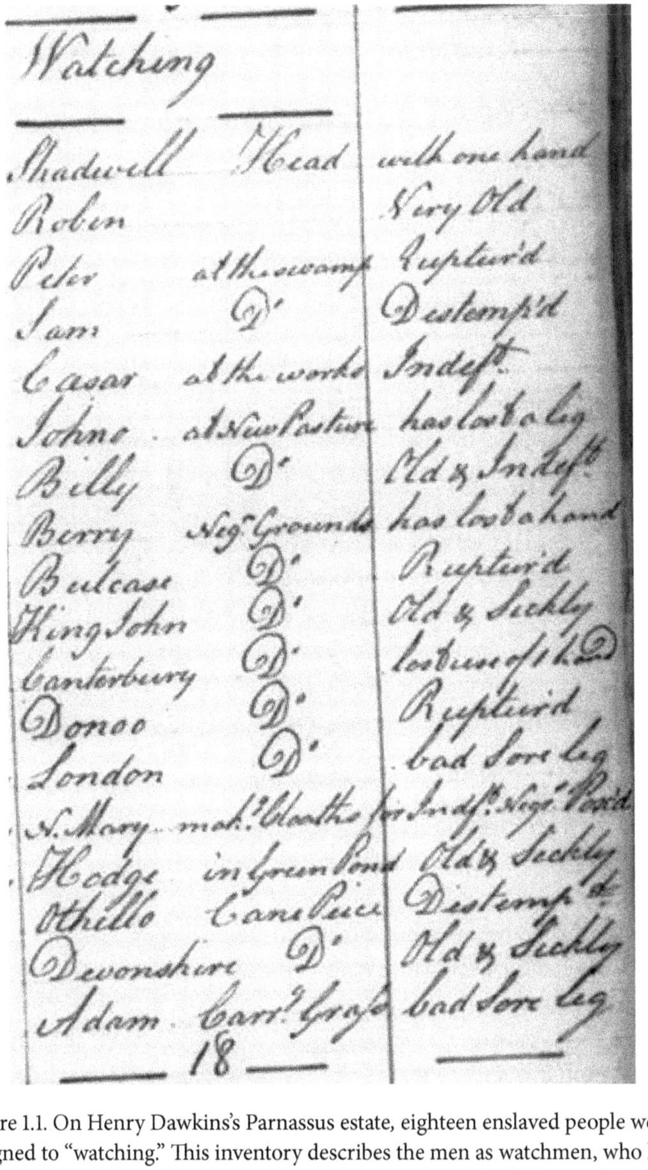

Figure 1.1. On Henry Dawkins's Parnassus estate, eighteen enslaved people were assigned to "watching." This inventory describes the men as watchmen, who kept security over various spaces. Many were elderly or injured and thus could not be assigned to other labor. Adam Matthew Digital, Slavery, Abolition, and Social Justice. Original held by Wilberforce House Museum.

condition of being placed in this duty. A newspaper correspondent identifying himself as "Measure for Measure" wrote that an enslaved man named
Quamina had been brutally punished using a stretching block, which dam-
aged his arms. "In consequence," he was "placed as a watchman on a slip of
uncultivated land."[11]

Almost all of those assigned to keep watch were men. The list for Parnassus appears to include one woman, N. Mary, herself suffering from pox, and
many plantations included no women keeping watch. The gendered division
of labor may also have reflected the fact that elderly women tended to be put
to work at alternative tasks—cooking, sewing, and watching children. Indeed, N. Mary seems to have been employed at multiple tasks at once—she
was assigned to keep watch while also sewing clothing. This gendered division of labor seems to have held across the West Indies—in 1790 a planter
named Alexander Willock advised that he owned "more males than fe-
males" because men were "necessary for boilers, tradesmen, carters, and
watchmen."[12] Female watchmen appear to have been employed to watch
over spaces or jobs that were typically assigned to women and children. N.
Mary would have been considered as among what Thomas Roughley, author
of a guide for sugar planters, described as "handicraft watchmen." Handicraft watchmen monitored the production of goods on the plantation, both
making goods themselves and depositing these "in the appropriate store, to
be had when wanted."[13]

The daily demands of "watching" varied widely. Planter Robert Thomas
testified that in St. Kitts and Nevis, "The office of watchman is to keep cattle
from intruding on cane-pieces, whilst the plants are young, and when mature, to guard them from depredations of negroes. Watchmen also attend
stores, &c. where any valuable effects are deposited."[14] The inventory for
Parnassus lists where each watchman was assigned. One or two were tasked
with keeping watch over most plantation spaces—"at the swamp," "at the
works," "at New Pasture," "in Green Pond," and at "Cane Piece." Some of the
watchmen probably spent most of their time watching cattle and also keeping a lookout for fire. They were responsible for making sure that cattle did
not break out of "their places of confinement, and to give the alarm should
any accidents of fire happen."[15] They also hunted for rats, which were the
"very great enemies" of the cane and had to be killed in "innumerable pro-
portions by the watchmen who are dispersed over the different parts of the
plantation."[16] On the inventory for Sutton's Estate some of the watchmen
were described as "ratcatchers."[17]

Watchmen's most important task seems to have been keeping surveillance over other slaves—monitoring them both as they worked and while they rested. On Parnassus, six men, the most assigned to any space, kept watch at the "negro grounds." While handicraft watchmen or those positioned "at the works" would have monitored work processes, these six men were tasked with monitoring enslaved people's living spaces and provision grounds. Still other men were tasked with watching the most valuable parts of the plantation, protecting them from "plunder." In his defense of the slave trade, James M. Adair explained that watchmen were "placed over each cane-field that is of forward growth, and near the mansion house and sugar works."[18]

These were some of the most vulnerable people on the plantation—individuals who could not rely on physical strength or a high market price to protect their well-being. And the fact that the work of watching could be performed by the injured and the elderly did not make it light work. In his *Descriptive Account of the Island of Jamaica*, author and planter William Beckford described the wind and the cold that plagued those who were "obliged to watch the cattle-pens upon the summits of the hills at night," a "tedious and necessary avocation." Observing their poor conditions, "shivering to the wind without raiment perhaps, and without food," he lamented the lack even of "temporary hovels" for shelter or "wrappers to keep their bodies warm."[19] Benjamin Moseley wrote in his *Treatise on Sugar* that when an enslaved person was afflicted with yaws, the planter would "separate him from the rest, and send him to some lonely place . . . where he could act as a watchman, and maintain himself, without expense to the estate, until he was well." By Moseley's estimation, however, recovery rarely came. Alone in a "cold, damp, smoky hut . . . he usually sunk from the land of the living."[20]

In using the aged and infirm as managers and watchmen, planters were both making efficient use of those who could not work in other tasks and also turning their infirmities to particular advantage. These slaves could be "trusted" in part because they had very limited physical capacity to escape or resist. In the collection of information, their vulnerability offered planters control.

Keeping Control

Plantation records and management reflect planters' concern with maintaining control over enslaved watchmen. Chief among these was the employment of a head watchman to keep watch over the watchers. Thomas Roughley, author of an advice manual on running a Jamaican sugar plantation, explained that "a head watchman is always a necessary slave officer on every property."[21] In the next line, he warned that "if such a person is not narrowly looked after," he would spend "the greater part of his time in gadding about" or "working a distant ground of his own." Tasked with preventing theft, the head watchman might himself take "an effective mule off the estate, to carry some provisions with despatch to market." In all of this, the head watchman could become "a bad example to the slave population, who are ever prone to catch infection of this kind."[22]

To prevent such "noxious influence," Roughley advised regular contact with the overseer, who should demand regular reports "of the state of the business." Constant reports would help the manager to quickly assign blame, both to watchmen and to those they were watching. Roughley prescribed that the head watchman was "go over the lines of the property once or twice a week, through the woods, and strictly observe that no damage is done there, or loss sustained by trespass; and report the same to the overseer." Roughley explained that the head watchman should take particular care when monitoring the provision grounds, ensuring that "no mischief is done, or trespass committed," and keeping the watchmen stationed there "most particularly to their duty."[23]

Though most sources seem to suggest that planters relied on elderly and infirm enslaved people to keep watch, a few sources suggest precisely the opposite. Keeping security sometimes required brawn. In a book published in defense of the slave trade, James M. Adair described watchmen as "the stoutest and most trusty of the slaves," even worrying that their particular strength might lead them to hurt men or women found searching for food. He also described arming them with "a cutlas, rarely a musquet."[24] Those who suffered from physical limitations could not have apprehended enslaved people. Other tasks also required strength—for example, a transcription from a trial after an insurrection described a watchman being sent out to ensure that a contested area is safe.[25] Indeed, some of the enslaved watchmen on the Dawkins properties were able-bodied. While Sutton's Estate and Parnassus Estate relied on the elderly and the injured, on nearby Friendship Estate both the head watchman and those working below him were all described as "able."

Weapons made them potentially threatening to their masters, but more often to their masters' property—for the men and the women they were watching were themselves valuable assets. As James M. Adair wrote about preventing robbery: "if any mischief is done, being responsible, they . . . sometimes destroy the culprit in the act of depredation."[26] Watchmen had to be held responsible for the spaces they watched but also prevented from hurting enslaved people in the process. Adair described one manager's practice of offering presents not only "to his own watchman," but also "to his neighbour's watchman, beside what the law allows, if in apprehending the runaway slaves they treated them with lenity. This had a good effect."[27] Weak or strong, the cooperation of enslaved watchmen was secured in part through "presents" of adequate provisions and, for head watchmen, occasionally even access to small luxuries. For example, Thomas Roughley recommended that "as an incentive to the principal headmen of an estate to do their duty well or reward their exertions" they be given "a weekly allowance of a quart or two of good rum, some sugar, and now and then a dinner from the overseer's table."[28] As he explained, these allowances could also be withdrawn in punishment.

Even as planters warned that watchmen might harm escaped slaves, they also feared that they would shelter them. Roughley claimed that they did this for their own gain, warning that a watchman might harbor "runaway slaves, whom he cheaply hires to perform some work for him."[29] More likely, watchmen simply took advantage of their unique ability to offer shelter to other slaves. In particular, watchmen stationed in remote areas had more opportunity to conceal those who had escaped without detection. In 1822, the *Royal Gazette* reported that an escaped man named Paris was "from negro information" being "harboured by a Watchman" at Hind's Bog in St. Ann Parish.[30] An enslaved man named William described being sheltered by a watchman during the second of his two escapes. William mentioned this in passing, as part of a deposition taken to gather evidence about the Jamaican Maroons, communities of escaped slaves who had entered into treaties with the British. In a published excerpt of his deposition, William testified that he had been "taken up" by three Maroons after leaving the watchman. But, given the stakes of admitting to any collaboration, it seems plausible—even likely—that this chain of events might have reflected broader networks of communication among the enslaved and formerly enslaved.[31]

Planters' fear did not stop at theft. In 1821, the *Barbados Mercury* reported a "barbarous murder," where a plantation owner was killed by an enslaved man named Jeffry. Jeffry had been held "in such confidence" that his master allowed him to "sleep in the same chamber every night." But this

trust was also Jeffry's opportunity, and the paper reported that he had con-
spired to the murder with several other enslaved people, including Jack
Grig, one of the plantation watchmen.[32]

Anxiety and Rebellion

Planters' many strategies for maintaining control over enslaved watchmen
reflected the slender but real power they held to undermine the slave system.
When watching broke down—or, more ominously, was wielded against
planters—the whole plantation structure threatened to collapse. In 1817,
after returning from fourteen years in Jamaica, Dr. John Williamson published his diaries of the time as *Medical and Miscellaneous Observations
Relative to the West India Islands*. Williamson's account, much of which
took the form of a monthly diary of his time in Jamaica, ranged across a
wide variety of topics, from protecting the health of Europeans upon their
arrival in the West Indies to reducing the mortality of enslaved children
to the management of plantation hospitals. The book also includes a shadowy retelling of a suspected insurrection in 1807. These reflections, a mix
of information with rumor colored by fear, suggest how important watchmen and the networks of information they represented were to order on the
island.[33]

According to the doctor's diary, the 1807 plot came to light when an
overseer was encouraged to leave the plantation by a group of the enslaved
people because his life was in danger. The doctor's account suggests that this
overseer was warned because he was well liked and the slaves feared for his
safety, but there were surely many reasons why enslaved people might wish
to be rid of an overseer. Several enslaved men were implicated in the "plot,"
and two of whom were identified as leaders came from Spring Garden Estate
in St. George Parish: the head driver, Anthony Gutzmer, and the head watchman, Adam Williamson. As head driver, Anthony Gutzmer would have been
the most prominent enslaved person on the property, and the doctor explained that the watchman Adam Williamson "stood in as great estimation"
as he did. As evidence of this high status, the writer explained that Adam
Williamson had been "permitted to assume the name of a highly respected
Lieutenant-Governor." The doctor wondered in his diary at Williamson
and Gutzmer's disloyalty, given the "luxuries" and "comforts" their positions granted them. Spring Garden Estate was a large property—one that

"excels almost any other," and the doctor's diary claimed that the estate be-
stowed many "comforts and luxuries" on the slaves. As head driver, Gutzmer,
the doctor claimed, had a house that "was not inferior in comfort to the
overseer's." And the head watchman purportedly also received "kindly"
treatment.[34]

Ultimately, it is very difficult to determine what, if anything, actually
took place. But after the supposed plot was uncovered, Adam Williamson
and Anthony Gutzmer were put on "trial for life." Remarkably, they were
acquitted, suggesting that their accusers could present no solid evidence.
Still, despite their innocence, "measures were promptly adopted as secured
the peace of the island." The lieutenant governor "exercised a prerogative" to
send the men "off the island," since they were "considered by the Privy
Council improper persons to be permitted to remain in that country." The
doctor recounted in his diary that the two men had "considerable influence
over the minds of the other negroes," and evidently they were sufficiently
threatening that this had to be carried out by "a party of about thirty soldiers" under the cover of night. As he explained, if the "business had been
conducted in any other manner, a great commotion would have been raised,
productive of consequences which it was impossible for us to conceive without horror."[35] As he explained, not only did Anthony Gutzmer and Adam
Williamson threaten the stability of the plantation where they labored and
the neighborhood around it, but "their intention was to extend a disposition
to outrages to other parishes at a greater distance."[36] Real or imagined, as
head driver and head watchman, their positions and their access to networks
of information may have enabled them to organize across great distances.

Whether there was a real plot or simply fear of one, we do not know. In
the end, the story shows the vulnerability of the enslaved, not their power.
As Randy Browne has written about enslaved drivers, theirs was a "fragile
authority" that depended on delicate—often impossible—negotiations.[37]
Acquitted at court, Adam Williamson and Anthony Gutzmer escaped with
their lives. The evidence against them must have been scant, indeed. But
their acquittal offered little real protection. They were sent off the island,
exiled and stripped of the status they had built and surely also of family and
community ties. Their influence was enough to terrify white planters, but it
was not enough to protect their well-being.

By contrast, the planters and politicians who had them sent away escaped without consequence. In October of 1807, the Jamaican colonial council
passed an act to "indemnify his honour the lieutenant-governor" for the

extraordinary action of banishing innocent men from Jamaica. On his order, "four slaves of a dangerous description" had been "transported from
this island." These men included Gutzmer and Williamson as well as two
others not mentioned in the doctor's diary—Peregrine and Captain, both of
Orange Vale Estate, also in St. George Parish. This was carried out on the
"unanimous advice of the privy council." It was also clearly illegal. Addressing the king, "we . . . humbly beseech your majesty," the act sought forgive-
ness for the action, explaining that the measures were "expedient and
necessary for the safety and welfare of the island." Further, it assured the
king that the owners of the slaves would "have ample compensation" for
their losses. The fate of the four enslaved men "transported" away is not
mentioned, and surely they received no reparations.[38]

Countersurveillance

The role that enslaved watchmen actually played in this and other plots remains murky, but it is clear that Jamaicans saw the figure of the watchman
as potentially subversive. In 1829, two free men of color, Edward Jordon and
Robert Osborn launched the *Watchman*. Jordon and Osborn were uniquely
prepared to run a paper: both had been involved in political and civil campaigns for nearly a decade, and Osborn knew the trade from an apprentice-
ship at the *Chronicle*, another newspaper in Kingston.[39] The men founded
the *Watchman* during a campaign for civil rights for free people of color on
the island, and, in a sense, they would turn the figure of the watchman
against the slaveholding apparatus in Jamaica. The paper advocated for the
abolition of slavery as well as for political, economic, and social rights for
persons of color. The *Watchman* offered a kind of countersurveillance—
providing crucial details to help locals to protect themselves from the violence and fear of the planter class. Candace Ward has persuasively argued
that the *Watchman* successfully "disrupted white planter control over print,"
"lending revolutionary significance to Jordon and Osborn's claim that 'ours
is a free press.'"[40]

The *Watchman* was not the first or only paper of the period to bear the
name, and the paper's title likely reflects both classical and biblical references to the question "Who watches the watchmen?"[41] And yet, in the context of Jamaican security, the immediate presence of tens of thousands of
enslaved watchmen across the island must also have been on the editors'

minds. Enslaved watchmen watched *for* the watchers, but with Jordon and Osborn's paper, people of color could also keep watch *on* the planter class. The paper's masthead was adorned with an image of a night watchman (Figure 1.2). Wearing a heavy coat and hat, he carries a lantern and a ratchet rattle to sound the alarm. At his feet lay scraps of broken chains, and below them the Latin phrase "Nunquam dormio"—never sleep.[42] The *Watchman* disrupted the planter class's near monopoly on information, both for local audiences and for those across the Atlantic. In an editorial on April 17, 1832, the *Watchman* described the landscape of print on the island. "There are, in Jamaica, supported and patronized by the planters, five weekly and two daily papers, ALL of them decidedly pro-slavery." By contrast, only the *Watchman*, published twice each week, differed in opinion.[43]

The dominant newspapers, which disparaged the *Watchman* as a "dingy little sheet," viewed this incursion on their monopoly with hostility. The *Watchman* regularly critiqued the coverage provided by other papers. For example, on December 8, 1830, the *Watchman* published an editorial decoding and critiquing an essay published in the Jamaica *Courant, another Kingston weekly publication.* The *Courant* had published an article purporting to support the progress of Jamaicans of color, devoting, said the *Watchman*, "not less than *forty two lines and a quarter of small pica*" to commending aspects of a bill being debated in the House of Assembly. The *Courant* called for people of color "to be satisfied" that "the respectable part of [their] class" was being "treated with every mark of consideration."[44] The *Watchman* responded by pointing out the hypocrisy of this supposed "liberality," and particularly the suggestion that Jamaicans of color were ungrateful. The editor replied, "The People of Colour are as grateful a body of men as any under the canopy of Heaven—Experience has, however taught them . . . to distinguish between real and pretended friends . . . [and] to judge of men, not by their professions but by their conduct." Further, the *Watchman* clarified, "the people of colour seek" not—as the *Courant* had implied—"a free and unrestrained association with the whites," but a free and full "participation in civil rights ONLY; any further association is to them a matter of perfect indifference."[45]

The *Watchman* had to tread carefully to stay in print, but even during times of crisis the paper disrupted the planter class's monopoly on information. Consider their coverage of the Christmas Rebellion of 1831–32. This massive uprising, also called the Baptist War, threatened the entire western side of the island as well as its sugar harvest. Led by a network of Baptist

Figure 1.2. The figure of a night watchman, holding a lantern and rattle, adorned the top of the *Jamaican Watchman*, published by two free men of color, Edward Jordon and Robert Osborn. Broken chains at the night watchman's feet signified the paper's abolitionist stance. Masthead, *Jamaica Watchman* (Kingston), January 1, 1831.

missionaries and converts, the attempted revolution was inspired both by rumors of emancipation and by particular hardships after a period of drought.[46] The *Watchman* rhetorically distanced itself from violence and re-volt while also reporting with a lens for free and enslaved people. Through-out the attempted revolution, the *Watchman* published detailed information on troop movements. Reports on the colonial militia were organized by par-ish, and they included the commanding officer, formation, and eventual destination. They also identified troops composed of Jamaican Maroons.

The paper couched these reports in terms of surveillance, explaining for example, that "the following intelligence was communicated to us, which we hasten to communicate with our readers."[47] This information would have helped free and enslaved Jamaicans to keep themselves safe amid the violence, and it seems possible that this information might even have aided the rebelling slaves.

The coverage was also carefully crafted to bolster the case for abolition abroad. As a letter to the editor from "you know who" exclaimed, "not only ascertains and published instances of cruelty, and oppression here, on the spot, but he goes to England by every Packet, and proclaims them at the foot of the Throne, and in both Houses of Parliament, and also excites the British Public . . . for the purpose of banishing slavery, injustice, and irreligion."[48] During the Christmas Rebellion, the paper continually reminded the outside world that the vast majority of blacks on the island, indeed even the majority of enslaved and free blacks in areas occupied by the rebellion, were not engaged in violence. The editors noted that instead of revolting, blacks in parishes around Jamaica continued working. In St. Mary, the situation was so secure that the *Watchman* printed only one line about the entire parish: "All remains quiet in this Parish."[49] After the crisis ended, the *Watchman* also exposed the despicable and arbitrary violence used by the governor to restore order to the island. For example, the *Watchman* quoted Major General Robinson of the colonial militia, who explained that "it is the governor's instructions and my positive orders, that every negro house be burned down, and all their hogs and poultry killed . . . and their provision ground destroyed."[50] These orders apparently were not limited to active participants in the rebellion.

Similarly, the *Watchman* both relayed and subtly questioned messages from the colonial militia explaining how to surrender. For example, they conveyed the instruction that "all who yield themselves up at any military post immediately, provided that they are not principals and chiefs in the burnings that have ensued, will receive his Majesty's pardon; all who hold out will be met with certain death."'[51] But along with this "intelligence," the paper expressed skepticism about the mercy promised to free and enslaved Jamaicans of color. It argued for lenience, calling for due process and a fair trial: "popular clamour has been excited, but as it is a fundamental principle of Jurisprudence to consider a man innocent until he be proven guilty, it becomes us, as impartial Journalists, to suspend our decision." The *Watchman* also worried that those not involved would be swept up in the wave of retribution that seemed certain to sweep the island after the rebellion was finally suppressed. As the editor cautioned, "the innocent should not suffer with the guilty."[52]

The *Watchmen* addressed not only people of color in Jamaica but also the British government abroad as a potential ally. Drawing on enlightenment rhetoric, the *Watchman* reminded the colonial authorities of their legal and moral responsibilities. After all, the missionaries and slaves who had supported the resistance were merely following the dictates of the Christian religion and the British constitution: "Enjoying freedom in its purity, associated as it preeminently is with all other blessings of the British Constitution, improved too by Christianity, it appears a natural consequence for fellow Britons to impart to their fellow creatures, particularly those within range of their political intuitions, those benefits they enjoy."[53] As long as slavery existed in the colonies, such revolts would naturally occur.

Throughout the Christmas Rebellion and the violent repression that followed, other publications called for the closing of the *Watchman*. The pressure culminated in Jordon's arrest in April of 1832 on a charge of "constructive treason" for an editorial published in the wake of the revolution. Osborn refused to testify on the grounds that it might incriminate him, and Jordon was acquitted, in part because doubts remained about who had authored the editorial. Within a month of the first trial, Jordon was arrested again, this time on a charge of libel. This time, he was convicted, sentenced a year in prison, and fined £100. Jordon's sentence was later overturned, but only after he had served half of the term.[54]

During Jordon's legal cases and eventual imprisonment, the *Watchman* continued its work. Amid this storm, a reader elevated the editor from the sobriquet "Watchie" to the post of "Captain Watchie." During the trial, the paper also dropped the subhead "and free press" and changed its masthead image (Figure 1.3). No longer standing free, the watchman is newly chained. And the rattle and lantern, formerly in his hands, are now scattered at his feet.[55] The fallen lantern and rattle surely symbolized the attempted censoring of the *Watchman*, but adorning the masthead of a paper that continued to print, the new image could also be subversive. The *Watchman* would continue to operate covertly—watching the planter class from under the cover of darkness. In her analysis of the surveillance of blackness, Simone Browne describes the lantern laws enacted in eighteenth-century New York City to make black bodies more visible and thus easier to regulate. City law forbid

Figure 1.3. After Edward Jordon's arrest and imprisonment on a charge of "constructive treason" for the contents of anonymous editorials, the newspaper changed its masthead. The figure of the watchman is now in chains, his tools at his feet. Yet the paper continued its work. Masthead, *Jamaica Watchman* (Kingston), June 20, 1832.

any "Negro or Indian Slave above the age of fourteen years" from venturing onto city streets without "a lanthorn and a lighted candle." A slave caught "unlit after dark" could be sentenced to a public whipping.[56] Such laws did not make all bodies visible, but rather shined "more brightly on some than on others."[57] While the Jamaican slave law of the time did not contain an equivalent lantern law, it did regulate the assembly of enslaved people in the darkness.[58] In the new masthead, a surveilling eye gazes down from a darkened sky. The watchman is in chains, without his rattle and lantern, but cloaked in darkness—unlit—and, shielded by his pseudonym, "Captain

Watchie" continued to write. The *Watchman* offered a marginalized community of free and enslaved black persons in Jamaica an opportunity to refocus light onto their oppressors.

Conclusion

Slaveholders used enslaved watchmen to keep surveillance over the thousands of men, women, and children laboring on plantations in the British West Indies. These workers—typically elderly or injured men—could be used as watchmen when they were too weak or ill for more physically demanding tasks. Their infirmity may have made them easier to "trust"—a sick slave would have had less ability to resist or negotiate. Their age may have made them more influential among other enslaved people, putting them in a position of both authority and precarity that planters turned to their advantage.

By contrast to the British West Indies, the position of watchmen was exceptionally rare in the American South. Though some enslaved people surely kept watch or gave reports, plantation inventories do not generally include anyone whose occupation was "watching." In some ways, this is unsurprising. In Jamaica and the broader British West Indies, where enslaved people vastly outnumbered free, slaveholders had little choice but to rely on the eyes and ears of their slaves to collect information. By contrast, in American South at the time of the 1790 census, enslaved people outnumbered free in only one state, South Carolina. And by 1800 free people in even South Carolina outnumbered slaves..[59] Only in the wealthiest plantation districts did the number of enslaved people outnumber free, and in these locations, a supply of free labor was readily available for plantation management and security.

And yet, the Jamaican story is valuable for thinking through the role of surveillance for plantation operations across the Atlantic world. While surveillance functioned differently in different places, in many settings information systems were essential to maintaining control and improving productivity. American and West Indian slaveholders relied on detailed recordkeeping to monitor supplies, to measure output, and to maintain control over the enslaved people whose labor they exploited. As slavery merged with modern business practices, planters sought to increase their domination over enslaved people by blending violence with information systems. The problem of trust created by planters' reliance on enslaved people to keep watch is also one that extends far beyond the British West Indies. Where business owners and managers have to extract information from watchers whose allegiances lie elsewhere, the information provided will always be fragile.

As planters' anxieties make clear, enslaved surveillance was not freely given. To maintain control, slaveholders used systems of incentives and reports to make sure that the networks of enslaved watchmen they created did not turn against them. Slaveholders sought to dominate the circulation of information, but their efforts did not set them at ease. They feared that watchmen might shelter escaped slaves, or, worse, that they might use their position to support resistance and rebellion. The nature of the sources that describe such deceptions—almost always filtered through the words of slaveholders—makes it difficult to separate real plots from conspiracies. Still, given what we know about enslaved resistance across the region, it seems likely that watchmen may have used their positions in these ways. Jamaica's abolitionist newspaper the *Watchman* reflects this subversive potential. A lone critic of slavery amid a host of pro-planter publications, the paper not only argued against slavery, it also offered subtle countersurveillance for free people of color on the island. The editor, celebrated as "Captain Watchie" by his readers, kept watch over the watchers.

CHAPTER 2

_____

The Information Bazaar

Mail-Order Magazines and the Gilded Age
Trade in Consumer Data

RICHARD K. POPP

In the 1880s, only the post offices of New York, Chicago, Boston, and Phila-delphia did a bigger business than that of Augusta, Maine. Contrasting the city's postal operations to its modest size, a Pittsburgh newspaper likened it to "Jay Gould running a bank in Skaneateles." The metaphor was not too far afield. Augusta could, in fact, count some of the nation's biggest publishing magnates among its residents. Home to E. C. Allen & Co., Vickery & Hill, Gannett & Morse, and several other publishers, the city of ten thousand was the indisputable capital of the mail-order magazine trade. By the late 1880s, the town's outbound traffic in periodicals and sales literature filled a railcar to near capacity each day. The incoming traffic in letters, orders, and pay-ments was no less impressive. At one point the largest private user of the U.S. mails, Allen alone received as many as 11,000 letters a day. For locals, this staggering volume was a clear source of pride. "The apothecary com-pounding your quinine pills," *Puck*'s Clarence Stetson joked about his visit to Augusta, "the grocer doing up your package, and the postman as he hands you your letters, all remark: 'As you are a stranger, perhaps you don't know that this is one of the largest post offices—' then you escape."[1]

Augustans could hardly be blamed for their boastfulness. For half a century, local boosters had worked at turning the sleepy state capital into a city of industry. The Kennebec River, which passed through the center of town, was already one of the country's premier ice harvesting fields. Others could see money in the Kennebec's running waters and began agitating for a dam that might transform Augusta into another Lowell. Completed in 1837, the waterworks seemed to hearken a new era.[2] Instead of industrial prosperity, though, the town saw one setback after another as a series of floods and fires consumed Augusta's budding factory district. Still hoping the dam would pay dividends in the 1860s, boosters lured the calico giant A. & W. Sprague to town, only to see it succumb to bankruptcy in 1873. By then, Augusta's industrial ambitions were changing. Around the same time the Sprague mills were under construction, so too was an impressive, six-story building on Water Street to house the operations of E. C. Allen & Co. Allen too would make use of the Kennebec's navigable waters. Rather than shipping in bales of cotton, he imported copious volumes of paper, ink, and other key commodities of the publishing trade, among the most vital of which were the names and addresses he bought by the thousands. Indeed, more than anything else, the commodity that made Allen's whole system go were the batches of secondhand mail exchanged by him and his confederates on a regular basis, knowing that each new cache might yield a handful of individuals willing to enlist as sales agents—and, in turn, purchase the sales kits and merchandise requisite to that line of work.[3]

This chapter explores that exchange. In so doing, it reveals a world where consumer surveillance was from the very start a constitutive feature of commercial media and where large-scale publishing operations and small-time mail-order hustlers were among the pioneers of surveillance capitalism. While historians have recognized the generative role played by such industries as life insurance and credit lending in the emergence of systematized consumer surveillance, mass publishing has largely been overlooked. To be certain, magazine publishers show up in the broader history of surveillance. But it has generally been their pioneering work in audience research that has garnered attention, not their mail rooms and addressing departments. Yet the mailing operations at magazine publishing houses were home to ledgers and card cabinets that stood among the largest repositories of personal data in existence in late nineteenth-century America. And unique among the institutions amassing such records, mail-order merchants and publishers built a lively market in them. Knowing full well that customer inquiries were strewn with information of value, Allen and his peers recognized that transactions were also sites of production.[4]

By bringing surveillance and data collection to the forefront, we gain a new perspective on how mass marketing and direct marketing worked in combination to shape consumer capitalism. While communication scholars have traced the roots of today's database-driven marketing to the mailing-list industry, they have largely left the formation of that earlier field unexplored. By digging into its intricacies, we can see that the harnessing of industrialized marketing with industrialized publishing looks very different from the offices of an E. C. Allen than that of a Curtis Publishing Company. In contrast to the synchronized factories, railcars, ad agencies, and middle-class homes brought to mind by the latter's *Ladies' Home Journal* at century's end, Allen's Reconstruction-era publishing empire was crafted on an ad hoc ensemble of junk mail, discount goods, door-to-door sales agents, and marginal households. What kept this more plebian version of mass marketing together was the tools and networks built by Allen and his peers to collect names and addresses from the margins of communities near and far.[5]

The Publishing Germ

Edward Charles Allen was born in 1849 to a farm family on the outskirts of Augusta.[6] Finding sales more to his liking than farm work, Allen began peddling at an early age, sourcing goods through the mail-order ads that filled small-town newspapers and selling them to townsfolk. A quick study, Allen soon recognized that it was the principals supplying the goods, and not the agents selling them, who really stood to gain. After a brief stint in Ohio, Allen moved back to Augusta in 1868 and found his first true money-maker—a simple, yet effective, formula for mixing up batches of soap. No bigger than a paragraph, the recipe could be printed on slips that cost fractions of a cent to produce but sold for as much as a dollar. Allen was less interested in selling the recipes himself than recruiting agents who bought bulk lots priced on a sliding scale: ten for $3, one hundred for $5, or one thousand for $25. The scheme was quite literally a formula for profits, as evidenced by an account book that recorded Allen's progress. Between 1867 and 1869, his yearly sales jumped from just $448 to $46,705.[7]

By then, Allen was in a position to place notices in newspapers nationwide. Intrigued by Allen's unusually large orders, the advertising agent George Rowell made the trek from New York City to Augusta in the late 1860s. There, the future *Printers' Ink* publisher found a distinctively plebian operation. "He had a room up one flight of stairs, in a barn-like loft," Rowell reported, "the chambers of what appeared to be a block of stores." Stationed throughout the room was a staff of six young women writing addresses, collating letters, and making stacks of postal currency. The detritus—"opened letters and torn envelopes"—were piled up in a coal bin in one corner of the room while Allen supervised from another. But Allen's shop was changing, and by the decade's end he was increasingly focused on publishing his own sales messages. In 1869, Allen's modest sales sheet morphed into a monthly magazine called the *People's Literary Companion*. Over the next two years, Allen made the *People's Literary Companion* a weekly, added a semimonthly children's magazine, and branched out into book and lithograph publishing. In a bid to attract subscribers, Allen began offering the latter as a premium. By the time Allen moved into the Water Street building, his shop was already the best-equipped printing house in Maine. The building hummed with activity. Six steam presses and a staff of seventy churned out copies of Allen's publications by the millions each month.[8]

As Allen's publications multiplied, the man behind them remained something of a mystery. As one correspondent put it in an 1874 R. G. Dun & Co. credit report, Allen "really belongs to that class of which you cannot say *how, when,* or *what.*"[9] Adding to the intrigue, he operated under a variety of names, some of which made their way into the credit reports even before their patron. "This is no more or less than E. C. Allen of Augusta doing business in the name of his foreman," a Portland correspondent wrote Dun of the city's True, Hallett & Co. "We have but little confidence in the enterprise." The same could be said of fellow Portlanders Geo. Stinson & Co. "Making $& pay very well," the report read, "but everything is owned by Allen & Co. is risky."[10] With or without creditors, Allen's firm grew. In the mid-1870s, he diversified into book publishing and, under the name of an associate, opened a second publishing house in Portland. He also expanded operations in Augusta, erecting a second six-story building across the street in 1880. A combined twelve stories, Allen's physical footprint outsized that of New York City's largest newspaper publishers. Formerly wary credit reporters could now only look on with awe. "He is a marvelous man," one correspondent reported to Dun's that year. At that point, Allen's physical plant included sixteen printing presses—seven of which were the largest and fastest on the market—an electrotype foundry, composing rooms, a bindery, a five-ton elevator, and a battery of steam engines to power it all. By then, Allen was publishing a whole array of titles, three of which boasted a combined circulation of more than 900,000 copies. By comparison, the circulation of the largest "quality" monthly of the era, the *Century*, topped out at 250,000, and it would take until the late 1890s for the new mass monthlies to reach a larger audience.[11]

Magazines had become the "great business of the city, completely over-shadowing everything else," recalled Frank Munsey, who before establishing his own publishing empire in New York headed up Augusta's Western Union office in the mid-1870s. Allen's plant was a corporeal presence in town. Munsey's office, just down the block, rattled with the vibrations thrown off by Allen's machinery. In the morning and the evening, a steam whistle fitted atop the annex could be heard for miles around, announcing the beginning and end of the workday—and more generally, marking time—for area residents. "The publishing germ gradually got into my blood," Munsey recollected.[12] Munsey was not alone in catching the bug. Others in Augusta, including the journeyman printer Peleg O. Vickery and local businessmen W. H. Gannett and W. W. Morse, followed him into the magazine business.[13] Together, they employed hundreds and accounted for more than twenty different maga-zines pouring off Augusta's presses each month by the late 1880s.[14] Allen died suddenly of pneumonia in 1891, and his successors dramatically down-sized the company, but the industry thrived well into the 1890s, with Gan-nett & Morse's *Comfort*, more or less a vehicle for selling their proprietary nerve drink, reaching more than 1.3 million homes each month.[15]

Allen's blend of mail-order marketing and magazine publishing clearly offered his townsfolk a model, but the industry's deeper roots were in the postal reforms of 1845 and 1851, which dramatically reduced the cost and inconvenience of sending letters through the mail.[16] Equally important to publishers like Allen was the 1852 elimination of distinctions between maga-zines and newspapers with regard to privileged postal rates, after which mag-azines under three ounces were charged just one-cent postage for delivery anywhere in the nation. Marketers dealing in cheap goods, or "notions," re-sponded by dressing up their sales literature as magazines. Thereafter, mass-produced sales matter, or "junk mail" as it would later be called, was a weighty presence in the nation's mailbags. Subsequent reforms, including the introduction of first-, second-, and third-class grading in 1863, were intended to staunch this flow, yet direct-mail agents proved savvy at eluding regula-tory efforts. The introduction of bulk-mail rates in the 1870s and 1880s, for instance, carried stipulations, such as a controlled subscription list, to gov-ern who exactly qualified for the one-cent-per-pound bulk rates afforded periodicals. Yet provisions within the same policies opened loopholes through which direct marketers found ways to qualify for rates designed, in

theory, to exclude them. For instance, although legitimate periodicals required a subscription list, publishers were permitted to send unsolicited
sample issues to nonsubscribers. In other cases, publishers learned to pad
their subscription lists with vaguely worded offers that roped in new customers. As more and more sales matter poured into the post, the volume of
second-class mail spiked from roughly 70 million pounds in 1881 to 315 million in 1895.[17]

If publishers like Allen could capitalize on an overhauled post office, they
could also leverage an expansive playbook of sales schemes written in the caveat emptor world of Barnum-age commerce. Allen relied on two in particular: premium schemes and work-at-home offers. The former was developed in
the 1850s by booksellers, jewelers, and small-time merchants keen on disposing of their overstock. Their great discovery was that consumers, in surprisingly large numbers, could be persuaded to buy two items—both of which had
problems selling otherwise—if one was offered for "free."[18] Work schemes offered employment in a range of supposedly lucrative enterprises, but among
the most common were sales agencies. When combined, premium and work-
at-home schemes functioned a lot like the "catch games" postal inspectors of
the era spent much of their time unraveling.[19] In their purest form, "catch
games" were essentially bait-and-switch operations built around some bar-
gain the seller had little intention of honoring. In some cases, the "seller"
simply pocketed the small, but for buyers, not insubstantial, payment of perhaps a nickel or a few cents' worth of stamps. More often, though, orders
were filled with inferior goods. For example, a widely advertised "dancing
skeleton," which by description sounded like a kind of mechanical automa-
ton, turned out to be nothing more than a paper cutout.[20]

Allen enjoyed a better reputation than such small-time swindlers, but
the magazines and premiums he marketed served a similar purpose. Though
cut-rate, his products had value to those who bought them, many of whom
were rethinking the place of material comforts in their lives. Most popular
in rural areas, Allen's lithographs and magazines offered decor and novelty
to households that had traditionally gone without.[21] The periodicals themselves encouraged this budding consumer consciousness outside the cities,
blending the poetry, serialized fiction, and trivia one might expect to find in
Scribner's or the Century with the agricultural advice proffered by the farm
press. The net result was a ruralized version of the family home magazine. A
typical issue of Our Fireside Journal from 1876 featured installments of a
Western by Buffalo Bill Cody, a melodrama by British novelist Pierce Egan,

several columns filled with jokes and curious asides, and household tips on everything from making custard to tanning leather.[22]

Interspersed throughout were notices publicizing Allen's sales agencies, usually occupying the better part of two full pages. "READ ALL OF THIS!!," implored one notice for subscription agencies in an 1876 issue of True & Co.'s *Fireside Journal.* "Kind readers, one and all of you, we desire to show you how to make money, and also how to extend the circulation of the paper of which you are a patron." In fact, the notice continued, "many of our agents are making even HUNDREDS OF DOLLARS PER MONTH at the business." "The HARVEST IS RIPE and the field is almost boundless and we must have more reapers at once. Reader, will you be one of them?" Those interested were directed to write True & Co. for terms. "Employment! Employment! Employment!," another ad rang out a few pages later. "Agents Wanted Everywhere to Canvass for Our Fireside Journal and Elegant Chabanneau Metal Jewelry."[23] Allen's agencies purportedly grew more lucrative with time. "YOU CAN MAKE $1,000 SPEEDILY!," trumpeted an 1882 notice in *True's Illustrated Magazine and Home Companion.* All that was needed was the modest capital of a quarter to pay for what the company called "the Largest, Most Magnificent, and Expensive Outfit Ever Placed in the Hands of Agents by any Publishers."[24]

The term "outfit" was a relatively new one in mid-nineteenth-century America, at least in the context Allen used it. At the turn of the century, "an outfit" was what someone needed to embark on a long journey, for instance, a sea voyage or overland expedition. "To outfit" was to provide someone with those materials. By midcentury, it crept into broader usage—clothes or even one's character could be an outfit—but the word still strongly conveyed notions of travel. Those connotations made "outfit" a good fit for the language of sales work, which in an era of peddlers, drummers, and canvassers, usually meant the day-to-day trek from house to house, town to town, and county to county. Yet "outfit" also had a more figurative relation to the journey, or venture. As Richard White has argued, the post–Civil War years were an era of migratory movement "both from abroad and within" that "combined wrenching change, dislocation, and dispossession with opportunity." Though it often took a willful act of imagination, to uproot oneself could be construed as the first step toward seizing the main chance.[25] Having transformed their own circumstances through sales, Allen and his peers capitalized on those sentiments in their recruitment efforts, filling their literature with testimonials (Figure 2.1).[26]

Figure 2.1. Drawing heavily on Reconstruction-era notions of self-ownership, Allen's promotional literature depicted his sale agencies as a means of personal transformation. "Find the Right Way; Then Push Onward" [1890]. Advertising circulars, True & Co., E. C. Allen business records, Baker Library, Harvard Business School, Cambridge, Massachusetts.

Romance aside, Allen's outfits were a tangible product, or rather several: product samples, preprinted forms, sales literature, and portfolios. The "magnificent outfit" advertised in 1882 included a set of True & Co.'s publications, twelve lithographs, subscription blanks, a certificate of authenticity, and directions for running the agency. The instructions Allen provided agents were primers on door-to-door sales: learn your prospects names; exude confidence; and so on. They also offered tips for making the most effective use of the outfit: carry the chromos flat in a portfolio rather than rolling them up over and over ("unless you wish to soon ruin them"); upon entering the home, blanket the floor with the images. As the new agents read on, they would have learned more about the terms of their employment. Subscriptions cost a dollar, seventy cents of which went to E. C. Allen & Co. and thirty cents of which went to the agent. Those terms improved as the agent enlisted more and more subscribers. Reading further along, the new agent would also have learned that those subscribers had no obligation to pay until their premiums were delivered. This may not have been problematic if not for the fact that Allen would not ship the chromos until he received payment in full. Agents, then, were expected to advance the money on behalf of their customers—an unlikely proposition given that many acquired the agency because they needed work. In short, the agents found themselves in a bind. Fortunately, Allen had just the solution: additional sets of the lithographs could be purchased by agents ahead of time at seventy cents per set. That way the agents could collect payment at the time of the sale and then pocket the dollar, the surplus thirty cents belonging to them. In effect, then, Allen's subscription agents were door-to-door lithograph salespersons.[27]

The Name Game

The purpose of the millions of magazines that left Augusta each month was to find that handful of individuals who would take the bait and scrape together what they could for bulk lots of chromos. Or better yet, to locate the even smaller number of people who might purchase an agency for Chabanneau jewelry, and with it the $42 sample set and carrying case.[28] The publications were a pretext for recruiting new agents. Within the scheme, Allen's current agents pulled double duty. First of all, they found new subscribers, a handful of whom might sign on as agents. But just as important, they continuously furnished the names and addresses populating the subscription lists that qualified Allen for second-class postal privileges, thereby permitting him to send sample copies to nonsubscribers, who in turn might yield additional sales agents.

The surest way to do so was to tap into a nascent economy of names. Along with the consumer credit bureaus and life insurance agencies of the late nineteenth-century, magazine publishers were the largest and most sophisticated compilers of personal data in the United States. The reasons were both obvious and not. At the most basic level, they did business at a distance and needed to know where to send their products. But also, publishers came to see the names and addresses they collected as assets with value independent of their original usage. Letters from prospective customers, generated from circular mailings or advertising placed in local newspapers and national periodicals, were the raw ingredients that made up the lists that mail-order houses used for mass solicitations. Once a letter of inquiry was received by an advertiser, it was fed into an intra-industry circuit in which it passed from one mail-order marketer to another. Standard practice was to ship bundles of letters, sometimes numbering in the tens of thousands, to one another. Upon their arrival, they were copied by a clerk and then returned. If purchased instead of rented, they were stored and perhaps sold to another house.

The discovery of such a circuit was something of a revelation to those new to the industry. In his 1902 memoir recounting twenty-five years in the mail-order trade, James Lee recalled that in his early days, burdened by a mounting cache of letters and unable to sell them for junk, he was on the verge of burning them all. As luck would have it, though, a letter from L. A. Kendall, a Boston broker who was looking for agents, arrived just in time. "Eventually I got over $50 cash for this lot of letters," Lee explained, "and I suppose since then I must have received several thousand dollars for old letters, as I certainly have received over a million letters and post cards and I have always found ready buyers at fair prices for them."[29] This trade in letters was essentially the connective tissue linking hundreds of mail-based merchants of various stripes—some large, some small, some legitimate, some illegitimate—into a national industry.

Allen had a voracious appetite for names and addresses, purchasing hundreds of thousands of letters from other mail-order concerns, some of whom he inked multiyear contracts with. The most direct tactic was to simply respond to their advertisements, querying whether the company would be willing to sell the names of those who responded. Not uncommonly, these firms, ostensibly his competitors, were perfectly willing to do so. To take one example, Allen contacted the Home Manufacturing Company (HMC) in late 1885 in response to that company's call for women interested in homework. A few weeks later, HMC responded, stating that it had received 20,000 inquiries, available for $3 per thousand letters provided Allen returned them in fifteen days. In early December, Allen bought another batch of 20,000 names and attempted to work out a long-term arrangement in which HMC would supply fresh inquiries on the tenth of each month. Having found a good source, Allen repeatedly contacted the company for additional lots over the months to follow.[30] In a similar manner, Allen quickly came to an arrangement with the Chicago Specialty Company to acquire its inquiries for "Lady Agents" at the much steeper price of $10 per thousand.[31] Indicating that others in the field employed the same practices, some houses declined Allen's offers only because they had already signed long-term contracts with other letter buyers.[32]

Of course, not all respondents were interested in selling their letters. Some simply ignored Allen's requests. New York's Barnum & Co, which had placed an ad for "Farmers' Sons or others, owning Horse and Buggy, and commanding $100 to $200," ignored four inquiries from Allen between November 1885 and May 1886.[33] Others were put off by Allen's blanket refusal to swap names himself.[34] In still other cases, previous dealings with Allen left a bad taste in their mouths. The bookseller B. F. Johnson of Richmond, Virginia, for one, was still unhappy with the shoddy merchandise he purchased from Allen a decade earlier. "Now of course," Johnson's representative wrote, "we do not care to give you an opportunity to treat others as you served him."[35]

More often than principle, though, merchants tended to cite proprietary motives when they declined Allen's offers. "We know that everyone is interested in our particular class of goods," replied an Erie, Pennsylvania, dealer in washing machines, ". . . and a good agent would bring us more money than we could get for a copy of our letters." Similarly, New York's S. H. Moore & Co. declined Allen's offer, stating that "our agents' names we regard as a prime stock."[36] Others were particularly interested in preserving the freshness of their inquiries for their own promotions. A. B. Gehman of Chicago, for instance, was not averse to selling his names, but he planned to "circularize them" on an upcoming book "before disposing."[37]

As Gehman's response suggests, the value attached to a name fluctuated depending on a range of variables. Like any other commodity broker,

mail-order merchants developed a classificatory schema for grading and assigning value to letters that were otherwise uniform. For direct marketers,
the most important variant was freshness, meaning how active an inquirer's
desire to purchase was, coupled with the likelihood that others had already
sapped those desires. Not uncommonly, Allen negotiated multiple rates for
large batches of letters, and differentials in price were generally pegged to
the date received. After paying a visit to the New York offices of Gay & Co.—
another mass purchaser of letters—Allen reached an agreement to pay $5
per thousand for letters that were up to two years old and $10 per thousand
for newly received letters. Unsure of the value of its names, Taylor Bros. &
Co., a Cleveland merchant dealing in rubber stamps, shipped them to Allen
in 1886 and simply asked for a fair price. After sorting the nine thousand
inquiries by date, Allen offered $2 per thousand for letters dated 1883 and
1884, $3 per thousand for 1885 letters, $4 for undated letters, and $5 for those
sent since the first of the year.[38] Those eager to do business with Allen thus
emphasized the freshness of their letters. W. C. Rogers, a Boston letter broker, badgered Allen throughout the spring of 1889 about buying a batch of
U.S. Medicine Co. letters he had gotten his hands on. "Now at 30M entered
on the 2 books & all received since Jan. 1 1889," he assured Allen, "so they are
fresh enough."[39]

In addition to freshness, characteristics such as gender and class were
incorporated into the letter brokers' calculus. Generally, men's names
fetched more than women's names. Industrial Art Exchange, for instance,
was informed that "your names being entirely, or almost entirely ladies are
not so valuable to us as such are largely from men." Given the number of
feminine names filling Allen's account ledgers, this may have reflected a
readier supply of women's names in the letter trade. Alternatively, the dis-
parity may have reflected gendered conceptions of women's fitness for canvassing work.[40] Class, faintly visible in the goods a respondent inquired into,
also influenced price. According to Allen's calculus, religious goods roughly
equated to middle-class respectability, which in turn justified a higher rate
per letter. As a whole, Allen appeared especially eager to gather names from
religious publishing houses.[41]

Above all other personal characteristics, though, Allen and his ilk prized
sales-mindedness. A track record of shopping for items through the mail
was not enough to warrant premium prices. Rather, a prospect needed a
demonstrated interest in purchasing items wholesale. Thus when C. J. Dem-
mer, a New Haven bookseller Allen contacted about agents, proposed to sell

him the orders received by a local rifle manufacturer instead, Allen unequivocally declined the offer. "It is our purpose to secure canvassers," Allen explained. On the other hand, those brokers who could supply a steady stream of agents' names were paid handsomely. Jay Bronson of Detroit, for instance, was offered the princely sum of $1,500 for 100,000 names, provided they were prospective agents only. Similarly, Allen was willing to pay $8 per thousand for names gathered by J. Hampton Johnston, the Pittsburgh operator of the Swedish Insect Powder Company and Hewett Manufacturing Company, among other businesses. Again, though, Allen specified that the names must be "in answer to your wanted advts or similar advts which offer inducements for money making."[42]

This characteristic, which, most charitably, might be called the entrepreneurial spirit, or less charitably, an inclination toward turning a quick buck, placed these respondents in a distinct class. However one defined it, merchants like Allen were not alone in prizing such instincts. Perpetrators of mail-order scams were also keenly interested in identifying those with a vulnerability to "inducements for money making." Indeed, swindlers operated something of an alternative mail-order trade that in many ways exploited the same aspirations and desires as agency outfitters like Allen.

The most infamous of these cons was the "green goods" scam, a scheme that revolved around mail-based offers to buy into surefire counterfeiting schemes. Marks who bit on the initial offer were gradually enticed to New York or other big cities, where they were promptly relieved of the buy-in cash they brought with them. Like the market for agents' names, there was a brisk trade in the names of marks.[43] Counterfeit schemes clearly crossed the boundary into illicit behavior. Yet they shared fundamental features in common with more legitimate, if also clandestine, enterprises like the letter trade in that both capitalized on the intoxicating appeals of easy money. At the heart of both was a recognition that the value of information lay in the access it granted to certain types of people. If and when a relationship was established, those individuals could then be incorporated into systems designed to carefully extract payment from them. Sometimes that system was the faux theater of the con, in which a set-piece narrative was put in motion; other times, that system was a standardized set of boilerplate mailings and wholesale goods. Either way, the goal was to dispel the clouds of skepticism, or outright suspicion, that might lead the mark or prospect to think twice.

The parallels did not stop there, however, considering that the networked nature of the letter trade rendered the line between the legitimate and the

illicit blurry at best. As such, legitimate operators found themselves trans-
acting with less scrupulous entrepreneurs and, as a result, handling letters
initially secured under questionable circumstances. Allen's relationship
with the Standard Silver Ware Company of Boston provides one such
example. After reaching an agreement on a price of $5 per 1,000 letters, Stan-
dard Silver Ware shipped Allen at least 43,000 letters between November 1885
and January 1886. After that point, Allen and Standard continued doing
business, but the relations soured once Standard expressed dissatisfaction
with the previously agreed upon rate, eventually demanding as much as $50
per thousand. This opportunistic move was perhaps in keeping with Standard proprietor Edgar W. Jones's established practice.[44] First appearing in
R. G. Dun's credit reporting volumes in 1880, Jones at that time operated
under the moniker Wildes & Co. and several other trade names, "all of
which," noted Dun's correspondent, "are said to [be] fraudulent and numerous complaints are heard of victims." Well known to authorities, Jones
had once already been arrested on obscenity charges, resulting in the seizure of his mail. After a quick name change, Jones was again arrested. In
1882, he resurfaced under the name G. W. Ingraham & Co., obscuring his
own poor reputation behind that of his bookkeeper. Under that guise,
Jones published the *Boston Gazette*, which itself was a shell for promoting
"whatever novelties he has for sale & these are continually changing," as
Dun's respondent put it. Investigated once again by postal authorities,
Jones "escaped blacklisting" only to be convicted of illegal use of the mails
in early 1884.[45]

For swindlers like Jones, the boxes of letters Allen inquired into were no
different from the notions and jewelry his customers ordered. Both provided a pretext for sly dealing. But why the letters themselves and not lists?
After all, a list, which could be placed in an envelope and mailed for just a
few cents, presented a number of advantages. For one, it was far cheaper.
And two, it would have been easier to handle for the recipient. Rather than
sorting through thousands of letters and straining to read thousands of different hands, an office worker could have simply transcribed a neatly presented list that had been written in the clear, uniform penmanship of a clerk
like him- or herself, or better yet, typed. This would have been a faster, more
labor efficient method. Indeed, exchanging lists would have been the *systematic* thing to do. Yet major mail-order houses turned down lists when
offered, insisting on the physical letters instead. When offered a list of 10,000
recent letter writers, alphabetized, and carefully assembled to exclude those

"of little account" by Eugene Pearl, a New York mail-order house, Allen turned them down. "The list of names we do not wish." Even as late as 1900, mail-order publisher Samuel Sawyer, himself well versed in modern organizational methods such as index files, advised new entrants to the mail-order field to insist on letters rather than lists.[46] Why the aversion to lists? The short answer is that in an industry so chock-full of mistrust lists simply could not instill adequate confidence. Letters were verifiable in a way that lists were not. One could see the individual behind the inquiry through the personal imprint of handwriting. Moreover, the dates written on a letter provided evidence of an inquiry's freshness. In some cases, Allen went so far as to ask for envelopes as well, which presumably, bearing a canceled stamp, added an additional layer of security.[47]

Successful businessmen like E. C. Allen likely cringed when thrown into the same category as habitual offenders like Jones. Yet large firms like Allen's were complicit in that they were perfectly willing to handle the letters yielded by such schemes and in so doing created a market and reward structure for their less scrupulous peers. This brings into focus the dual nature of a mail-order industry that essentially sold two distinct products to two distinct markets. On the one hand, they were retailers who sourced goods from vendors and sold them to distant customers. On the other, they were information brokers who extracted data from consumers and sold it to other marketers. In conducting the first line of business, they created the product for the second. But whereas mail-order houses were obligated to pay the vendors who plied their wares, the customers who supplied their second line of merchandise—names and addresses—went uncompensated.

If value attached to personal information and characteristics, which it clearly did, was its appropriation from individuals without remuneration an act of theft? Not in the eyes of the law. Postal authorities and law enforcement might look askance at shady mail-order houses, but that owed to infractions in the first line of business, not the second. Yet at roughly the same time and in similar contexts, courts were ascribing property status to one's privacy and self-image. Individuals whose likenesses were used without authorization in advertisements, for instance, were newly recognized as having their rights violated on the grounds of property law. According to this logic, the use of one's name or likeness in a marketing campaign indicated that it had commercial value; in using that likeness without authorization, the advertiser had deprived its rightful owner—the individual—of her or his opportunity to capitalize on that property.[48]

For those whose names ended up on mailing lists, however, those hypo-thetical property rights were legally nonexistent. That does not mean, how-ever, that their names never took on the status of property. Indeed, names and personal data, such as a customer's purchasing history, were fully recog-nized as assets to which marketers had sovereignty in intra-industry dis-putes. When mail-order partnerships went bad, for instance, adjudicators recognized that mailing lists were among the most valuable assets—if not *the* most valuable asset—at stake. The list's status as property could also be seen in instances where mail-order merchants stole names from each other.[49]

The most direct example of this involved New York City publisher W. Jennings Demorest, owner of *Demorest's Monthly Magazine*. In 1888, De-morest brought suit against Gerrit S. and Frank M. Scofield, charging the two with having illegally obtained tens of thousands of names from his of-fice. The Scofields, neighbors of Demorest, sold sewing machines via mail order and had previously licensed rights to Demorest's name. Without Demor-est's knowledge, the Scofields contracted with a clerk in his employ, paying him $278 for more than 55,000 names. The presiding justice in the case, Charles H. Truax, appointed an investigator to whom the Scofields were ordered to re-turn the names. They ultimately produced only 811, claiming that Demor-est's names had become indistinguishable from those obtained elsewhere. In their defense, the Scofields pleaded ignorance as to the source of the names. An unconvinced Truax, however, laid down an injunction against their fur-ther use, as well as any inquiries that had resulted from earlier mailings. Further, he castigated the defendants for "having done as dishonest a thing as he ever knew a man to do, and in a manner which no honorable business-man would use."[50]

Later cases were met with even greater reprimand. In 1913, a pair of clerks, Robert Friendly and Charles Swett, were caught smuggling 25,000 names from the offices of their employer, the Chicago catalog house John Magnus & Co. Having set up a mail-order operation of their own in the backroom of a saloon, Friendly and Swett snuck the index cards out in lots of one thousand, carefully selecting customers who purchased often and paid quickly. "Only gilt-edged accounts were taken," the *Chicago Tribune* summarized in its report on the incident. With the names valued at $50,000 (equivalent today to roughly $1.3 million), Friendly and Swett were charged with conspiracy to commit larceny.[51] Such incidents occurred with enough frequency that one New York state assemblyman introduced legislation in

1905 to criminalize both the theft and receipt of "lists of customers or subscribers." As one supportive publishing manager put it, such measures would force buyers, surely aware they were "getting stolen property," to ask the all-important question: "where did you get these names."[52]

By framing name theft as something that happened to marketers rather than to consumers, such incidents helped shape an emergent logic of property rights in personal information that would largely go unchallenged until the 1960s. From this perspective, sovereignty over whatever value personal data might command on the market belonged to its compiler rather than its flesh and blood bearer. In essence, ownership rights in the facts of individual identity were born of paperwork, not biological processes. The marketers and publishers who captured that data might well choose to broker it to another firm. But when denied exclusive use without recompense, those compilers—in the eyes of the law—were illegitimately deprived of their property. In a post–Thirteenth Amendment United States, marketers could no longer hold property rights in human beings. They could, however, claim ownership in the capacities for value generation that attached to descriptions of them: name, address, sex, income level—what marketers today call data points.[53]

Conclusion

Returning to Augusta, we might say that Allen's world—marked by pinpoint marketing, an ethically ambiguous trade in personal information, and precarious employment schemes facilitated by new communication technologies—sounds a lot like ours. And it is true that publishers like E. C. Allen & Co. open a window on the long history of the truck and barter in consumer identities. Indeed, in the same postbellum decades when many marketers were learning to see the national populace as one great mass, others were learning to find individual women and men within it. In contrast to a later era of target marketing, it was not the affluent they were after, but the vulnerable. Part publisher, part direct-sales impresario, Allen and company saw opportunity in the uncertainties of Gilded Age life, laying the groundwork for later efforts at mass-marketing sales work to those with few other options. Locating such individuals required a veritable blizzard of paper—magazines, lithographs, letters, envelopes, sales kits, forms, bills, and so on. What it all amounted to was a system for finding people in distant communities, coaxing small payments from them, and enlisting those individuals in the larger project of finding others like them.

Along with the growing life insurance companies and consumer credit bureaus of the day, mail-order publishers like Allen were in the business of transforming paper and facts into new forms of commoditized identity. For insurers and creditors, personal information was less a commodity, in and of itself, however, than a vital input that shaped the crafting of the products made available for purchase. The insurance coverage one was offered and the terms of credit one could secure bore the imprint of one's personal biography, physiological characteristics, and demographic classifications. Making use of actuarial models and scoring systems, markers of individual identity enabled insurers and creditors to place consumers within larger populations of risk. Yet it was the policy or loan that was for sale, not the bits of personal information those businesses had so assiduously collected and stored away. In fact, when approached by buyers interested in purchasing consumer data, insurers and creditors consistently rebuked such offers deep into the twentieth century.[54]

In contrast, the network of mail-order merchants E. C. Allen dealt with harbored no such qualms. For them, the bits of personal data they harvested were objects of exchange. As a result, on any given day in the 1870s or 1880s, boxes and barrels of secondhand mail—bought and sold for access to the personal details it revealed—were routinely loaded onto mail cars or express wagons and hauled halfway across the continent. This willingness to not just hoard personal information but trade in it stemmed from a qualitatively different understanding of information's capacity to yield profits. If the credit bureaus and insurance agencies were animated by the burgeoning spirits of bureaucracy, Allen's mail-order industry operated more like a bazaar. As Clifford Geertz observed, the bazaar economy could best be understood as a kind of ongoing "information game." "Capital, skill, and industriousness play, along with luck and privilege, as important a role in the bazaar as they do in any economic system," Geertz explained. "But they do so less by increasing efficiency or improving products than by securing for their possessor an advantaged place in an enormously complicated, poorly articulated, and extremely noisy communication network."[55] Allen and his ilk were prodigious producers and voracious consumers of information. But unlike their more bureaucratized contemporaries, they were less concerned with ordering and analyzing information than with quickly deploying it for transactional advantage.

Allen's never-ending search for agents brings another issue to light: for several decades after the Civil War, the development of direct-sales networks and the production of mass culture were joint projects in places like Augusta. They related to each other in the same way that mass advertising related to mass publishing—as a source of revenue and a means of orienting readers toward a nascent consumer economy. Yet selling lithographs or costume jewelry door-to-door was a very different experience of consumer modernity than a trip to the department store. On a day-to-day level, the mail-order magazine model was geared more toward mass-producing marketers than mass-marketing goods. Its purpose was to locate individuals in communities across North America (and eventually beyond) and convince them that, whatever the outcome of their prior run-ins with it, the market could be made to serve their ends. Plausible or not, such appeals resonated with many Americans, who in the decades after the Civil War faced few alternatives.

CHAPTER 3

The Case of the Competing Pinkertons

Managing Reputation Through the Paperwork and Bureaucracy of Surveillance

JAMIE L. PIETRUSKA

In 1867, Pinkerton's National Detective Agency, with offices in Chicago, New York, and Philadelphia, published a slim volume titled *General Principles* that established management principles and operating rules for the agency that had been founded in 1850 to prevent and detect crime. *General Principles* asserted the existence of a new "modern Detective" and a "more scientific" form of crime.[1] Central to this modern detective work and scientific crime fighting were the paperwork and bureaucracy of surveillance. Few organizations or sectors of the economy in the late nineteenth- and early twentieth-century United States could boast of a broader commercial surveillance network than detective agencies. After the founding of Pinkerton's National Detective Agency, famously known as "The Eye That Never Sleeps," the industry exploded, with hundreds of private detective agencies operating by the turn of the twentieth century.[2] Increasing competition forced agencies to explicitly manage professional reputation, which the Pinkertons did in part by conducting surveillance of other agencies. This essay demonstrates how the paperwork and bureaucracy of surveillance constructed information systems, managerial order, and the "control through communication" identified by JoAnne Yates in her pathbreaking study of American management, yet could also destabilize the professional reputation and bureaucratic rationality of American detective agencies in the late nineteenth and early twentieth centuries.[3]

This essay focuses on an early twentieth-century legal battle between Pinkerton's National Detective Agency and its lesser known competitor, Pinkerton's United States Detective Agency, over the latter's use of the Pinkerton name and reputation. Genres of detective paperwork were at the center of this case, as both Pinkerton agencies turned their methods of surveillance on each other in their attempts to claim their legal right to the Pinkerton name and its authority. As the original Pinkertons pursued their imitators in the courts and across the country, they each relied on far-reaching networks of surveillance and material documentary practices through which the bureaucratic authority and professional reputation of both agencies were constructed. However, the power of Pinkerton surveillance had its limits, as these networks of commercial surveillance also revealed the contingency and fragility of that authority and reputation. Ultimately, the competing Pinkerton's United States Detective Agency reinvented itself as a collection agency—engaging in another form of commercial surveillance—in an attempt to escape the original Pinkertons and legal punishment.

Detective work has long been a familiar feature of American capitalism and culture, made famous by the literary escapes of detective novels and the recurring role of the Pinkertons in violently suppressing labor uprisings in the Gilded Age. Shifting away from the figure of the detective as dime novel hero or capital's mercenary, this essay examines detective work through the lens of the mundane and routinized but nevertheless consequential technologies of paperwork and bureaucracy in the first professional detective agency in the United States. Following scholarship in the history of capitalism, history of science, and media studies that considers the genre of paperwork itself as a form of knowledge production, this essay focuses on the quotidian material practices of detective agencies, taking as its point of departure Lisa Gitelman's formulation of "documents [as] epistemic objects" that are not merely used by bureaucracies but rather constitute them.[4] This essay examines how detective agency paperwork actively produced knowledge (rather than simply recording it), and how (and how well) it constructed bureaucratic rationality and professional identity, reputation, and authority. In so doing, it de-emphasizes the agency of individual detectives, focusing instead on bureaucratic practices and the detective paperwork that circulated as "paper technologies of capitalism."[5] Detectives and their agencies are best understood as actants linked to myriad others in a network that included wanted posters, application forms, business cards, operatives' reports, detective agencies' training manuals and newsletters, tin badges, railroad companies, newspapers, courts, and injunctions.[6] An actor-network framework reveals the processes of "extracting, organizing, stabilizing, interpreting and circulating information" that Kenneth Lipartito has identified as the constituent elements of surveillance—and how such commercial surveillance networks were constituted and contested.[7] It is important to note that the seemingly banal paperwork and bureaucracy of surveillance simultaneously obscured and undergirded the nonstate violence associated with the Pinkertons and Gilded Age capitalism more broadly. The Pinkertons who wielded paper technologies instead of pistols—typing correspondence, mailing reports, and organizing files—were in that respect typical corporate employees, thereby legitimizing Pinkerton business practices. Yet the same business practices also supported the anti-union violence unleashed by Pinkerton men by, for example, coordinating attacks on strikes, relaying intelligence gathered by labor spies, and accounting for revenues and expenditures—all of which involved different genres of detective paperwork.

Genres of Detective Paperwork

The organizational structure of Pinkerton's National Detective Agency and other large detective agencies in the late nineteenth and early twentieth centuries was in many respects identical to the bureaucratized corporate form. As Frank Morn's classic study of the Pinkertons observed, "At mid- and upper-management levels, . . . Pinkerton's became a carbon copy of their clients, the business community."[8] Each Pinkerton office had four departments—clerical, criminal, operating, and executive—with the clerical and criminal departments characterized by the routinized practices and paperwork of a Weberian "bureaucratic enterprise."[9] Clerical department personnel included a custodian, an "office boy," a cashier, a bookkeeper, stenographers, a chief clerk, and the office superintendent. The criminal department relied on bureaucratic technologies to classify and organize the paperwork of detection: the "Rogues' Gallery" and a card index file with typed entries for employees, suspected criminals, and gangs.[10]

Different genres of detective paperwork were essential to the business of investigation, from code books and training manuals to case notebooks and wanted posters. The secret operative's daily report, which John Walton has recently termed "a palimpsest through which several layers of action are discernable," not only relayed details of union activity in a railroad town or a mining camp, but also facilitated agency control of far-flung and otherwise unsupervised operatives.[11] A summary of the operative's weekly reports, which a former Pinkerton operative described as "often a choice bit of realistic art," was sent to the client in order to provide, for example, a list of suspected labor organizers and suggestions for suppressing unionism.[12] In addition to the Pinkerton operatives' weekly summary report was the "General Business Letter," a sixty-page, single-spaced report compiled every two weeks to provide a summary of all operatives' canvassing and a financial accounting of agency activities, which was incorporated into a division business letter and sent to the general manager and his staff of assistants, who devoted much of their time to "the reading of the voluminous general business letters."[13] The operative's daily reports, which were summarized, aggregated, and often embellished in these other reports, constituted managerial order as an instrument of surveillance—by and of the operative. These lengthy reports also constructed professional authority and reputation in the hands of agency superintendents and clients themselves. However, as a case from the Pinkerton archives reveals, as detective paperwork circulated through the marketplace, it could also undermine managerial order and bureaucratic rationality.

"Two Kinds of Pinkertons"

The paperwork and bureaucracy of surveillance were at the center of an early twentieth-century legal battle between Pinkerton's National Detective Agency and the unrelated Pinkerton's United States Detective Agency, a Milwaukee competitor that claimed to be "without question the largest Private Detective Agency in the West."[14] The identity of the person running the Milwaukee agency was a mystery to the sons of agency founder Allan Pinkerton, Robert and William. They initially assumed it was Matthew Worth Pinkerton, born in 1852 and raised in Wooster, Ohio, where he worked as a machinist and foundry and mill superintendent before coming to Chicago in 1877 to work as a collector in the Pinkerton Protective Patrol (or Night Watch Department).[15] But, as William Pinkerton later lamented, Matt repeatedly made "false statements" claiming to be a Pinkerton relative, and, after Matt's "irregular" accounts were brought to light, he was fired in the early

1880s.[16] William Pinkerton later denounced Matt as a "blackmailer" and "a fakir and a crook" who had been engaged in "dirty work . . . throughout the country."[17] After leaving Pinkerton's National Detective Agency, Matt opened the agency Pinkerton & Coe in July 1883 with Fred Coe, another former Pinkerton employee. When Coe retired from the agency within a year, it was conveniently renamed Pinkerton & Co.'s United States Detective Agency.[18] As an 1886 history of Chicago remarked admiringly of Matt Pinkerton, "Possessing the name of Pinkerton, he embodies all the import of a name which is a cause of terror to evildoers everywhere."[19]

Yet the United States Detective Agency's letterhead revealed that the Pinkerton of the competing agency in the early twentieth century was not Matthew W. but rather David W., who was born in Scotland in 1881, migrated to Canada in 1902, and subsequently began working for the International Detective Agency of Milwaukee. After that agency hired David Pinkerton—on the conditions that he allow his last name to be used and pay $1,000 for a share in the agency—it was incorporated in June 1904 as Pinkerton's United States Detective Agency.[20] At first William and Robert Pinkerton dismissed D. W. as "a fake" and "a myth," and William insisted, "Pinkerton's U.S. Detective Agency never did exist."[21] But D. W. Pinkerton and his U.S. Detective Agency did indeed exist, with D. W.'s business card claiming sole authority of the Pinkerton name: "Don't Wait for Detectives from Other Sources."[22] Nonetheless, Robert and William Pinkerton spent a good deal of time in the early twentieth century trying to determine who was the real Pinkerton impostor, Matt or the mysterious D. W.

Despite this confusion over the agency's origins, Pinkerton's United States Detective Agency was highly visible in the early twentieth century, advertising in about twenty different cities across the country, including Kansas City, Brooklyn, Toledo, Salt Lake City, Cincinnati, Philadelphia, Denver, St. Louis, and Chicago, as well as in Montreal.[23] Alongside its newspaper advertisements, Pinkerton's United States Detective Agency produced paperwork that performed different functions as it circulated through the economy: it promoted the agency and its reputation, solicited prospective applicants, and was ultimately collected by Pinkerton's National Detective Agency as legal evidence of fraud. Applicants to Pinkerton's United States Detective Agency completed a membership form by indicating their age, weight, height, eye color, hair color, marital status, nationality, current occupation, and relevant experience.[24] The question about nationality was but one indicator of the racial exclusion at the core of the private detective industry, as Black detectives represented the tiniest fraction of the rapidly expanding ranks of the profession.[25] Applicants could also fill out a form to enroll in Pinkerton's United States Detective Training School, which offered correspondence courses on topics including shadowing, department store and hotel detective work, and commercial, criminal, and civil law. These forms not only functioned as a bureaucratic mechanism within the agency for identifying and classifying potential operatives but also constituted the agency's public legitimacy and professional reputation.[26]

Prospective applicants to Pinkerton's United States Detective Agency could consult official publications that, similar to those of the original Pinkertons, explained the agency's scope and structure and whether an aspiring operative would be suited for the organization. For example, a pamphlet entitled *Brief Explanatory Notes to Prospective Operatives*, similar in form and content to the original Pinkertons' *General Principles*, included a section on "Objects of the System" that defined the agency's broad purview as "all classes of civil, criminal and commercial work, embracing forgeries, embezzlement, blackmailing schemes, threatening and anonymous letters, robberies, safe-blowing, horse-stealing, rape, murder, to ascertain the habits of employees and their associates, the authenticity of wills and deeds, tracing heirs and establishing their connection or identity."[27] This catalog of criminal and commercial activity did not merely signal but actively constructed the organizational reach of Pinkerton's United States Detective Agency. At a time when a fledgling detective agency would have faced myriad competitors, enumerating its activities helped Pinkerton's United States Detective Agency establish the scope of its professional authority and bureaucratic power.[28] As Lisa Gitelman has observed, "bureaucracies don't so much employ documents as they are partly constructed by and out of them."[29] In this way, in describing "Objects of the System," the pamphlet was constituting the system itself.

Once prospective detectives filed their application and fee, they received, in addition to a six-pointed nickel-plated badge emblazoned with "United States Detective Agency," a set of documents conferring professional authority and reputation upon them, including a membership certificate, a traveling card, and an identification card with "the official seal of the Agency." As the *Brief Explanatory Notes* explained to a new operative, the card would "entitle him to the trust and confidence of all good citizens, and . . . insure to him all the privileges usually accorded the profession."[30] New operatives also received an instruction book entitled the *Detective*

Adviser and the official agency newspaper, the *International Detective Review*, which advertised the agency's correspondence courses.[31] These advertisements in particular drew the ire of Pinkerton's National Detective Agency, which faulted its competitor for "advertising promiscuously, and undoubtedly misleading a great number of people."[32] As the six-pointed badges and paperwork legitimized Pinkerton's United States Detective Agency, they simultaneously destabilized the professional identity of the original Pinkertons.

Local police departments entered the Pinkerton versus Pinkerton battle, when, in response to public confusion, they issued statements distinguishing between the Pinkertons and the pretenders. Pinkerton's United States Detective Agency, headquartered in Milwaukee, drew the attention of the local police department, which issued a circular after receiving hundreds of letters from across the country inquiring about "the standing and reliability of various so-called 'Detective Agencies' located in Milwaukee." The police chief insisted that no "legitimate" detective agencies in Milwaukee would advertise for operatives and reminded the public that "no law exists in Wisconsin supervising or licensing the business of private detectives or detective agencies."[33]

The archival record contains an epistolary paper trail left by aspiring detectives—some unemployed, others seeking a new line of work—who claimed to have been defrauded by Pinkerton's United States Detective Agency.[34] A Syracuse man named John Winchell, upon discovering that he had paid three dollars but was not an official Pinkerton detective, wrote a letter explaining how he had replied to a newspaper advertisement and then received, along with his business cards and certificate of membership, assurance that he "had the power to arrest and carry guns . . . because I was a Pinkerton man." Suspicious, he went to the local police station and discovered the fraud, whereupon he wrote angrily to Robert Pinkerton, asking "if you permit people to [use] your name to defraud others. I think you ought to inforce the law to wipe them off the earth."[35] A Virginia applicant suffered worse consequences, as he described in a letter to Pinkerton's National Detective Agency that demanded to know, "Are you all the same detective agency?" He complained that he was "signed up by them as a Private Detective to do Detective Work anywhere in the US an[d] I was arrested on it and found it to be more of a fraud than anything else so I want pay for the trouble that I have gone through."[36] The many letters echoing these reflect the extent to which the paperwork of Pinkerton's United States Detective

Agency generated confusion and consternation over which Pinkertons were which.

After receiving many such letters, Pinkerton's National Detective Agency systematized the bureaucratic process and the paperwork for collecting reports of fraud. All Pinkerton offices were instructed to prepare a separate report for each victim that included the following: "Date and name of the newspaper victim read advertisement in," "date victim responded," "papers received by victim," "did victim forward money, if so, how much," "has he a . . . money order receipt, registered letter card, or express receipt," "what did he receive for his money," and "did victim believe that he was corresponding with us from the start."[37] Pinkerton operatives also answered advertisements for Pinkerton's United States Detective Agency; they were instructed to use their home address, their own handwriting, and different stationery, and they were required to keep copies of any correspondence they received from the other Pinkertons.[38]

This anti-fraud paperwork became the key to the Pinkertons' legal attack on their competitor. Indeed, Robert Pinkerton vowed to spare no expense in fighting Pinkerton's United States Detective Agency, which he deemed "a fraud pure and simple, on the public," a "get-rich-quick scheme," and a threat to the reputation his agency had built over fifty years.[39] The agency collected many pieces of evidence like John Winchell's letter and certificate of membership in Pinkerton's United States Detective Agency to present as evidence at a hearing with post office officials and the assistant attorney general in Washington, D.C., in July 1904.[40]

The legal consequences of the original Pinkertons' attempts to protect their name in 1904 were twofold. Postal inspectors, determining that the United States Detective Agency's promotional newsletter, the *International Detective Review*, should not have been mailed under second-class newspaper rates, issued a fraud order in June 1904 that returned a reported $3,000 to unsuspecting Pinkerton applicants. The following month, the U.S. District Court in Milwaukee issued a preliminary injunction preventing the United States Detective Agency from "using the name or word 'Pinkerton' or 'Pinkerton's,' or any variation thereof, in connection with the words 'United States Detective Agency,' or any of such words, in any publication or advertisement, or upon any letter head, sign or star, or in any manner tending to mislead the public to believe the defendant to be identified in any manner with the plaintiffs, or their established business known as 'Pinkerton's National Detective Agency.'"[41] The original Pinkertons charged that the Milwaukee Pinkertons were operating "a dishonest, unfair, and illegitimate business" that had already cost them $10,000 in business, and newspaper coverage described the injunction as "a big victory" after "a bitter fight in the courts."[42]

In late July 1904, Pinkerton's National Detective Agency published a circular, designated as "Form 154," to announce these developments, emphasizing that Pinkerton's United States Detective Agency had no official connection with theirs.[43] Thousands of copies were distributed to police departments, judges, and would-be Pinkertons across the country,[44] and many newspapers alerted the public to what one journalist termed "two kinds of Pinkertons."[45] Robert, William, and Allan Pinkerton hoped that this case would thwart Pinkerton's United States Detective Agency, along with any other "bogus detective companies who are not using our name but who are a disgrace to the detective business."[46]

Although Pinkerton's United States Detective Agency was headquartered in Milwaukee, the original Pinkertons imagined national and particularly rural implications of fraud. It would not be easy to determine which Pinkertons were which in areas out of the original Pinkertons' reach, as William Pinkerton acknowledged when he warned that the United States Detective Agency was purposely advertising in "country newspapers, as they do not think we will hear of them unless it is in some place where we have an office."[47] Pinkerton agent James McParland confirmed that United States Detective Agency advertisements "have been scattered through nearly every newspaper in the West."[48] Robert Pinkerton estimated the scope of the problem, writing to his brother William, "There is no question that probably over 1,000 of these badges have been sent out by this firm" and that "nine out of every ten who answer this advertisement, think they are writing to us."[49]

Robert Pinkerton's fears were confirmed by a July 1904 *Los Angeles Times* headline that announced, "Tin Stars Are Thick. Humbug Detectives Growing Too Numerous. Suckers Paying Out Coin for Worthless Toys. Police on the Track of the Pretenders." The article reported that "these near-Pinks come butting up into the real Pinkerton office and demand the use of the office."[50] In one instance, Elijah Carter of Louisiana wrote to Virginia's Baldwin Detective Agency to inform them of his surveillance of a "desperate man" who had somehow wrecked a passenger train and killed the engineer on the Norfolk and Western Railway. Carter claimed he was a Pinkerton operative and promised to deliver the suspect for six dollars per day plus expenses. The Baldwin Detective Agency notified Pinkerton's National

Detective Agency and the Norfolk and Western, who sent Carter a stern rebuke: "You have evidently been reading trashy novels and have the Detective Fever."[51] The proliferation of tin stars suggests that there were many Elijah Carters operating in a nation-spanning army of unofficial Pinkertons conducting unauthorized surveillance.

As Pinkerton's National Detective Agency would discover, shutting down the "near-Pinks" would not be so easy. Pinkerton's United States Detective Agency issued its own circular to explain the legal ramifications of the fraud order and injunction, noting that it had abandoned the name "Pinkerton." But the agency still claimed to be "in a measure the successors of 'Pinkerton's United States Detective Agency,' but as such assume no responsibility for their contracts, promises or agreements." Of course they were perfectly willing to reinstate former members and reissue identification cards and badges to anyone who filled out a new application and paid a two-dollar fee, warning, "Take advantage of this offer at once . . . the credentials you are now working under are unlawful, and if you continue to use them you will get into serious trouble, as their authority has been cancelled."[52] Ironically, the other Pinkertons profited from their own exposure as frauds.

"Put the Name Pinkerton . . . Entirely Out of Business"

In July 1904, a frustrated William Pinkerton acknowledged that he had his "hands full with these different Pinkertons."[53] Indeed, the proliferation of would-be Pinkertons posed an administrative problem, as Pinkerton "offices in eighteen different cities . . . were besieged with individuals who had answered the advertisements."[54] Spokesmen for Pinkerton's United States Detective Agency estimated that between 2,500 and 5,000 applicants had sent in their $3 application fee, but admitted that only four people were paid the promised rate of $4 per day for their work. The lawyer representing Pinkerton's United States Detective Agency justified such an imbalance between fees and wages when he "said that this concern was operating just the same as what a collection agency was; the idea was to have men appointed all over the United States so that if a man received some work to do in Oregon, which had to be performed in New York, the Oregon agent would write to his headquarters at Milwaukee, and the Milwaukee concern would give it to one of their New York agents."[55]

In this model of a decentralized network of collection agents, the other Pinkertons proliferated in a manner at once elusive and highly visible. After Pinkerton's United States Detective Agency moved out of its Milwaukee office (and William Pinkerton fumed that Matt, the *other* other Pinkerton, was publicly credited with shutting it down), it reappeared in different guises.[56] Upon learning of the brand-new Sullivan and Pinkerton International Detective Agency, a furious William instructed his lawyers, "We want the name Pinkerton obliterated. . . . We want you to put the name Pinkerton, as far as other detective agencies are concerned, entirely out of business."[57] Pinkerton's lawyers, citing the July 1904 preliminary injunction, filed a motion for contempt, but the judge held the motion in abeyance, deciding to give the defendants the chance to omit the offending "Pinkerton" name.[58] Of course, this seemed unlikely, since, as the attorney for Pinkerton's United States Detective Agency admitted, "Pinkerton's name was used to give the concern a high-sounding reputation."[59]

Surveillance of their competitors' paperwork became central to the original Pinkertons' strategy. The Milwaukee police chief had admitted in June 1904, "I do not see that anything can be done at this end to suppress these fakes except to keep watch for some circumstance upon which to base a charge of fraud," after which Pinkerton superintendents were instructed to "have a watch kept for the advertisements in newspapers relating to the International Detective Agency."[60] Pinkerton clerks nationwide collected newspaper clippings and advertisements revealing that Pinkerton's United States Detective Agency had reinvented itself under several different names— Pinkerton's International Detective Agency, Sullivan and Pinkerton International Detective Agency, and the Milwaukee Co-Operative Detective Service—all of which sought "Detectives—Every locality; profitable. Inexperienced Applicants trained."[61] These clippings reflect a typical turn-of-the-century gendering of classified advertisements. Since detective work was considered a masculine profession—with a few high-profile exceptions like Kate Warne, the first woman known to be employed as a private detective, and Cora Strayer, who ran a Chicago detective agency focused on women clients—the vast majority of newspaper advertisements did not specify gender or, like an ad in the *Syracuse Sunday Herald* for the International Detective Agency in Milwaukee, appeared in the "Help Wanted—Male" section.[62] In rare instances, women were mentioned in newspaper ads like the one for the National Protective Agency in St. Paul, Minnesota, that appeared in the *Philadelphia North American* in August 1904: "Detectives—Men

Everywhere; Also a few right women."[63] Pinkerton offices were instructed to watch newspapers for these "or any other suspicious advertisement, every day" and have clerks reply to them.[64]

No doubt to evade this surveillance, the other Pinkertons engaged in selective erasure of the Pinkerton name, but ironically, this strategy only drew more scrutiny. The other Pinkertons ran newspaper advertisements with and without the name "Pinkerton," as in the *Seattle Post-Intelligencer*, which featured identical copy for both Sullivan & Pinkerton's International Detective Agency and the International Detective Agency, both of Milwaukee: "Detectives—Every locality: profitable. Inexperienced Applicants trained."[65] The Chicago office of Pinkerton's National Detective Agency answered the International Detective Agency advertisement to see if the concern would use the Pinkerton name in its correspondence, but the other Pinkertons did not fall into the trap. A circular from Pinkerton & Sullivan deleted "D. W. Pinkerton, Manager" so that the letterhead read only "The International Detective Agency."[66] Replies to the International Detective Agency advertisement yielded correspondence in which, as manager Edward S. Gaylor observed, "the name of Pinkerton is left out in every particular. They are using their old letter heads, but are blotting out the name of Pinkerton as manager, and using only the name of Sullivan as General Superintendent."[67] Although the other Pinkertons resorted to these cross-outs to avoid charges of fraud (and likely the cost of reprinting letterhead), this strategic erasure was turned against them when Robert Pinkerton presented to the assistant U.S. attorney general in Washington, D.C., letters with the word "Pinkerton" crossed out in red as evidence of the agency's awareness of its wrongdoing.[68]

The original Pinkertons' attempts to create an archive of fraud highlight the tension between the ostensible permanence of paperwork and the ephemerality of the material culture of these "so-called Pinkerton Detective Agencies."[69] Pinkerton offices, following instructions from superintendents and managers, carefully watched the newspapers and collected many detective ads with no mention of the word "Pinkerton."[70] Upon discovering that the office in Spokane, Washington, had discarded circulars and correspondence from the International Detective Agency in Milwaukee that did not include the Pinkerton name, Allan Pinkerton was indignant: "I cannot see why they were destroyed and not sent to Chicago as they should have been. We surely have room enough and files enough to record such matters as this. If the circulars were worth writing, for they were worth filing. In future matters such as this must not be destroyed; it is a very careless way to do things."[71] Allan Pinkerton's insistence on the collection of all paperwork produced by competing Pinkertons, whether it actually contained the word "Pinkerton" or not, reflects a bureaucratic logic that aspired to comprehensive surveillance during a time when private detective agencies as well as Pinkerton imitators were proliferating.

Although the original Pinkertons' fraud archive contained many reports of aspiring operatives cheated by Pinkerton's United States Detective Agency, numerous stories also surfaced of the other Pinkertons exploiting their professional identity for power and profit. In St. Louis, they posed as official detectives at the 1904 World's Fair; a Pinkerton's United States Detective Agency operative collected $25 (nearly $700 today) from a Bostonian; and a man in Detroit opened his own branch of Pinkerton's United States Detective Agency.[72] One Pinkerton's United States Detective Agency operative reportedly showed his star and extorted money from sex workers in Los Angeles, and William Pinkerton confirmed that "in a number of cities men wearing their stars have attempted to blackmail people. Employees of our agency do not wear stars or badges."[73] William Pinkerton's agency was tracking the activities of Pinkerton competitors who were conducting their own surveillance in the name of extortion and blackmail, appropriating the Pinkerton name as well as the threat of violence it evoked.

In December 1904, six months after a permanent injunction had been issued in Wisconsin, Pinkerton's National Detective Agency had seemingly tracked down their adversary after receiving a tip that D. W. Pinkerton was operating Pinkerton's Union Detective Agency in Des Moines. The tipster, a former police chief who headed the American Detective Agency, noted that "they are using the Pinkerton name very strongly among the unsuspecting."[74] This was indeed the case, as their business card claimed to be the "only legitimate secret service for corporations, attorneys, steam, street and interurban railways, business firms and private individuals. All Service Under Personal Supervision of D. W. Pinkerton."[75] A Pinkerton's National Detective Agency lawyer advised that while such advertising did violate the injunction, D. W. Pinkerton could not be arrested on that charge outside Wisconsin state borders, so the Pinkertons should file a similar lawsuit in the United States District Court in Iowa.[76] Robert Pinkerton notified the assistant attorney general for the U.S. Post Office Department about the Iowa situation, and so began a game of cat and mouse in which the other Pinkertons stayed one step ahead of the original Pinkertons as they kept moving west. In the coming years, Pinkerton's United States Detective Agency and its principals would appear under different names in different places, from Detroit to Los Angeles as well as the South.

Not surprisingly, Pinkerton's National Detective Agency archives produce a narrative depicting the agency as both victim and moral victor. In the original Pinkertons' telling, their competitors were complete frauds, merely operating a scam in which they ran ads using the Pinkerton name and reputation to convince unwitting applicants to send in three dollars, which the agency kept without sending a detective badge or anything else in return. And, indeed, this did happen, according to the letters that Robert and William Pinkerton collected as evidence of mail fraud in 1904. But the tin stars that are sold online today by antique dealers and gun collectors confirm that the Pinkerton United States Detective Agency did in fact operate as a detective agency, if one more decentralized and short-lived than Pinkerton's National Detective Agency.

"Good Collectors of Bad Debts"

As D. W. Pinkerton tried to evade surveillance by the original Pinkertons, he reinvented his firm as a collection agency. In October 1904, the National Detective Service of Milwaukee alerted Pinkerton's National Detective Agency to an advertisement for "Good collectors of bad debts—try us. Pinkerton's Claim Adjustment Bureau, 50, 51, 52, 53 Exchange Building, Fifth and Grand Avenue. Tel. Main 2302. D. W. Pinkerton, manager." This address was identical to that in the advertisement for the United States Detective Agency (which did not include the Pinkerton name).[77] The same month, a Pinkerton superintendent in Buffalo discovered two newspaper ads for concerns based in Milwaukee, one proclaiming "DETECTIVES-EVERYWHERE; experience unnecessary; $5.00 per day earned. United States Detective Agency" and the other, "COLLECTORS, AT ONCE, EVERYWHERE; good pay. Pinkerton's Claim Adjustment Bureau."[78] Suspicious, Pinkerton general manager George D. Bangs had one of his managers apply to the collection agency to "develop what fraud there is in connection with it."[79] But in the subsequent correspondence, the agency apparently, and no doubt strategically, never mentioned Pinkerton's Claim Adjustment Bureau. Nonetheless, the original Pinkertons were convinced that the new collection agency was "a mere subterfuge," with Allan Pinkerton deeming "the correspondence sent out by the Company . . . most misleading and . . . just as much a fraud as the Pinkerton's U.S. Detective Agency."[80] According to Pinkerton attorneys in Milwaukee, this advertisement did not violate the injunction, but they promised to "try and keep watch of this matter and see if we can learn of anything that will enable us to properly claim a violation of the court's order."[81]

Their surveillance would take a long time to pay off, for several reasons. Pinkerton's United States Detective Agency shifted its focus to collections, a line of business the original Pinkertons were not in, and it took careful steps to avoid another legal battle and fraud order.[82] And, most important, there was not one but rather two Pinkerton collection agencies with the name "United States Detective Agency," one launched by D. W. Pinkerton after the 1904 injunction and the other by Matt Pinkerton a decade later.[83]

Pinkerton & Company United States Detective Agency touted its new commercial department as part of the agency's "scientific detective work among modern lines" while simultaneously trading on yet distancing itself from the reputation of Pinkerton's National Detective Agency, just as D. W. Pinkerton had previously done (Figure 3.1). Matt Pinkerton based his agency's reputation on the ostensible uniqueness of its collections department and its distinction from the more famous Pinkertons. An advertisement in the *Los Angeles Herald* in June 1912 declared that the agency "has never been in any way connected with the Pinkerton National Detective Agency. We operate all over the civilized world and also are the only detective agency to operate a commercial department."[84] But such disclaimers could not keep the original Pinkertons at bay.

I have pieced together the story of the Matt Pinkerton collection agency from trade journals and newspaper sources from the 1910s, which tell a story not of what one Pinkerton manager had deemed "the rankest kind of a swindle" in the case of the D. W. Pinkerton collection agency but rather of a flexible competitor adapting to legal constraints and new business opportunities.[85] In 1914, Montana representatives of Pinkerton & Co.'s United States Detective Agency denounced the original Pinkertons for using "unfair and disreputable tactics," namely, having sent a circular warning of a rival agency using their name—as they had commonly done a decade earlier—to the Missoula Chamber of Commerce. A Pinkerton & Co.'s United States Detective Agency representative named Gilkey emphasized that the agency's circulars plainly denied any affiliation with Pinkerton's National Detective Agency, insisting, "We not only do not misrepresent ourselves, but take

PINKERTON & COMPANY

UNITED STATES
DETECTIVE AGENCY

Chicago, Ill., -   -   Ever Since 1883

N͞O connection with or relation to the Pinkerton National Detective Agency. Scientific detective work along modern lines.

Our Commercial Department

finds the criminal intent in criminal accounts and reduces it to a practical basis. A criminal account is one that can pay but won't. When the criminal feature is exposed it wants to pay.

Figure 3.1. This advertisement for the Pinkerton & Company United States Detective Agency's new commercial department distanced itself from—but also traded on—the Pinkerton reputation. *United States Investor*, October 24, 1914, p. 113. Google Books, https://books.google.com/books?id=NJotAQAAMAAJ.

particular pains to get squarely before the public prior to attempting to do business." Gilkey cited "hundreds of testimonials from satisfied clients in all parts of the United States and Canada," including one from the *National Banker* in Chicago, which reported, "they are thoroughly reliable and responsible regardless of what Pinkerton's National Detective agency says about them."[86]

These testimonials signaled the second Pinkerton collection agency's business acumen as well as the size of its enterprise. The *Bulletin of the Commercial Law League of America* reported that the scale of the agency's collection business was considerable, with over one million dollars in accounts. With offices in California, Nevada, Oregon, Washington, and reportedly "almost every state in the Union,"[87] the agency entered into contracts to collect overdue accounts, promising "to collect four times the amount of retainer fees." As the *Bulletin of the Commercial Law League* noted, "A majority of the claims upon which the company contracted to collect were old accounts and in some instances were 'loan shark,' easy payment furniture claims and old liquor accounts."[88] An article in *Rand McNally Bankers' Monthly* lauded "the detective's place in business" and explained "how Matt W. Pinkerton has applied scientific detective work to an acute business problem." The article went on to note, "No one is surprised that this novel idea should emanate from Pinkerton & Co. United States Detective Agency, for it is in keeping with their usual alertness; nor is anyone surprised at the amazing success the agency has had in reducing this novel idea to a practical basis, for everybody knows that they get what they go after, and that this reputation can only be attained by born detectives."[89] Such success depended in no small part on paperwork: the Pinkerton collection agency sent letters on Pinkerton & Co. detective agency letterhead to remind a debtor that they owed money and warn that an investigation would be opened if they did not pay.[90] Presumably the Pinkerton letterhead was also vaguely threatening to recipients who recalled the brutality of late nineteenth-century Pinkerton strikebreakers that culminated at Homestead Steel Works, near Pittsburgh, in 1892.[91] In this way, detective paperwork, surveillance, and violence remained entangled into the twentieth century.

And so another round of Pinkerton versus Pinkerton commenced about a decade after the first legal battle. In August 1913, Pinkerton's National Detective Agency issued a circular titled "WARNING" that declared, "We have no connection whatever with Pinkerton & Company, and we do not conduct a Commercial Department or Collection Agency" and denounced the "other parties . . . endeavoring to secure business on the strength of our name and reputation."[92] The accused fired back in an unsuccessful December 1913 lawsuit alleging "business libel" and asking for $150,000 in damages, and the legal tide turned further against them when the postmaster general issued another fraud order in March 1915.[93] The fraud order was reported in major newspapers and in commercial trade journals for retailers and lenders, with the *Retail Grocers' Advocate* pronouncing Pinkerton & Co.'s United States Detective Agency a "fake detective firm" and a "so-called Pinkerton detective agency."[94] And ironically, Pinkerton's National Detective Agency, which had issued "hundreds of thousands of circulars and notices in the public press" over the previous three years to disavow any association with the Pinkerton collection agency, issued a circular to explain that the fraud order they had sought did not apply to them and that they had never been engaged in the collection business.[95]

The question of whether an "imitation Pinkerton agency" was illegal was raised in the courts once again in late 1916 and early 1917.[96] The J. W. Hoodwin Company had sued Matt Pinkerton, his wife Ann Emma, his son Ralph, and general manager J. W. Rankin to recover the fifty dollars the company had paid to an agent of the U.S. Detective Agency who claimed that the two Pinkerton agencies were in fact the same one. The Municipal Court of Chicago initially found that the Hoodwin Company had indeed been hoodwinked by Matt Pinkerton's agency, but in March 1917 the Chicago First District Appellate Court ruled in favor of Matt Pinkerton's wife and son (Matt had died in January 1916) and the general manager. The appellate court cited the lack of sufficient evidence "to show that certain defendants, appellants, were connected in any way, as partners or otherwise, with a certain detective agency."[97] With this ruling, Pinkerton & Co.'s United States Detective Agency had finally established its legal legitimacy and, at least in this particular case, escaped charges of fraud. In the end, it was Matt Pinkerton's death, not Pinkerton's National Detective Agency, that put Pinkerton & Co.'s United States Detective Agency out of business for good.

The case of the two—and ultimately, three—Pinkerton agencies was in some respects not unusual in the context of intensified campaigns against commercial fraud in the late nineteenth-and early twentieth-century United States.[98] But this case is different in its emphasis on the multiple and shifting registers on which paperwork functioned as both an instrument and a product of commercial surveillance. Detectives' identification cards, for example, constructed professional authority and reputation. But paperwork, like membership applications, that circulated through the marketplace also created new opportunities for fraud, which in turn generated new standardized methods for collecting and classifying evidence thereof, like the Pinkerton National Detective Agency's Form 154. In this case, the locus of fraud was not in a material object akin to a commodity such as sugar or patent medicine, nor was it simply a fraudulent advertising campaign. Fraud in the case of the two Pinkerton agencies emerged from the circulation and contestation of different genres of paperwork during a time when Pinkerton's National Detective Agency had not yet trademarked its famous logo, which did not happen until the 1950s.

Emphasis on the paperwork and bureaucracy of surveillance should not efface the murderous anti-labor violence that was synonymous with the Pinkerton name in the late nineteenth century. Rather, it broadens this traditional interpretation to include not only Pinkerton operatives but also the managers and clerks who performed the paperwork that managed professional reputation, constituted a corporate organization and culture, and created a bureaucratic infrastructure for state-sanctioned violence. The case of the competing Pinkertons was solved not by detectives brandishing pistols but with the materials and practices of commercial surveillance.

CHAPTER 4

_____

Mystery Shoppers and Self-Monitors

Managing Emotional Labor to Improve the Corporate Image

DANIEL ROBERT

In February 1908, just days before William G. McAdoo opened the first sub-way line connecting New Jersey to Manhattan, he gathered his employees together to explain to them exactly how his new line would operate. "Safety and efficiency of the service are, of course, the first consideration," McAdoo told his workers, "but, among the things of the highest importance are civility and courtesy in your dealings with the public." Employees would undoubt-edly encounter "rude and offensive" passengers, McAdoo admitted, "but . . . you must learn to take such things in good temper; it is a part of your job."[1]

McAdoo's new courtesy policy had nothing to do with beating the com-petition. He had none. His line possessed a monopoly on subway traffic be-tween Manhattan and New Jersey, slashed commute times compared to taking the ferry, and was undoubtedly going to see immense ridership. Yet McAdoo opened his line directly on the heels of the Panic of 1907 and just as progressive antimonopoly sentiment among New Yorkers was reaching a cre-scendo. The timing could not have been worse. On the New York side of Mc-Adoo's line, the Panic had exposed a massive stock watering scheme involving another New York streetcar line. Residents had also just elected Governor Charles Evans Hughes, who promptly legislated against monopoly utilities. On the New Jersey side of McAdoo's line, residents would soon elect Wood-row Wilson as governor, partly because Wilson promised to regulate com-muter trains, which he did. And all over the country, Americans were reading muckraker Lincoln Steffens who used streetcar companies as his primary example of how monopolies corrupted municipal government.[2]

In response to this political economic climate, McAdoo coined his famous phrase, "the public be pleased." The phrase was an obvious reference
to William H. Vanderbilt's infamous outburst of 1882, "the public be
damned." "The day of 'the public be damned' policy is forever gone," declared McAdoo in 1908. "It always was an objectionable and indefensible
policy, and it will not be tolerated on this road under any conditions."[3]

McAdoo's "public be pleased" policy had one major problem, however.
Neither McAdoo nor his managers could observe all their employees all the
time to ensure they were minding their manners. This lack of surveillance
was a problem recognized by executives to exist at all large corporations.
Unlike the owners of early nineteenth-century workshops who lived and
worked with their charges, managers of large firms could not directly oversee all of their employees. Discussions of this problem occupied a great deal
of the management literature of the early twentieth century, with some
managers advising being more "friendly," though not "chummy," toward
employees, while others recommended an open-door policy with respect to
the manager's office.[4]

McAdoo devised his own solution. He enlisted his customers into the
surveillance of their own corporate servants by posting signs throughout
his subway stations soliciting customer feedback. "One has only to report
the number on the cap of the offending employee to assure redress," Mc-
Adoo explained to an audience at Harvard Business School in 1910. McAdoo
and his managers might not be omnipresent, but passengers were, and now
passengers would help oversee employees—and without pay. McAdoo's employees now had supervisors at both ends of the corporate spectrum, from
managers above and customers below.[5]

McAdoo's strategies of courtesy and customer feedback had enormous
implications for the extent of surveillance at American corporations. Mc-
Adoo's "public be pleased" policy proved a huge success in undermining
antimonopoly sentiment toward his subway. The public, press, and politicians positively lauded McAdoo's efforts and contrasted his monopoly with
others that had not reformed themselves.[6] As a result, hundreds of executives,
not only in the streetcar industry but also in the electricity and telephone industries, adopted and refined McAdoo's ideas. Their logic was simple: Public
opinion now ruled the political economy of the United States. No franchise
permit, regulatory body, or rate hike could survive if it violated the court of
public opinion. "The world today is ruled by public opinion," declared AT&T
vice president Nathan Kingsbury in 1912. And since it was axiomatic among

executives that public opinion was simply the aggregate of individual customer opinions, executives set out to improve public opinion, one courteous
customer interaction at a time.[7]

I call this strategy "courteous capitalism" and it profoundly influenced
the managerial strategy of executives, the work experience of clerks, and the
antimonopoly sentiments of customers. Managers at utilities began compelling their clerks to exude "courtesy," "friendliness," and "sympathy" toward
customers. Executives wanted "obliging" clerks who "cheerfully" attended
to patrons. Supervisors instructed clerks to display "a smiling courteous demeanor," exhibit "a world of patience," and emit a "ray of sunshine during
the entire day." Only then would customers warm up to the corporate mo-
nopolization of crucial utility services.[8]

As the strategy of courteous capitalism matured, nearly everything
about clerks' job "performances" became subject to managerial prescrip-
tion, including clerks' phrases, gestures, eye contact, posture, voice inflection, clothing, even their combed hair, trimmed nails, and fresh breath. By
the late 1920s, public opinion had improved, but the cost to low-level employees was high. Their plastered smiles and scripted pleasantries represented a loss of emotional autonomy and a new level of managerial control.[9]

The use of employee emotions at monopolies bore similarities to what
sociologist Arlie Hochschild has called "emotional labor" in her insightful
study on the work of flight attendants in the 1970s. But courtesy at utility
monopolies was not simply commonsense business strategy to beat the
competition. Monopolies had no competition. Rather, courteous capitalism
was a political strategy, designed to fend off government ownership, rein in
regulation, and change public opinion regarding the structure of the market
itself.[10]

To obtain this courteous conduct, executives expanded their surveillance of both clerks and customers. Close managerial supervision, solicited
customer feedback, hired "mystery shoppers," and electronically listening
in on customer-service interactions enforced courteous behavior, all in an
effort to improve public opinion toward monopolies.

The advent of courteous capitalism, and its twin, surveillance, can therefore help answer an important question of American political economy:
why did antimonopoly sentiment in the 1920s decline? In the decades surrounding the turn of the twentieth century, urban Americans became
strongly critical of monopoly streetcar, electricity, and telephone monopolies that treated customers in a high-handed and contemptuous manner,

even while ultimately depending on voters for franchise permits and rate hikes. But on the eve of the stock market crash of 1929, thousands of street-car, electricity, and telephone monopolies existed, yet popular protest was muted. Courteous capitalism and surveillance partly explain this political economic change of heart. This essay will trace that surveillance as it grew to cover utility employees and customers—nearly every urban American—and analyze how this surveillance innovated methodologically and burrowed deeper into public and private spaces.

When utility executives first adopted McAdoo's "the public be pleased" strategy, they also began experimenting with additional surveillance methods besides customer feedback. Executives called their own companies and impersonated customers or sent people to district offices to see how face-to-face service appeared from the other side of the counter. In 1921, the vice president of public relations for the Southern California Edison Company, Samuel Kennedy, established a more formal program to watch his employees. He called it the "Department of Greater Service." Kennedy handpicked forty men—no "young fellows" or "fly-by-nights" permitted—gave them a good salary, and "patiently schooled" them in all aspects of the company. Kennedy then assigned each employee to one of his company's local customer-service offices where they functioned as Kennedy's eyes and ears in the field. Although they had a desk at their assigned office, they bypassed the normal chain of command and reported directly to Kennedy rather than to the commercial office manager. This way, Kennedy could carry out surveillance not only on his clerks but also on his managers.[11]

Employees of the Department of Greater Service also called on six hundred customers a month at their homes and interviewed them to "obtain the mental attitude of each customer." While McAdoo waited for customers to contact him, Kennedy actively surveyed customers to improve customer service. After each interview, Kennedy's employees filled out a card that categorized the customer's attitude as: "in accordance with the company," "indifferent," or "antagonistic." After listening to Kennedy describe his new department, an executive from another utility observed that "the knowledge that men are travelling over the territory, talking with customers and checking service, must put the employee on his mettle." It did indeed, Kennedy assured him; low-level employees were now "much more alert" and "tuned up to a higher point" since they knew they were being observed and talked about by customers. Many other utilities established similar programs.[12]

Yet these and similar programs failed to provide an accurate measurement of employee behavior and public opinion. Employees taking field surveys found that customers were reticent to share the details about their customer-service experiences, or that too much time had passed since the customers' last visit, making their recollections vague. Managers still read letters from customers, as McAdoo had, but managers realized that these usually did not reflect the average level of customer service.

By the late 1920s, executives were getting frustrated with their inability to accurately observe their employees. William Durgin, a manager at Chicago's Commonwealth Edison Company, expressed this frustration to colleagues at an electricity industry conference in 1929. Durgin had been trying to observe his clerks' customer-service habits, but his very presence changed his clerks' behavior. It had "a most distorting influence," which made "unbiased measurement" impossible, Durgin huffed. "We must have some technique which will get the measurement through the eyes of the public rather than those of anyone associated with the company."[13]

With this goal in mind, Durgin began hiring mystery shoppers, who went around to customer-service offices and secretly graded clerks on their courtesy. To find these mystery shoppers, Durgin placed ads in newspapers soliciting "housewives for interesting, part time work." Armed with a concealed "Service Sampling Check List," these mystery shoppers rated utility employees in four categories: appearance, information, speech, and politeness. Under "Speech," shoppers were asked if the clerk's voice had a "disagreeable or patronizing inflection." Under "Politeness," shoppers were asked: Did the clerk "give you a pleasant greeting? Look at you while he talked? Remain seated while you were standing?" Did the clerk "address you by your name," and say "'Thank you,' 'you are welcome,' 'good-bye'?" For "Appearance," shoppers determined if employees needed "a hair cut [sic] or shave," had "soiled" hands or nails, and if their desks were "orderly."[14]

These surveillance efforts provided a slightly more accurate picture of customer service, but with the survival of monopolies hinging on public opinion, executives wanted even more intensive surveillance methods. To obtain this, executives turned to outside consultants, including one of the nation's leading business consultants, psychologist J. David Houser. Houser's namesake firm boasted the capability of carrying out consumer-attitude surveys across a company's service territory, and employee-attitude surveys within a company itself. To gauge customer service, Houser employed mystery shoppers to systematically rate utility employees on their job performances.[15]

By 1930, Houser's firm had collected data on seventy-five utility firms from across the country using mystery shoppers. "[The data] is the most fascinating single set of generalizations on public relations that I have ever laid my eyes on," Houser enthused at a utility industry conference in 1930. The study included interviews with "probably a hundred thousand customers, actual customers, bona fide customers, interviewed in regard to what they thought about public utilities," Houser continued. In an irony of the Progressive Era, as consumers scrutinized corporate monopolies for their poor service and demanded reforms, they themselves became the scrutinized, which helped monopolies thrive and municipal ownership decline.[16]

Initially, however, the results of Houser's surveys were not encouraging to executives. His survey of "public attitude" indicated "a degree of favor toward private ownership of about 26" out of 50. According to Houser, barely a majority of Americans favored private ownership of utilities in 1930. Houser also measured "customer attitude toward service," which focused on "the way employees treat the public as they come into the various utility companies." In that category, utilities performed even worse, earning only 26 points on a 100-point scale. Surveys carried out by the telephone industry produced only slightly better results. In 1929, Bell service observers found that only 43 percent of customer-service interactions at branch offices were free of defects. In 1930, that number had increased to 53 percent. Executives believed these numbers were accurate since the Bell System had just standardized their observation methods.[17]

The results of these studies only confirmed to executives that more courtesy and surveillance were needed in order to improve public opinion toward monopolies. But what else could executives have concluded? Could they admit that public distaste for utilities stemmed partly from the fact that utilities monopolized markets and resources, sent profits to distant headquarters and holding companies, and were often weakly overseen by compliant and usually nondemocratically selected regulators? These were precisely the criticisms leveled by critics of corporate utilities, but for executives to admit to them would have been heresy. It would call into question the entire framework in which corporate utilities operated. Instead, executives intensified their extraction of emotional labor and the surveillance of clerks and customers that supported it.

Surveillance helped executives control clerks, but it would be much easier if employees internalized the demands of courteous capitalism and controlled themselves. To develop such self-monitoring employees, executives used several methods, including promoting a corporate ideology that down-played traditional American values such as independence and individualism and stressed instead ideals helpful to the corporation such as subservience and loyalty. To legitimize this ideology, managers frequently quoted the Bible. Indeed, if clerks could be convinced that a higher power beyond the corporate executive required courteous service, surveillance itself might become unnecessary. It was "a sin" not to provide good customer service, employees at the Southern Bell company learned from their employee mag-azine in 1921. "Remember the words and teachings of the Savior as our greatest example," exhorted the editor of an electric company employee magazine in 1915. "His was a life of service—'Servant of ye all.'" Samuel Kennedy was fond of quoting Solomon to promote courtesy, especially the proverb, "a soft answer turneth away wrath, but grievous words stir up an-ger," and Kennedy was not the only executive to cite the wisest man ever. Even some lower-level employees used the Bible to buttress the demands of courteous capitalism. In 1929, a chief operator quoted the biblical passage of Martha serving Jesus and then exhorted her fellow operators to "take heart and be assured, for the Great Executive has approved your course." Chief executives could not have said it better themselves.[18]

The idea that companies wanted clerks to internalize the demands of courteous capitalism and become self-monitoring is no mere repetition of French critical theory; it was the explicit statement of executives. A manager at a Bell Personnel Conference in 1922 acknowledged that "the eye of the management" had limits and stressed instead the "self-supervision by [the] employee." At the same conference, another Bell manager, Verne Ray, ob-served that "an employee, under close supervision, may be made to conform to proscribed mechanical processes . . . of courtesy," but that that was not a "full measure of ungrudging and whole-hearted service." To obtain that, Ray argued, the employee must be led to "self-convert" to the company's way of being. Once "self-converted," the employee would carry "the idea into his daily work as his own, with an enthusiasm which he would not have if the conclusion were forced on him." Managers should not order an em-ployee to convert, Ray instructed, since that would not obtain genuine con-version. Instead, employees should be "unobtrusively guided toward and allowed to reach a conclusion by their own thought." Ray promised that once employees absorbed the company's doctrines, they would not only per-form their jobs more enthusiastically, they would "usually take an interest in propagating it further" by proselytizing their coworkers. The sources indicate that some utility employees did experience this self-conversion and became self-monitoring.[19]

In addition to creating self-monitoring employees, utilities used architecture to enhance surveillance of workers and customers. In the early twentieth century, a typical utility office where customers went to sign up for service, pay their bills, or dispute a charge featured iron bars, high counters, and glass partitions. Utilities inherited this design from bank teller windows. Yet in the first decade of the twentieth century utility executives came to believe that these barricaded offices expressed secrecy and bred suspicion among customers that utilities had something to hide. In response, executives tore down the bars, counters, and partitions, and replaced these "closed offices," as managers called them, with new "open offices." Executives reasoned that if customers could see and hear what was going on in the office, and physically move around within these spaces, the widespread suspicion of monopolies would be replaced with confidence that corporate utilities represented the best way to provide needed services. "If you look a consumer squarely in the face and he looks you squarely in the face," Samuel Kennedy taught, "you are going to feel different toward each other than if you are dodging back and forth, looking through a pigeon hole." Enhanced observation through architecture would shape public opinion.[20]

Visibility of employees to customers was therefore a key design feature of the new open office. The design allowed customers to survey employees and managers as soon as customers entered the office. The new open office was "so arranged that the district agent and his assistants are at all times visible and accessible to the company's customers and the public," boasted an employee magazine article published by Kennedy's Southern California Edison Company in 1914. Yet after the advent of the open office, Samuel Kennedy noted that some managers were hiding "probably in a back room." The problem was visual. "You can't see him. A customer can't see him," Kennedy complained. The manager was "not visible." "Now then," Kennedy demanded, "in business hours, he should be visible; he should be accessible to take care of customers who want to see him."[21]

The open office not only made employees visible to customers, it also made lower-level employees visible to their supervisors. A typical open office included several rows of desks with customer-service clerks, usually women, sitting in the front and performing the most emotional labor. Directly behind them sat their supervisor, known as the chief clerk, as well as a bookkeeper or two. Behind them sat their supervisor, the assistant manager. Finally, at the very back sat the manager, literally overseeing the office. The disciplinary hierarchy was therefore finely graded and spatially embedded in the office layout. Surveillance and control ran all the way down the line, with each position supervising the position below it.[22]

When customers entered an open office, they could see all the faces of the employees. As a Bell employee magazine noted, open offices were designed with "each associate's desk facing the entrance." This contrasted sharply with the old closed offices. From the manager's perch in the back of the open office, he could see the faces of customers, as well as the backs of his employees, though his employees could not see him without turning around. The open office layout therefore provided excellent surveillance of clerks due to the asymmetry of vision. Executives believed that this led to better customer service. "By all means, let the manager be in a position to see everything that is going on in the office," Kennedy instructed executives in a talk about how to improve public opinion. "Direct, on the job, personal supervision is the most effective form of supervision and control," declared a Bell commercial office manager in 1926. "The first and most important factor in business office management is 'viewpoint.' The correct viewpoint sees the problem first." Jeremy Bentham never built any of his panopticons, but utility executives built hundreds of open offices.[23]

Although the new open offices appeared to show customers the entire office, at many offices, an unseen back region made this transparency an illusion. This back region facilitated greater surveillance. A Bell open office in New Orleans, for example, featured a "public office" where a manager dutifully stationed himself so that "those wishing to see him can do so conveniently." Yet behind this public office existed an "interior office," where various workers labored, including a "service observer." The service observer listened in on customer-clerk interactions occurring in the pubic office via microphones embedded inside customer-service clerks' desks. This technique was a logical extension of Bell's long-held practice of listening in on telephone operators and telephone subscribers using employees called "monitors." But as direct-dial phones became more popular and clerks at branch offices became the literal face of the company, Bell began focusing more on the courtesy of its customer-service clerks and the surveillance of them. By 1930, 70 percent of Bell's face-to-face customer-service transactions at large offices were under surveillance, up from 45 percent the year before.[24]

The constant surveillance from customers and managers made the work experience of clerks difficult. Historians of white-collar culture have often asked why these workers tolerated such conditions. One answer is that, although surveillance made lower-level jobs difficult, it also motivated employees. That was because promotions provided not just an increase in pay or prestige but also a reduction in one layer of supervision and a decrease in the amount of emotional labor one had to perform. Yet getting promoted partly depended on internalizing the discipline given by one's superior, or at least appearing to. Once employees received a promotion, they immediately began disciplining those occupying their former position. Employees did this because it was better than doing the job themselves, and, if they did it well enough, they might be promoted again, until someday, they could sit in the back, where they did not have to engage in much emotional labor at all and no one could see them. "The new employee who holds the lesser position is required to 'service his time' in the disagreeable job of waiting on the public or at the 'complaint window,'" a New England gas executive told colleagues. Therefore, he continued, "the ambition of the recruit is to hurry up and get promoted, so he, too, can go to the rear, have a nice, quiet, private office where he will not be bothered by customers with grievances and requests for information." Each rung in the corporate ladder came with a new desk location and more privacy.[25]

In addition to commercial office design, Bell Telephone also used the design of telephone operating rooms and switchboards to maximize the surveillance of the employees. Designers did this because they believed that greater surveillance of operators would improve customer service and thereby improve public opinion. Scholars have shown that certain factory layouts and machines were designed not only to increase production but to individualize employees and sow discord among workers. The design of telephone operating designs presents a different case. In the telephone industry, operating rooms and switchboards were designed to increase supervision of workers and thereby shape the political economic sentiments of customers. Improving operator supervision and public opinion were not the only design criteria for switchboard engineers, of course. Cost of ownership, user connectivity, call-connection speed, and reliability were also important design considerations. But engineers also considered how to increase supervision and thereby mold public opinion by design.[26]

By the turn of the century, the goal of high operator supervision resulted in a switchboard and telephone operating room layout that maximized operator surveillance (Figure 4.1). Unlike previous designs, operating room layouts by 1900 featured switchboards located against three walls of a room, forming a U shape. Operators sat on the inside of the U facing outward toward the walls, while several supervisors stood directly behind the operators. The monitor and the chief operator sat at the top of the U and enjoyed a panoptic position where they could see everyone without easily being seen.[27]

This design commonly existed since at least 1906 but was not inevitable.[28] Many alternatives existed. "There were almost as many kinds of switchboards as there were central offices," recalled one operator about the early days of telephone. In one early design, known as a "lamp-shade" layout, four operators sat facing the four sides of a central column mounted with switchboards. This design limited the number of lines that could be connected, but also made supervision difficult because seeing the operators required walking around the column. In another early design, operators faced each other across boards parallel to the floor, as if playing chess. This resembled the layout at large telegraph offices, but in terms of supervision, the operators on one side could easily see supervisors on the other side. Another design from the 1890s placed all switchboards on a single wall, which turned the operators' vision away from supervisors, but the switchboards were located on two floors, which made supervision difficult. Another design resembled the U-shaped pattern that would eventually dominate, except that the operators sat on the outside of the U, rather than the inside. There was a still a monitor observing the workers, but the operators could see her more easily, and the monitor's view of the operators farthest away was obstructed by nearer operators.[29]

None of these early designs persisted. At a switchboard design conference in 1889 an AT&T engineer explained one reason why—surveillance. "It is better to have the operators work from the inside of a circle [rather] than around the outside," he explained. That way "all operators are at once within view of the chief operator." The monitor's desk should also be located so that "all [switchboard] sections may be easily seen." Not only could the monitor easily see the backs of all the operators, but the operators could not see her. Finally, the engineer offered, the operating room "should be free from elevator shafts or other obstructions," such as additional lampshade switchboards that had sometimes been installed in the middle of the U. Engineers wanted enough space for supervisors to do their "patrolling," which previous designs lacked. The desire for improved supervision of operators even provided one motivation for engineers to consolidate the small exchanges, which had

Figure 4.1. A U-shaped Bell System telephone operating room, 1914. "The Reality—A Typical Exchange," *Pacific Telephone Magazine*, October 1914, 14, AT&T-TX. Courtesy of AT&T Archives and History Center.

once been scattered throughout cities, and combine them into one large exchange in each city.[30]

In addition to the telephone operating room layout, the design of the switchboards also enhanced surveillance. In 1895, engineers added a small light on the front of each switchboard tellingly called "supervisory signals." These lights helped supervisors know when an operator was not on a call so there could be no pretending to work. Engineers also designed switchboards so that monitors could listen in on any operator without her knowledge.[31]

By the early twentieth century, these switchboards arranged in the U-shaped layout became the standard. This layout hurt the work experience of operators since it permitted multiple layers of surveillance. First, supervisors stood directly behind operators, literally breathing down their necks. These supervisors oversaw just six to twelve women. Next came the "monitor" who sat at a special desk where she listened in on operators. The monitor reported errors to the "chief operator," who sat at the top of the U and could also listen in on calls anonymously. If operators slipped up, they could expect a reprimand from at least one of their bosses.[32]

In addition to observing their clerks in the office, utility managers also examined their employees' "home life" by visiting workers' and prospective workers' homes. "This, of course, must be done tactfully so as to avoid having the employee think that his privacy is being violated," a manager advised colleagues. Yet such "personal, kindly investigating work" represented a "good investment," a Bell employee argued, because lack of courtesy at work sometimes had its origins at home. This Bell employee then boasted that the Ford Motor Company was not the only corporation involved in "welfare work." The extent of surveillance at utility corporations in the early twentieth century was truly extensive.[33]

As for McAdoo, his "public be pleased" policy that initiated much of this surveillance proved so popular that it brought him into the national spotlight. As a result, in 1913 President Woodrow Wilson selected McAdoo to serve as secretary of the treasury, and McAdoo went on to become Wilson's son-in-law. Then during World War I, McAdoo served as the secretary general of the railroads during the period of railroad nationalization. By that point, however, McAdoo no longer hated government ownership of monopolies; he promoted it. That was when McAdoo's own policies came home to roost. The public had come to expect courteous service and had learned to complain about employees when it was not forthcoming. In one case, a telephone user mistakenly sent a letter of complaint to McAdoo, even though the letter should have gone to Postmaster General Albert Burleson, who oversaw the telephone network, which had also been nationalized. McAdoo and Burleson both favored long-term, if not permanent, nationalization of the nation's utility monopolies, such as telephone and railroad lines. The customer wrote that employees at the Bell-affiliated Pacific Telephone & Telegraph Company were "insolent" and "very impudent over the phone without reason" and that this all began "since the Co's have been taken over by you [the government]." This was not an isolated incident, and partly due to rude service, public opinion during World War I turned firmly against government ownership of utilities. When the war ended, the railroad and telephone networks were quickly returned to private control. The public was pleased. Yet they failed to realize how much their own surveillance of emotional laborers had affected the return. And Americans seldom if ever commented on how much they themselves had come under surveillance by corporate monopolies on the phone, at commercial offices, and at home.[34]

CHAPTER 5

The Watchful Gaze Behind the Welcoming Smile

Surveilling the Guest in American Hotels
in the Interwar Period

MEGAN J. ELIAS

In 1921, a woman using the name Mrs. Dunn found herself abandoned by
her companion at a hotel in Oklahoma City. The companion, registered as
Mr. Dunn, but not actually her husband, had borrowed and not returned
her diamond ring. He had also borrowed and not returned $10 from the
hotel, written checks at the restaurant that later bounced, and sneaked off
without paying his substantial bill of $68.43. Hotel room rates were typi-
cally $2–3 per night at this time. Mr. Dunn had committed three of the
most vexing crimes to plague the hotel industry at the time—"skipping,"
"bouncing," and taking a room for "immoral purposes." It is tempting to
think he packed some of the hotel's towels with him to complete his vil-
lainy in style.[1]

The story of Mr. and Mrs. Dunn was reported in a regular column in the
industry journal *Hotel World* titled "Way of Transgressor." The column existed as a form of public service for the hotel community. Having read the
piece, desk clerks and managers in the area might take a longer look at anyone registering as Mr. Dunn and might be more careful about accepting his
checks or acceding to his requests for loans. This column and other more
sporadic reports on fraud against hotels helped hotel managers and employees both to share useful information and to experience a sense of common
cause. "Way of Transgressor" only occasionally included physical descriptions of people who had defrauded hotels, and no photographs were ever
published. This left the desk clerk to protect the hotel's interests with only

the weakest of tools—a name that was probably false and a vague idea of likely behaviors. Most important, any attempt to identify the potential crook had to be conducted within the strict boundaries of good customer service, complete with smiling deference to the guest's every whim. Suspicion had to operate under the deep cover of a genuine welcome.

The interwar period was a pivotal moment in the business of hotel keeping and the hospitality industry more generally. During this period hotels became much larger and, central to this essay, the notion of customer service was born. New technologies in construction that gave the modern city its skyscrapers and apartment buildings also made possible large hotels with centralized heating, cooling, laundering, and cooking systems. Historian Molly Berger argues that the notion of personal service was born to counterbalance the potential "impersonality of these enormous structures."[2] The expansion of scale made it possible to serve more guests with more amenities and thus to make more money than hotelkeepers of past generations. Supply, of course, was only half the equation. The same forces that had helped to produce the hotels—industrialization and urbanization—had created a new demand for hotels. New modes of transportation—auto and air travel—joined rail travel to set Americans in motion, especially between the new urban centers. Linked to these developments, the culture and conduct of business of all kinds also became more mobile. Business travel began to supplement written communication.

And most crucial to the development of modern hospitality, traveling salesmen helped to shape the very structure and services of the hotel during this period.[3] Hotels were built with whole floors dedicated to sample rooms that allowed salesmen to show off their wares to potential clients. These floors were typically on lower floors, often mezzanines, to make it easy for customers to find the sample rooms. This arrangement brought local business professionals through the doors and into the heart of the new hotels, giving them ideas about what to expect when they themselves should have a chance to travel. Visually striking lobbies after the style of great halls in European mansions gave the business conducted in hotels an air of importance. A pervasive emphasis on "the latest" conveniences made them also seem future-focused. Within these institutions, a new kind of hospitality emerged that focused on the convenience of the guest. This was in contrast to the older inns where the convenience of the innkeeper had been privileged. In the few hotels for wealthy travelers that existed in the United States before World War I, excesses of comfort were the ideal. The interwar hotel stood somewhere in between, offering close but not subservient attention to the traveler's needs.

The managers of these new hotels saw themselves as a new breed of professional and styled themselves "hotel men" rather than innkeepers. They were typically American-born, in contrast to most of the chefs, who emigrated from Switzerland and France. They had worked their way up through the ranks from bellboy to desk clerk into management, and some were also able to become hotel owners. Through this process they developed thorough understandings of the workings of hotels. From the earliest days of the transformation, beginning with the first issue of *Hotel Monthly* in 1893, journals dedicated to the industry published articles about the many facets of hotel management, from the very material—how to make bedsheets last longer—to the more abstract—how to keep employees loyal. The industry journals themselves helped to construct the hotel man by telling him what his concerns should be. Reporting on issues of concern to larger urban hotels, country resorts, and smaller town hotels, the journals reveal the matters that mattered to a wide range of people in the business.

Where in the past innkeepers offered a bed and some food in the tavern, new hotels could offer a private room with a bath and the choice of several dining places. Hotels could now include small shops to keep the guest's money very local. Barbers, manicurists, candy shops, cigar stands, and even stockbrokers could be found in little indoor alleys in the modern hotels. The spirit of convenience shaped both the physical and the emotional landscape of the hotel.

Within the industry, hotelier Ellsworth M. Statler was credited with almost singlehandedly inventing the key features of the modern industry: streamlined convenience and the motto that "the guest is always right." This introduced a new notion of service into the industry and into commercial life more broadly that is still at the heart of relationships in the service industries today. Statler had worked his way from bellboy in a hotel in Wheeling, West Virginia, to the ownership of a string of hotels in the Northeast, including the huge and influential Hotel Pennsylvania. Looking back at his career shortly before he died in 1928, Statler noted that in his first hotel, a temporary structure built to accommodate visitors to the St. Louis World's Fair in 1904, he had posted a manifesto for customer service. The announcement read: "1. The policy of this house is to please. 2. No guest should be permitted to leave this house displeased. 3. No employee is to be retained who cannot please."[4]

The modern hotel was subject to modern problems that grew directly from Statler's innovations. In emphasizing convenience, the new hotels created an expectation that was not always easy to provide materially. Likewise, in letting the guests know that they were "always right," hoteliers created an unbalanced power dynamic. The newly entitled and empowered guest stood in a new relation to the hotel manager and staff. Higher expectations left more opportunities for disappointment than had been possible in the old share-your-bed inns.

Because the new hotels provided so much more in the way of service, they democratized access to treatment and material experiences that had not been available to regular travelers before. One no longer had to be "somebody" to be welcome in the kind of hotel that had a grand lobby, clean sheets for each guest, and ice water running in the taps. Opening up the experience to more people also opened up the opportunity for some to take advantage of hotels. If no one checked your pedigree at the door as you came in or your bags as you left, you could quite easily walk out with a set of towels and a bedside lamp. Indeed, the line between hospitality and private property seemed blurred in the new hotels.

Larger hotels with numerous staff members also created opportunities to become anonymous that in turn made (literal) room for new kinds of behaviors, some of them merely outside contemporary norms, others actually criminal. Hotels became places for sexual rendezvous, for drinking parties during Prohibition, for gambling, and for suicide. Hotel staff noticed that people behaved differently in hotels than they might at home, despite the widespread commonplace that hotels offered a home away from home. In his essential guide to hotel management, hotelier Lucius Boomer (of the Waldorf-Astoria) noted that "all sorts of people use hotels for all sorts of purposes." While most were law-abiding, "not a few people resort to hotels [to] throw off certain restraints which dominate them when at home."[5]

In his *Hotel: An American History*, Andrew Sandoval-Strausz noted, "The tense and unruly environment of the hotel was a microcosm of a broader problem of social control that accompanied the advent of modernity in the Atlantic world. By the early nineteenth century, the penetration of capitalist logic into human relationships was well under way." Where a world of small communities had once policed their own, new mobility and urbanization freed people from their neighbor's watchful gaze. "In much the same way that modern societies struggled to find ways to manage the behavior of strangers, hotelkeepers who presided over establishments filled with transients had to find solutions for both accommodating and controlling guests . . . as a result, every hotelkeeper's welcoming smile beamed beneath vigilant eyes."[6]

Hotels of the early twentieth century required staff to function with loyalty to the institution but simultaneously to project a warm welcome to the guest, straddling the line between true and commercial hospitality as gracefully as possible. In practical terms, what this meant was sizing up each guest as they approached the front desk for the first time, moved through the lobby during their stay, and finally checked out. Was this person likely to break the rules in some way? Would they skip out on their check? Would they bring to their room and have sex with a person to whom they were not married? Would they appropriate an ashtray or blanket as a souvenir?

This essay explores that work as it was defined and managed in the interwar period. This period was a turning point for hotels, including the rise of the large modern hotel, a phase of overbuilding, and the readjustments of the Depression era. After the Second World War, the industry changed again, both in terms of material and ideals of customer service because of larger trends in American and global cultures. The interwar period deserves special attention because it allows us to see the negotiations that laid the groundwork for our contemporary understanding of service as something provided within the paradox of paid hospitality. Outside of the business context, hospitality has been understood across cultures to be something freely given with no expectation of immediate compensation.

Within the industry, each type of transgression was approached in a different way, not just in terms of policy, but in how it was seen to fit into the industry as a whole. Because hotels dealt in reputation as well as in money, these things mattered. In past lore, hotels had been dens of dishonesty as well as iniquity. Pockets got picked while people slept and innkeepers charged the rates they wished to. As one historian of hotels wrote in 1930, "the policy of the innkeeper was, in the main, 'take it or leave it.' The old-time landlord did not believe in catering to the whims of travelers. They were not entitled to any whims and must put up with whatever Mine Host provided for them, which was usually an irreducible minimum of comfort and service."[7] Hotel men of the early twentieth century saw an opportunity to make more money if they could establish their institutions as honest and safe—not a den of thieves and whores. Unfortunately for this plan, thieves and sex workers continued to be eager consumers of the hotel's services.

To handle these problems, larger hotels developed credit departments and hired security agents and even detectives. These departments were included in hotel management guides, indicating how essential they were thought to be. Their existence also suggested that the amount of money lost to fraud and theft was large enough to justify the expense of the protective department. Beyond this, clerks and other "greeters" were encouraged to think of themselves as not just the eyes and ears of the hotel, but students of human nature.

As Josh Lauer explained in *Creditworthy*, a range of consumer businesses had "credit men" on staff by the late nineteenth century. Where earlier generations of merchants had typically had local knowledge of their customers, the era of industrialization created larger communities and set more people in motion among them, making it harder for a merchant to have personal knowledge of any one customer's financial position. Credit managers became researchers and reputation monitors, holding and updating information about individuals' likelihood of paying their bills. From these site-specific efforts emerged independent credit bureaus that shared information across businesses to categorize consumers as either creditworthy or a risk.[8]

Although Lauer found that by the 1920s "credit managers had established sophisticated systems for compiling, analyzing, and rapidly transmitting consumer credit information within their own stores and to the local credit bureau," hotels do not seem to have joined in this collective project until after World War II. Indeed, from the industry literature they seem to have been unaware of it and even unaware that other business sectors faced similar challenges.[9]

In 1933, hotel greeter Clyde Douthat offered his colleagues a reflection on the undesirable guest. In general, the undesirable was "one whose reputation, conduct or condition is such as to affect adversely the reputation of the house or the comfort and rights of its desirable occupants or to place in jeopardy lives or property." Undesirables could be of any gender or class and their status could change from day to day: "A guest may be desirable one day and on the next be undesirable for some reason, and then revert back again to the desirable status." A businessman might appear at the hotel one night with his wife, for example, and the next with a known sex worker. Some of the qualities that might make a person undesirable, Douthat argued, were "drunkenness, disorderliness, disease, insanity, filthiness, color, nationality, creed, gambling, skipping, passing bad paper, prowling, loud parties, unreasonableness, temper, fighting, profanity, bootlegging, commercialized vice."[10] Douthat lumped together voluntary antisocial behaviors, such as fighting and bootlegging, with the involuntary attributes of nationality and race as well as the seemingly pro-social choice of religion, reflecting a world in which the concept of civil rights was only just beginning to emerge. As urban historian Thomas Sugrue explains, in his study of segregation in the North, "the exclusion of blacks from hotels, stores, restaurants, and recreation centers in the North operated in a strange gray zone, blurring distinctions between 'private' and 'public.'" While some states' civil rights laws promised equal access to public accommodations, discrimination was so widespread that "most black travelers did not risk the humiliation of being rebuffed at a hotel."[11]

Similarly, the 1938 updated version of the popular guide *Hotel Management* noted that although "civil rights laws have been passed chiefly for the protection of colored persons . . . admission of such persons is often objectionable to other guests in the house and the hotel-keeper should instruct his employees to use tact and care to maintain the good-will of the house without violating the law."[12] No direct suggestions followed for how to provide inhospitable hospitality, but an example was offered of a residential hotel that won a legal case to keep an African American visitor from riding in the passenger elevator. The larger message was that "the customer is always right" only truly applied when the customer was always white. For this reason, beginning in 1948, African American mail carrier Victor Hugo Green published his now famous *Negro Motorist Green Book*, which listed black-owned hotels and restaurants for black travelers. Green's guide offered an alternative experience to the white hotel industry's Red Book, a national catalog of hotels. The Red Book did not overtly discriminate, but its very failure to address the issue of discrimination reflected the pervasive notion that segregation was both normal and acceptable throughout the nation.[13]

In cases in which the hotel determined that a potential guest was undesirable but law prevented them from being turned away, Douthat suggested some strategies. He advised, "The outstanding method of handling these unwanted ones, if the cause is clearly apparent at the time of their arrival, is for the room clerk to turn them down (tactfully) or to raise the price to a prohibitive price (legally); or, failing in these, to assign a room in a place where the occupant can and will be under control and not be a nuisance."[14] Even while lying to a guest or assigning them second-class status, however, a veneer of hospitality must remain in place for financial rather than ethical reasons. Douthat advised, "No matter what is said or done by the offending party, the hotel's representative should control his temper or there will be an immediate absence of tact. Once this control is lost, the undesirable has a big advantage and will likely take advantage of it subsequently by filing suit for damages or slander." Sometimes, Douthat claimed, people set out on purpose to antagonize a hotel just to get themselves ejected so that they could sue. Because hotels were so leery of bad publicity, they would be likely to settle out of court, providing the antagonist with a nice reward for bad behavior.[15]

Surveillance of guests was of two general categories—assessment and evaluation—performed by two different types of clerks. The desk clerk was tasked with processing first impressions of the potential guest, while the floor clerk was responsible for the guest's behavior once they had checked in. While desk clerks were typically male, floor clerks were typically female. Floor clerks, because their sphere was more limited and because there were typically more of them, ranked below desk clerks in the hotel's hierarchy. Gendered divisions of labor in the hotel business are rich material for an entirely other essay, but it is worth noting how the work of surveillance was assigned along gendered lines here since the work itself was credited as both intellectual and intuitive, almost emotional work, categories that were also typically gendered but here were combined.

Assessing the Potential Guest

The desk clerk's assessment focused on two facets of the person before him: creditworthiness and morality. Assessments of creditworthiness addressed the individuals' status within the capitalist economy and their adherence to its particular ethics, while guesses about morality addressed their potential divergence from broader cultural norms. Because cultural norms change and were notably in flux during the interwar period, this kind of judgment was extremely difficult to make. Since no one traveled with a marriage certificate, clerks had no way of knowing whether a heterosexual couple standing at the desk was married. Ironically, for all the worry hotel managers expressed about unmarried heterosexual couples sleeping together, the industry press never mentioned the same-sex partners who doubtless rented rooms together in this era, often in violation of state laws against homosexual sex but perfectly in compliance with hotel policies that allowed same-sex travelers to stay in the same room. Certain hotels, such as the St. George in Brooklyn Heights, became well known in the queer community as places to cruise. Of one St. George resident, Brooklyn historian Hugh Ryan noted, he "liked living at the hotel because it was anonymous yet lively, making it easy to bring home tricks without putting himself in danger."[16] Other hotels, typically smaller and cheaper, drew unwelcome attention from reformers and police if they became *too* well known as places for same-sex sexual activities.[17]

As with wedlock and sexuality, creditworthiness was hard to determine from visual clues, and appearances could be deceiving. One report of a known check skipper described the man as "very finely dressed; claims to be a college graduate."[18] The skipper's air of success made him less suspicious in the eyes of those who distrusted the poor more than the rich, positing economic success in the capitalist system as proof of righteousness. Upper-class markers served as camouflage. In 1927, William Lowe, manager of two hotels, advised that when guests reserved their rooms by mail, "it is generally possible from the letterheads on which they write to determine whether or not they are credit risks."[19] Lowe gave no further explanation, leaving modern readers to guess that a heavy paper stock or address in a "good" part of town might be taken as clues. Calling on a new science for help with preemptive detection, in 1928 the American Hotel Association Protective Committee suggested keeping registration cards for later handwriting analysis.[20] The article did not elaborate, but perhaps the plan was to compare the handwriting of known skippers to that of honest customers to determine some patterns. Once dishonest handwriting had been discovered, clerks would be able to prevent the fraudster from even registering.

Credit could be established finally through phone calls, telegrams, and repeat business, though some of this process could seem at odds with the spirit of hospitality and in the case of communications cost the hotel money. The mere act of requesting confirmatory information before cashing a check could easily be taken as an insult, so clerks often skipped it and just hoped for the best. Eventually, after World War II, the advent of the credit card would make this assessment work less important because it mostly moved the risk from the hotel to the credit card company. Until that innovation, however, the desk clerk engaged in socioeconomic profiling. In a 1919 guide to employment, the coauthors noted that the desk or room clerk's job was "a responsible position, for the room clerk must remember the guests who make the hotel their home while in the city and be able to size up people applying for rooms and be a splendid judge of human nature. The room clerk's position is not an easy one."[21]

If the clerk judged the visitor a risk either morally or financially, he could claim that the hotel was fully booked. As Clyde Douthat advised, "if the arrival is disgustingly drunk, or obviously insane, or beyond a doubt a prostitute, the policy should be to state courteously that all rooms are occupied, or reserved, or out of order; and to give reasonable assistance in getting them located somewhere else."[22] Even in the case of not providing services, the hotel employee must still provide services.

Also lurking in the back of the desk clerk's mind as he assessed the traveler was a kind of psychiatric scan: was this person likely to commit suicide on the premises? A listless demeanor or a very light suitcase or a request for a room on a high floor might suggest that the person had tragic plans. In 1927, a man escaped from a mental hospital, eluded the police, and entered the Waldorf-Astoria. He carried with him two boxes. One of them contained a rifle with which he killed himself in a basement bathroom of the hotel. A report of the event noted, "no one had seen him enter, nor noted the two packages which he carried. If they had been seen probably they would have been taken for Christmas packages," the event having taken place in late December. While reporting that the man had not been noticed, the writer simultaneously referred to the mechanisms of surveillance that existed within the hotel: his packages would have been assessed, not just noted. Further, the reporter explained that there was nothing "in the actions of the well-dressed young man to show that he was being sought by the police," implying that the visible badges of his economic class as much as his personal behavior spoke to anyone watching him, reassuring them that his presence in the fine hotel was not transgressive.[23]

In the summer of 1929, Cornell University, which had opened the first university-based hotel school in 1922, offered a course in psychology especially designed for the hotel worker. As a writer for *Hotel Monthly* reported, the course would be useful for anyone in a managerial role, but also for all employees "whose job is to please the large number of persons with whom he comes in daily contact." Among the topics to be studied was "Methods of measuring personality" which would presumably aid in assessing the potential guest's probability of being disruptive.[24] Certainly the last two arts, if performed well, concealed the clerk's simultaneous work of suspicion and possible discouragement.

William J. Stuart, a self-confessed "hotel crook" who had served time in jail for his crimes attempted to help the industry by describing the usual habits of a hotel thief—in his case one who stole from guests rather than from the hotel itself. Guests' property was legally under the care of the hotel so theft could hurt the house's reputation. Thus, thieves like Stuart stole more than they seemed to. Stuart explained, "The professional thief, having picked his 'spot' will usually drive up to the hotel about six o'clock attired in dinner clothes. He will check his hat and coat upon entering the lobby, thus giving the impression that he is a guest of the hotel. He may loaf around the lobby—buy a paper here, a cigar there—and chat with the employees—all the time keeping his eyes peeled for the house officer."[25] The thief waited until the house detective was in the lobby, then proceeded to explore the higher floors for opportunities. Another of the tricks of the crook was to study the habits of the night watchman, surveilling the surveyor, to establish when the best times to act might be. Too often, Stuart advised, night watchmen followed the same routine night after night, making the thief's job easier. As Stuart described him, the crook was intensely aware of the surveillance systems of the hotel. He presented himself as the opposite of a sneak—chatty and prosperous. Stuart even advised that once his work was complete the thief would call for the elevator, tip the operator lavishly, and refer to a great card game he was just leaving. In the lobby he might repeat the story, establishing himself as a bon vivant with nothing to hide. In fact, Stuart mused, "strangely enough, the professional thief is usually less suspicious in appearance than many hotel guests."[26]

Evaluating Guest Behavior

Once guests had been granted access to the hotel and assigned rooms, floor clerks evaluated their behaviors during their stay. Floor clerks were common in the larger urban hotels that set standards for the industry. As Lucius Boomer, owner of the Waldorf-Astoria, explained, "The floor clerk is an agent for protection, both for patrons and for the hotel. She should be watchful to guard property of patrons . . . as well as that of the hotel. . . . No less dignified and important is her function of upholding the moral and social standing of the hotel." The floor clerk's office was set up on each floor for maximum visibility and, "from the strategic location of her office she can observe the conduct of those coming from or going to the elevator, also while passing through the corridors; without being unduly inquisitive or meddlesome she can often detect intolerable conduct of persons in rooms which annoys patrons in nearby or adjacent rooms."[27] In the small time and space of the guest's walk down a hall, a floor clerk could evaluate all kinds of aspects of the guest's appearance, including whether the guest seemed drunk and if the guest's current companion was also on the register.

Floor clerks could help guests, particularly single women, feel safe in the hallway, and they were available to convey requests for any element of housekeeping—extra towels, new soap—as well as to make recommendations about local sites. Floor clerks also served the hotel by keeping watch on guest behaviors. Industry literature defined both desk and floor clerks as living a life of divided loyalties in which both the hotel's reputation and the guest's privacy were equally valuable. As Boomer explained, "The management desires to give to its patrons unlimited freedom of conduct so far as is consistent with law, morality, and the rights and comforts of others. But unrestrained conduct contrary to the decorum of a well-kept home injures the hotel's reputation and business and must not be allowed to pass unnoted."[28] Unlimited freedom of conduct consistent with law proved a difficult standard to maintain as the hotel press regularly reported on bouncing, skipping, and theft of property, hardly acts of decorum.

Bouncing and Skipping

Before the twentieth century, hotels had been among the few public institutions in most towns. The innkeeper knew everyone local and knew regular visitors too. He or she could be assumed to be a practiced judge of solvency if not character and to have larger sums of money on his or her premises than most other people did. For these reasons, the innkeeper often functioned as a bank, loaning money to travelers who might find themselves short. This expectation continued even as the institutions became much less locally focused and it became harder for staff to judge whether a check issued by an unknown business in an unknown town would be legitimate.

Hotelkeepers found it very difficult to drop this role because they had made the commitment to the guest's convenience and "rightness." To refuse to cash a check or grant a loan could inconvenience a guest at best and insult them at worst. It did not take long for mischief-minded people to realize the opportunity in this ill-matched combination of expectations and assurances.

Because checks had to travel by mail to the banks that had issued them in order to be processed, people who bounced checks intentionally usually had a significant amount of time to enjoy their stay in a hotel and move a safe distance away before their lack of funds was discovered.

In 1935, the editor of the *Western Hotel Reporter* lamented that the problem persisted: "When hotel men go out of their way to be bankers, no objection is raised by bankers themselves, for the boniface who does so is generally taking a chance that the bank would not take. What we mean specifically is that hotel folk often cash checks that they should not cash and lend money that they should not lend."[29] The author suggested that hotels charge fees to cash checks and charge interest if they insisted on loaning their customers money. Else all that remained to them were the "forlorn trunk or suitcase," usually empty, that bouncers, skippers, and deadbeats left behind. Walking through the lobby with a suitcase indicated that one was ready to check out—an impression that skippers wished to avoid. Furthermore, a trunk or suitcase left in a room sowed some doubt about whether the guest had really checked out, giving them more time to get away. The presence of these items then created a new problem for hotel staff. Throwing away someone's luggage was a kind of theft, but keeping a trunk you were sure no one would ever come back for took up valuable storage space as well as serving as a bitter reminder that the hotel had been bilked.

The rise of the traveling salesman resulted in a complementary rise in people pretending to be traveling salesmen. Assuming this persona gave one an aura of solvency—the traveling salesman's expenses were paid for by his company, so it did not matter if the individual seemed trustworthy because the company would be good for the funds. Blending into the new cohort of men in motion, the pretend salesman also supplied himself with a good reason to be in motion: not on the lam, but on the job.

In 1921, for example, a person traveling under the name C. M. Slocumb checked in at a series of hotels where he informed staff that he would be able to send payment for his hotel bill when he reached the next town on his itinerary, fifty miles away. His company would have wired funds to him there, he assured the clerks. When no money arrived, the hotels sent their bill to the company he had named, only to be informed they had no such employee. The company assured hoteliers that all of their real employees were supplied with travel funds to take on the road. Enough other businesses, however, did not operate this way for the hotel's staff to have accepted Slocumb's explanation and allowed him to depart without paying.[30]

Slocumb's representation of himself as associated with a particular firm enabled him to pass the hotel's preliminary surveillance test. By identifying himself with a known category of traveler (salesman) and a source of capital, Slocumb removed himself a step from suspicion. Salesmen and their expense accounts were known entities. Slocumb's clever ploy of not just skipping but of explaining why he would not be paying might well have reinforced the impression that he was reliable.

The veneer of trustworthiness could be purchased quite cheaply, as one T. W. Maloney demonstrated, also in 1921. Maloney paid his hotel bill of $2.25 and then asked to cash a check for $75. His request granted, he left the hotel and it was not till several days later that the hotel learned the check had bounced. By establishing himself as a person who paid his hotel bill— not a deadbeat—Maloney was neatly able to avoid doing so and to make money in the process.[31]

Although they were theoretically in competition, some hotel owners and managers realized that cooperation could serve as a kind of protection against the Slocumbs and Maloneys of the world. The "Way of Transgressor," mentioned above, was one attempt to enrich the regular, unfocused practice of surveillance with live details, even if these were mostly just aliases and ploys. In 1926, T. Charles Milton, who was special agent for the Kansas City Hotel Association, compiled a list of 1,400 names and aliases of alleged "swindlers" and sold it for $1.50 per copy. The names were listed alphabetically, for easy cross-checking with hotel registers. If a hotel employee were to find a name in the register that matched one on Milton's list, Milton would share a physical description of the person to aid in identification and, possibly, apprehension.[32] Because it was easy to come up with aliases, however, the list was limited in its usefulness. In 1928, a man was arrested for bouncing checks who had twenty-nine aliases and thirty-five business cards, suggesting that the line of work was lucrative and the chance of detection low.[33] The article announcing his arrest was titled "Catch a Bad One."

The hotel clerk who diligently read reports of fraud in other local hotels would be able to make a better assessment of potential guests, politely turning away anyone whose name appeared on a list and then rushing to inform those previously defrauded of the person's current whereabouts. The proliferation of telephone lines after the First World War made this easier, but communications also went by telegram and sometimes by mail. Big city hotels had resident detectives and even arrangements with local police. In 1927, the local hotel association and the New York Police Department set up the Hotel Squad, created to "cooperate in protecting New York hotels against skippers and bad check artists," an acknowledgment of the public/private nature of hotels.[34]

Smaller towns had only their own staff in close proximity. Whatever the situation, detaining a customer in public was not at all consistent with the ethos of modern hospitality. The vision of someone being handcuffed in the lobby both worried customers about how they might be treated and suggested that the hotel attracted criminals. Admitting that there were criminals in the "house," even if you were having them arrested, complicated hoteliers' mission to establish hotels as respectable. As much as they might like to help out their colleagues at other hotels, most managers prioritized getting the transgressor quietly out of the building over bringing them to justice.

By contrast, in 1926, an organized group of hotel owners in South Carolina vowed to share information about bouncers and deadbeats and to ask local courts for tough punishment for those caught, specifically "road sentences," meaning work on the road gangs.[35] This group set themselves apart from most other hotel owners who chose not to pursue criminal charges against bouncers or skippers if they received restitution.

This behavior deeply troubled Joseph Buch, head of the American Hotel Association's Protection Committee. Working hard to establish networks to share information about criminals preying on hotels, Buch advised his colleagues that they were partly to blame for the losses they suffered from check bouncers because they were so reluctant to prosecute. He urged them to seek retribution: "Each and every hotel proprietor defrauded should swear out a warrant for the arrest of the bad check passer and prosecute in each and every instance and in the event that he is sentenced on some other charge, file a detainer warrant so that upon his release he will be confronted with a warrant for his arrest in connection with all other bad checks passed."[36] As modes of transportation shifted from rail to road, Buch also advised hotels to keep track of guests' license plates as a way to track them down if they skipped out on or bounced a check.[37]

Corwin Lewis recounted a conversation about this subject between two hotel managers: "We all have too much personal pride that is really false pride when it comes to reporting bad checks received and hotel skips. . . . If we would just park our pride, and send in a report to the Secretary (no one else in the association sees it anyway) and if we did this at once upon discovering the action of the skip or bad check passer, our losses would be fifty to seventy-five percent less."[38] Hotel managers and owners were balancing the tangible and sizable losses from fraud against the intangible but potentially even greater potential losses from damage to the hotel-guest relationship and/or defamation lawsuits brought by guests wrongly accused of stealing services. Bouncing a check was not then or now a crime, nor was simply not paying a hotel bill unless the offended party could prove intent to defraud. In each case, the perpetrator could plead sudden unexpected loss of funds and promise to repay the debt. Once away from the hotel, an honest guest might well send in the money, whereas skippers were hard to trace and expensive to retrieve.

Registering at the hotel with the intent to skip out on the bill was a crime but essentially impossible to prove. One particularly insouciant defrauder routinely took loans from hotels, then told staff he was just driving over to another town for a day. He never returned but sometimes would "write back to the hotel that he did not get back on the day specified, but will start back in a day or two," preserving the facade of good intentions that was crucial to avoid an arrest for fraud.[39]

Hotel owners and managers were eager to protect their businesses from those who preyed on the industry, but they wanted to do it as privately as possible. In 1928, the Michigan Hotel Association formed a partnership with the American Bankers Association to get information flowing more quickly between banks and hotels about bounced checks.[40] Members of the ABA would undertake to telegraph to hotels (at the hotel's expense) whenever a check from a guest bounced. Members of the Protective Committee of the American Hotel Association reported that this kind of communication saved individual hotels significant sums and could prevent losses to the whole industry in the millions of dollars each year.[41] It also created a confidential communications channel; managers need not broadcast their own gullibility to their peers.

To prevent matters from even reaching the point at which banks would need to call hotels, the Protective Committee recommended the use of what they called "credit cards." These were cards held in the hotel's offices that established a guest's creditworthiness for future visits. The guest would be invited to apply for a card, which would be completed through a combination of the guest filling out a form and the hotel staff checking references.

Once the credit card existed, the clerk could theoretically feel safe in cashing a guest's check or even giving the guest a loan. Joseph Buch argued that an honest person would not mind the extra time and effort of filling out the card. In contrast, "those unworthy of credit usually fight shy of the credit card and upon one pretext or another defer the filing." The guest's response to the invitation to apply for credit then became a character test.[42]

Sex Outside Wedlock Inside Hotels

In his history of the American hotel, Andrew Sandoval-Strausz notes that "the hotel's distinctive combination of privacy, anonymity, and transience made it a highly sexualized space."[43] Recalling the old days of innkeeping, for example, writer Chic Sale noted that "the lobby of the Commercial House was the center of sin. Or at least it was thought it was." The transience of traveling salesmen in particular was assumed to attract sex workers to the hotels where they stayed, a reasonable assumption.[44]

While extramarital sex, whether for hire or for free, had always been part of the hotel's life, the new hotels provided more privacy and more types of public meeting places than old inns had offered, enhancing their use for sex. This proved problematic for hotel owners because they could be held liable for renting out rooms for "immoral purposes." The couple who booked a room for commercial sex or even for adultery, depending on the state, effectively made the hotel a party to their crime. As *Hotel World* editor Henry J. Bohn complained, "When it comes to 'cleaning the hotel' by statute the burden is always saddled onto the hotel man. The hotel operator and his staff are penalized for allowing things to happen. Well, maybe . . . the Purest can tell by looking a man or woman in the face whether they are married or not . . . but they should go into hotel service and test the matter." Because it was impossible to tell, Bohn argued, it was unfair to penalize the hotel for not being able to do so: "To ordinary sense it seems as if the person who is guilty of an illegal act is the one who should be penalized and not the innocent victim. But much of the hotel legislation is not conceived and drawn on that basis."[45]

Despite Bohn's complaint, hotel industry journals spent much less time discussing sex in hotels than they did worrying about bouncers and skippers. The difference, presumably, was that in most cases, people who came to the hotel for sex paid their bills. There were also opportunities for symbiotic relationships between hotel staff and sex workers or people who visited the hotel for other kinds of illicit sex. One sex worker who served clients in a hotel explained that her customers paid her for sex and paid the hotel bartender for the rooms where she provided it.[46] This suggested an additional partnership between the bartender and the room clerk to determine which rooms would be for available for hire.

In spite of the generally well-known and potentially lucrative connection between hotels and prostitution, when regular hotel visitor B. D. Gibson brought it up in a letter to *Hotel World*, managers reacted with outrage at the mere suggestion. Just as they were loath to pursue skippers and bouncers for fear of bad publicity, hotel owners and managers feared even to acknowledge a connection between sex work and hotels. In 1922, Gibson, wrote a general query to the industry: "I have been in many of the best hotels in which not only the bell boys but the elevator men also tried to 'sell' me a prostitute." Clearly, he argued, this could not be going on entirely behind the management's back. Why, he asked, did managers allow it?[47]

In response, editor Henry Bohn claimed never to have been solicited for sex in his forty years of travel. Bohn tellingly accused Gibson not only of lying but both of actually seeking out commercial sex *and* of being a prohibitionist, the hotel industry's worst enemy. Edwin Young, steward of a hotel in Chicago, dared Gibson to try to "get a woman in his room" at any of the more well-known hotel chains of the era. If he dared to try, Young claimed, "the Greeter at the desk would ask him for his key, and inform the gentleman that he could perhaps get a room to suit him in some massage parlor in the Tenderloin district."[48] Even while kicking the guest out for bad behavior, the clerk must perform perfect customer service by suggesting another, more appropriate hotel.

Other readers, however, acknowledged Gibson's complaint. One promised that "the proprietors and managers are fighting every minute to keep the business clean and honorable" and that if Gibson were to report solicitation by staff to the manager, the staff member would be disciplined. Help with surveillance was welcome.

While hotel men did not typically discuss the issue with Gibson's frankness, at least in print, they did suggest that policing illicit sex was becoming more difficult because of changes in culture. The increasing trend for women to travel alone caused difficulties for an industry developed with the single male traveler as paradigm. Because women alone in public were automatically considered both suspect and vulnerable, their accommodations were not always smooth.

In 1925, for example, hotel staff searched a woman's room because she had registered at the front desk with her initials, L. L. Corbett. She may well have done this as a protective measure because hotel registers were often open books during this time. Anyone could see that a female guest was staying alone in a particular room and come up with a ruse to force entry. Whatever her reasons, the evening clerk who came on after she registered assumed that the person registered was a man. On learning that there was a woman in the room, the manager had the room searched. Sources do not reveal how the desk clerk became aware of Corbett's gender, but the floor clerk might well have been involved, innocently reporting on the occupants of the floor. Because most hotels did not allow single female guests to "entertain" unrelated men in their rooms, management was prepared to evict the assumed male guest for keeping company with an unregistered woman. Corbett sued the hotel and the case was reported in the industry press as representing an issue that hotel managers should look out for.[49]

In the same year, Henry Bohn complained that women who kept their own names when they married created needless trouble for hotel staff. He referred to such women as "freaks" and imagined a scenario in which a married couple assured a clerk that they were married despite their different names: "'But,' replies the clerk, 'any two people could come along here and claim that, and my only assurance that they are married is their proper registration; what would the manager or proprietor say to me when he notes I roomed Mr. Straight and Mrs. Bentley in the same room the same night, and what would the public and our employees say and think?'"[50] Because marriage was not a visible state, apart from wedding rings, which could be taken on and off so easily, surveillance of the heterosexual couple was extremely difficult. Getting it wrong could have costly consequences.

In 1936, a man sued the hotel because he and his legal wife had been evicted from a hotel for immorality. For reasons not disclosed, the man had registered himself and his wife under the comically false names of Mr. and Mrs. Doe. The hotel detective happened to know the man's true name but had never seen his wife, so he assumed the name had been taken for the sake of illicit sex and had the guests thrown out. When the couple sued, the hotel quickly settled the case, hoping to avoid bad publicity. Although it was the responsibility of the hotel staff and especially the detective's role to know all repeat customers by sight and name, this could sometimes backfire.

Recognition

Knowledge of the guest—a positive kind of surveillance—was encouraged constantly in the industry press as readers were reminded how much people loved to be recognized. The surveillance work that could help to protect the property from damage to material or reputation was also a form of service, elevating the ordinary guest to a kind of local celebrity. As one anonymous writer in the *Hotel Bulletin* noted, "It is amusing, but nevertheless true and only human, perhaps, that every individual wants recognition. Each one is the most important personage in the world to himself." All guests must be treated as if they were special. Creating that sense involved the kind of attentiveness that also served to protect the institution from frauds of all kinds.[51]

Hotel staff were to be constantly vigilant for threats to property and reputation but also maintain the highest level of tact. In 1936, Ralph Hitz's industry guide recommended extreme tact in dealing with suspected sex workers: "A most careful watch must be kept on undesirable women or solicitors." Noting the new spaces created by the modernization of hotels, Hitz reminded clerks to keep moving through those spaces: "It is important that not only the lobby, but also the Mezzanine Floor, the Public spaces on the Ball Room floors, and the lower elevator lobby, should be inspected and undesirable people asked to leave." Especially when dealing with women, "courtesy should be shown, since an unwarranted action on the part of a House Officer may become cause for litigation."[52] Accusing a woman falsely of soliciting could create a terrible situation for a hotel. If those asked to leave resisted, a floor or night manager might be called. Police and bodily removal were the very last resort because of the injury their presence could do to the hotel's reputation. No guest wanted to see the inhospitable side of the business.

This obsessive focus on tact, courtesy, and service regularly functioned at odds with the immediate financial interests of the hotel and yet persisted. Because the modern hotel was established both materially and conceptually as a purveyor of convenience as a commodity, most of the systems that were established in this transitional era were shaped by the need to please customers. In this process, they created needs and expectations that had never factored into hospitality in the past. The physical plant now included industrial laundries, for instance, as well as suggestion cards that actually solicited complaints. Shoes left in the hall would be shined overnight and dirty dishes whisked away by unseen servants. By selling a sense of entitlement, hotels then created for themselves many of the problems that plagued them. For employees throughout the house, this meant hypocrisy as modus operandi, distrust disguised as welcome. That this approach can be deeply problematic for both employee and guest is hinted at in the American Hotel and Lodging Education Institute's training course about unconscious bias, offered for hotel employees in 2019.[53] The greeter as judge remains both a feature and a bug in the field.

CHAPTER 6

Seeing Straight

Policing Sexualities in 1930s Manhattan Nightclubs

JENNIFER LE ZOTTE

In July 1931, New York City police commissioner Edward P. Mulrooney summoned more than three hundred midtown Manhattan nightclub owners to a gymnasium at police headquarters. There, he demanded across-the-board adherence to new regulations designed to eliminate "the type of club and dance hall pictured . . . on the screen and in fiction."[1] After a highly publicized gang-related stabbing and shooting at Midtown's Club Abbey that January, Mulrooney vowed to remove the criminal operatives at the helms of nightclubs. This was the second wave of ordinances toward that end.[2] However, rather than concentrating efforts on crime operatives, Mulrooney directed his attention to "pansy" acts popular in midtown nightclubs, declaring in January: "There will be a shake-up in the nightclubs, especially of those which feature female impersonators." By February *Variety* and New York newspapers were already boasting of the "'Pansy' Stuff Dying."[3] Commissioner Mulrooney's July "commandments," as newspapers termed the numerous rules, continued the anti-pansy crusade.

Far from limiting gang involvement in popular nightspots, the multiplying restrictions concerning gendered and sexualized appearances in the 1930s created new opportunities for organized crime, which expanded interests in illegal sex work and nightclubs catering to gay and gender-nonconforming patrons. When Prohibition ended late in 1933, organized crime substituted some of its lost liquor profits with revenues from prostitution, taking violent command of the business and turning established madams into middle management of sorts. Mulrooney's regulations discouraging "freelancing" prostitutes from using nightclubs or dance halls as recruiting grounds for clientele drove marginalized sex workers to seek the dubious protection of mobsters.[4] While authorities increased their means of surveilling sex workers, proposed legislation punishing customers of sex trade ("johns") failed, in a pattern repeated throughout modern American history.[5]

At the same time, anti-cross-dressing ordinances encouraged the growth of mob-controlled nightclubs catering to homosexual clientele. Historians assign the rise of exclusively gay spaces in the 1940s and 1950s an important role in the creation of cohesive gay rights activism.[6] The history of the creation of spaces segregated by sexual preference in the 1930s, however, is not a tale of liberation. Instead, such clubs represented the increasing isolation of queer urban recreation following the comparative heyday of the 1920s, formed as they were by their patrons' exclusion from "straight" venues. Carving out centers of nighttime recreation designated as strictly heterosexual, gender conforming, and sexually nondeviant required intensified surveillance of potential patrons and employees, and this form of recreational segregation paralleled patterns along racial lines, especially after violence in Harlem and increased policing of the district discouraged white "slumming" by 1935.[7] In Midtown, the resultant legislation trained officials and business owners to "see straight," to recognize freshly prohibited material details of queerness and promiscuity, and to block offenders from employment and enjoyment in midtown Manhattan clubs. After the repeal of Prohibition in 1933, the New York State Liquor Authority (SLA) efficiently used the threat of liquor license loss to deputize owners and employees of nightclubs in the battle to eradicate visible gender and sexuality nonconformity in midtown Manhattan.[8] This chapter examines the context in which laws passed in the rapidly changing regulatory landscape of early 1930s New York City created specific internal guidelines for policing dress and appearances, guidelines that articulated modern exclusionary codes for respectable dress and for "straight" appearances.

The word "straight" appears early in the twentieth century as a casual descriptor of heterosexuality, though officials often used nonspecific terms for opposing assumptions, such as "perversion" and "deviance" describing same-sex preferences, as well as other unsanctioned sexual practices. For example, in 1920, the Committee of Fourteen, New York City's premier anti-prostitution vice squad, referred in its annual report to an increase in "perversion."[9] This ill-defined term covered a variety of possible behaviors, but in the context of the group's aims, most likely indicated homosexuality and oral sex—the latter as a component of prostitution seemingly (and to some, shockingly) on the rise.[10] By at least 1950, "straight" consistently signified a broader identity category, one indicative of a normative, vice-free lifestyle, absent of sexual and gender deviance—an opposite corollary to the word "queer," which in the United States suggested nonstraight sexual orientation sometime early in the twentieth century, though not usually in reformers' lexicon.[11] New York City regulations in the 1930s helped create a visual and material rule book for "straightness," one that went beyond cues of heterosexuality and was suited to the project of extending nightclubs' welcome to affluent and middle-class businessmen and "clean-minded" young people.[12] The clear quest of drafting a top-down, rule-bound, citywide image of nightlife resulted not only in increased racial segregation but also the geographic divorce of queer recreation from its gender-conforming counterparts.

Regulating Dress

A focus on the regulatory details about dress in this period underscores how societal views often put ideas about feminine promiscuity alongside notions of masculine "deviance." Rules about acceptable appearances also show how criminological theories influenced societal response.[13] For decades, as William N. Eskridge points out in his study of laws addressing homosexuality, the "rules used to police gender nonconformity were laws prohibiting crossdressing and prostitution." In the 1920s, though, these laws mostly focused on offending behaviors enabled by appearances, rather than appearances themselves. Even the decades-old laws prohibiting public appearance in "a dress not belonging to his or her sex" were usually used to prosecute *gender fraud*, most often committed by women looking to procure the social, sexual, or economic advantages of manhood.[14] A fresh regulatory emphasis on the specifics of dress and appearances as themselves deviant arose in the 1930s and focused on recreational consumption of various types. For example, Hollywood's film industry succumbed to the Motion Picture Production Code, commonly called the Hays Code, whose dos and don'ts censured dress deemed promiscuous or gender nonconforming.[15]

Coinciding with the new self-regulations of the movie industry, a sort of Hays Code of daily (or nightly) life emerged.[16] As it was with movie producers, club owners and managers were themselves monitored; Mulrooney's restrictions required club personnel to have fingerprints and photographs on file at the police department even as they were given chief responsibility for enforcing the statutes within the club, at the risk of losing their liquor licenses. Assessing physical aspects of midtown Manhattan nightlife, including building structures and spatial organization of the nightclubs themselves and the expected and recorded dress and appearances of patrons and employees, allows us to follow how the material culture of popular recreation affected and reflected expectations about gender, sexuality, and race. While race is not a central part of this chapter's analysis of midtown Manhattan, Harlem's social and economic relationship to nightlife is tightly entwined with the steps taken to homogenize New York City's nightlife visitors. More broadly, to appreciate criminal profiling's effects on marginalized groups, the material details of its development need closer examination. In the late 1920s and 1930s, sociologists and criminologists recommended practices of crime prevention, a broad ideology addressing potential criminal behavior based on all aspects of individuals' lives, including dress and comportment. Scholars have paid little attention to how laws and social standards regarding gender presentation reflected these recommendations.[17]

Increasingly, nightlife laws put responsibility for maintaining establishments' sartorial respectability onto nightclub owners. In addition to targeting gender nonconformity, these regulations also monitored gender-conforming female appearances as part of the city's ongoing (and perennially unsuccessful) attempts to control the sale of sex in the midst of a burgeoning quasi-legal sex industry that included striptease, burlesque, and taxi dancing (where men paid women by the dance). As Elizabeth Alice Clement notes in *Love for Sale*, the 1920s witnessed the commercialization of a broad array of sexual practices, from casual dating to professional prostitution.[18] In the 1930s, dress regulations extended to male and female performers' attire, gender conforming and not, resulting in the effective end of burlesque shows by the 1940s. Commissioner Mulrooney's July 1931 directive demanding "no more rouged and beskirted male entertainers" extended an order passed six months before, not long after the incident at Club Abbey, which insisted that "men are no longer allowed to lift their skirts in 'pansy clubs,'" demonstrating a progression from legislating actions to proscribing dress.[19]

Many of Commissioner Mulrooney's 1931 regulations drew upon the 1926 Cabaret Law targeting fraternization between patrons and performers, cross-gendered dress, and apparent homosexual activity.[20] But the 1931 laws passed the power to regulate clubs and dance halls to the police commissioner, whereas throughout much of the 1920s, the commissioner of licenses had managed such affairs, beginning with dance halls and extending to cabarets in 1926. Commissioner Mulrooney himself gained broad authority over dancing venues in hotels of fewer than two hundred rooms and over all nightclubs organized within the past five years—in other words, since the passage of the Cabaret Law.[21]

Two years later, a major portion of that authority would shift again, to distributors of liquor licenses after repeal—and, perhaps coincidentally, at the same time Mulrooney left his commissioner post to serve as chairman of New York's State Alcoholic Beverage Control Board. An efficient progression of regulatory control based on the threat of liquor license removal secured the fading away of "horticultural lads" from midtown entertainment by the end of the 1930s. In 1938, the State Liquor Authority (SLA) forbade "homosexual-themed bars" and threatened "tolerant establishments with closure." In 1940, the city ordered the fingerprinting of all cabaret employees and required them to hold special identification cards. This expedient measure directly policed mainly the owners and employees (with SLA inspectors running on-site spot checks), holding owners, in turn, accountable for censuring the dress habits of the broader population.[22] This close relationship between the new state authorities controlling liquor licensing and the enforcement of regulations unrelated to alcohol consumption shows how surveillance of commercial sites expanded without direct justification and without comprehensive reliance on law enforcement officials.

Regulating "Vice"

Vice regulation in the 1920s, amid Prohibition, was a mammoth, corrupt, and incomplete undertaking, one increasingly concentrated on nightclubs by the end of the 1920s. With streets brightened by electric light, a large mobile population thanks to Ford's Model T automobiles, and increasing discretionary income for many Americans, nighttime recreation enjoyed a commercial boom throughout much of the 1920s, despite and sometimes encouraged by the prohibition of alcohol by the Eighteenth Amendment to the Constitution. The Volstead Act, which provided enforcement for the amendment, prohibited the manufacture and sale of alcoholic beverages but not the consumption. Therefore, many restaurants and clubs adapted, charging higher cover charges for entrance into establishments and giving away "free" drinks to patrons, sometimes masking the content with teacup service.[23] Organized crime, whose hold on the city's prostitution and illegal gambling was already marked, coalesced even more through covert manufacturing and distribution of alcohol, weathering local raids, padlocking, and in the late 1920s, the federal government's "war on nightclubs."[24] Though Prohibition initially closed reams of smaller nightclubs (of disproportionately nonwhite ownership), the city soon rallied. New York City had more than 30,000 speakeasies and nightclubs by the mid-1920s, despite intermittent municipal padlocking of establishments found in violation of liquor laws.[25]

For at least all of the twentieth century, alcohol reform went hand in hand with efforts to control prostitution, an aim adjunct to monitoring gender presentation. In 1905, members of the New York Anti-Saloon League founded the Committee of Fourteen, dedicated to the abolition of Raines Law hotels. Raines Law, passed in 1896, restricted saloons from selling liquor on Sundays but permitted hotels with more than ten rooms for rent to offer alcohol every day of the week. Savvy saloon owners quickly remodeled upstairs areas to fit the ten-room rule. Increasingly, Raines Law hotels let those rooms to prostitutes, encouraging the spread of sex for sale in the city.[26] In 1910, the committee expanded its purview to include the suppression of all commercial immorality or "vice as a gainful business," which soon came to include cabarets featuring provocative, often interactive dance that broke down lines between spectacle and observers. The Committee of Fourteen forged, especially after World War I, a tightly cooperative relationship with law enforcement, acting as investigative reporters as well as advisory board and lobbyists. The committee took proud responsibility for the passage of several laws concerning prostitution, mostly in conjunction with vagrancy laws—though their efforts to pass a "customer's amendment" to vagrancy laws in order to prosecute johns procuring prostitutes' services was a telling failure.[27]

Early vice reports show that working-class bawdy houses, including some Raines Law hotels, took expert management and organization. By the 1920s, such houses had been all but suppressed. Commercialized sex, like alcohol consumption, adapted after a brief decline. The files of the Committee of Fourteen report a shift from house-based operations to individual entrepreneurs.[28] Automobiles and telephones helped prostitutes keep appointments in secrecy, so that they were able to meet clients in hotels or take men back to their own room in a boarding house. Landladies often allowed for such goings-on, happy to take the additional charge for "privileges" allowing

the entertaining of men.[29] At the same time as these technologically supported changes in prostitution, broader varieties of sex as entertainment
populated Manhattan in the form of taxi dancing, striptease, and burlesque.
This proliferation succeeded in racially segregating sex work, as legal venues
barred the employment of nonwhite women, relegating them to the riskier,
illegal sex work—a still-extant inequality of sex work. Throughout the 1920s
and 1930s, vice laws disproportionately targeted nonwhite club owners and
workers.[30]

While stripping and burlesque dance were at least semilegal until the
1930s, vice investigators trumpeted warnings against nightclubs' "hostess
evil," whereby hostesses subtly steered johns toward "call girls" who stayed
off the streets and used apartments, boarding rooms, or hotels for assignations, thus connecting nightclubs and the new, domestically housed
varieties of prostitution.[31] The new formats for sex workers minimized
streetwalking and made anti-prostitution enforcement difficult. Again, this
applied unevenly across race, with sex workers of color having fewer unsur-
veilled options. In 1927, the Committee of Fourteen trumpeted the chief
moral dangers of nightclubs, and in 1929, New York City police commissioner Grover Whalen used the growing concern over hostesses and prostitution, as well as clubs' popular cross-dressing acts, to justify another series
of nightclub raids and closings—after the federal government's massive 1928
raids failed to limit illegal alcohol consumption and sex work.[32] To further
bolster their own legitimacy and in keeping with the times, the Committee
of Fourteen emphasized their "scientific" analyses leading to these conclusions, which, by 1927, included comprehensive records of alleged prostitutes'
dress.

Fickle Fashions

The Committee of Fourteen's dress analyses, however, are peppered with
ambiguities and inconsistencies over what visually indicated sex work. The
multiplication of spaces in which prostitution was conducted by the 1920s
made it difficult to distinguish between "respectable women" and prostitutes. The new, nighttime inclusion of heightened numbers of young,
unescorted women looking for fun—but not necessarily peddling sex for
profit—confused time-tested cues of prostitution. In courtrooms, sartorial
distinctions were openly debated. Some witnesses claimed they could tell a

prostitute by sight. When pressed by prosecution one man said: "Well, she was dressed what I would call loud." When asked what that meant, he described a not-unfashionable mode of dress for the time: "Well, she had on a red hat with red trimmings, a long tan coat, black lapels, brown dress, princess gown."[33]

By the mid-1920s, visual markers such as face makeup, exposed lower limbs, certain furs, and bright color palates were no longer predictably relegated to sex workers. Fashionable, ready-made clothing was more accessible to New York City women than in any other time or place before in America. By 1920, almost two-thirds of all ready-to-wear clothing produced in America came from New York City, whose central shopping district coincided with Midtown's nightclub scene. And while wealthy women might identity cheaper—and often "louder"—versions of fine clothing, young immigrants and native-born women working in factories as well as taxi dance halls embraced mass-produced offerings as the height of democratic fashionability.[34] Details of class and generation distinctions in fashion are often mischaracterized in historical recollection, however. The popular image of the "flapper" pervades American memory with numerous inaccuracies, "sexing up" the fashions of young, adventurous women, portraying them as more fringed, less covered, and cut for more suggestive movement than the original models. Dresses made for nightlife notably emphasized comfort and even masked secondary sex characteristics with dropped waists, high necks, and exposed backs—at the same time correlating menswear favored nipped waists and slim tailoring. The androgynous *garçonne* look exemplified by New York City fashions signaled complex relationships with urban environments and personal identity.[35]

Yet amid increasing difficulties in categorizing women's sartorial intent in the nighttime context, the Committee of Fourteen committed to the value of identifying links between prostitution and manners of dress. Between 1927 and 1932—the committee's final years—investigators compiled more than two thousand "personal description cards," cataloging the appearance and apparel of suspected or verified prostitutes. Committee records offer no indication of the purpose for which these files were retained, but the close attention to dress might have been part of a plan to determine something like sex workers' uniforms or particular stylistic proclivities (or, possibly, something more like prurient interest). The description details included locations (hotel, speakeasy, or tenement), recorded price of services, and nation of origin and/or race, but the bulk of attention was on apparel.

Color, cleanliness, cut, style, and fabric were specified on nearly every card. Distinctions were made between types of fur—rabbit, squirrel, caracul, fitch, raccoon, and mink—and whether they were imitation or genuine, indicating that the male investigators were at least passably acquainted with women's clothing's distinguishing characteristics, even if ill-equipped to interpret their meaning. Amid the Committee of Fourteen's concerns about the access to higher-end operations due to budget constraints, especial detail was paid to those prostitutes listed as securing higher prices. Specific shades ("orchid," "cream," "maroon," "rose") were recounted, as were hat types ("Milan straw," "turban," tamashanter" [sic]). Even haircuts—"Dutch bob"—were sometimes detailed.[36]

This precise accounting of dress dovetailed with regulations newly attentive to such details, even as other indicators insist that sartorial distinctions between "respectable" women and prostitutes were increasingly unreliable. At the same time, scandal further compromised the legitimacy of New York City prostitution regulations. In 1930, in the midst of compiling personal description cards for alleged prostitutes, the Committee of Fourteen found itself tainted by Women's Court scandals revealed by newspaper investigations. Charges that members of the New York City police department were racketeers compelled Commissioner Mulrooney to fast-track trials for twenty-eight officers after a "go-between" admitted to having been hired by detectives of the vice squad in a lucrative entrapment scheme, whereby the police extracted tribute from accused prostitutes and madams.[37] Widespread details about the court-and-police graft committed in the name of vice regulation compromised the usual anti-prostitution proceedings—perhaps another factor in encouraging rules concerning feminine dress in clubs as a stopgap measure to control sexual behaviors.

Identifying homosexuals by their apparel at the dawn of the Great Depression also grew less reliable. Significantly, nightlife observers, including sociologists, found that in the 1920s cross-dressing no longer served as a reliant indicator of homosexuality. In fact, reformers, after noting cross-dressing in reports frequently in the years following World War I, did not themselves "rely on the presence of gender reversal to classify homosexuals."[38] As George Chauncey shows, during the interwar period, societal notions of binary sexual identities strengthened, particularly in New York City. Previously, homosexual behavior, while still often disapproved of, was seen as an action rather than a stable, personal characteristic. Its acceptability varied a bit depending on the role of the participant (with men, the receptive "fairy" or the masculine "trade") and the frequency of the activity, but over the course of the early twentieth century, "homosexual" became a noun, something one *was*, often presumed by not only sexual activity but gender comportment, even as sex and gender became unbound in medical analyses of sexuality.[39]

The shift in perceptions of homosexual identity from an apparent gender category marked by "inversion" and often discernible by dress and comportment to a sexual identity reliant on choice of partners alone threw attempts to visually recognize sexual "deviants" into doubt. Shifting fashion standards further complicated any prospect of quickly recognizing queerness based on attire. Effete male fashions with careful attention to accessorizing detail and bright splashes of color grew in popularity among even the most public (and heterosexual) of figures. For example, Mayor Jimmy Walker, a well-known nightclub regular elected to city office in 1926, dressed flamboyantly with tailored, pinched-waist single-button suit jackets that clung to his slight frame, "toothpick"-pointed shoes, a wide collection of fedoras and derbys, and modishly narrow cravats—much of which dipped into a garish palate of emeralds and purples, including his favored lavender handkerchiefs (Figure 6.1).[40] Theatrical elements of color and cut preferred by Walker might have correlated to reliable cues of homosexual preferences in years past, but by the early 1930s, they were simply fashion-forward.

As Americans encountered ideas of binary sexualities, they simultaneously observed an uncoupling of gender presentation from those expectations alongside more rapid and experimental fashion cycles. Somewhat inconsistently, then, a major shift in perceptible gender and sexuality identity in America tracked with the increasing regulation of appearances in addition to behaviors. As both homosexuality and prostitution became more visually elusive, authorities grasped at methods to at least eliminate the appearance of deviance in New York City—a goal that escalated later in the 1930s, when Mayor Fiorello La Guardia honed an urban utopian vision in preparation for the New York World's Fair in 1939.[41] These obvious inconsistencies arose because regulatory failures severed previous avenues of vice control at the same time New York City officials wanted to cultivate a global image of a safe, "straight" urban commercial scene. Ultimately, the enforcement

Figure 6.1. Mayor Jimmy Walker of New York City in Boston (circa 1930). Walker's elegant style was the height of urban fashion and employed elements such as a trim cut and bright colors, formerly associated with effeminate men. Courtesy of the Boston Public Library, Leslie Jones Collection.

of dress conformity in midtown nightclubs represented attempts to manage consumer impressions, rather than a full-throated, morally motivated effort to eliminate sex work or public homosexual activity.

Crime Prevention and Spectacle

The centering of reform advice on the problem of nightclubs, the reorganizing of regulatory standards and their locus of control, and the economic imperative for robust and apparently "wholesome" nightlife offer some practical reasons for focusing on dress and appearances in 1930s Manhattan. Further justification for using dress as a trackable indicator of bad behavior comes from emerging theoretical trends in criminology. In the late 1920s, sociologists and criminologists foregrounded the new concept of crime prevention and undertook more comprehensive detailing of the life histories of verified or potential deviants in order to chart patterns enabling observers to hypothesize as to a subject's criminal potential. Related methodology grew by the 1960s into criminal profiling practices, but in the 1930s existed as a spreading belief in the collaborative nature of criminal indications; dress showed tendencies. Sociologists lobbied for measures in schools and communities to forestall future deviant behavior, and the "life-history approach" developed by criminologists in Chicago took a comprehensive view of at-risk youths' assessment. If a youth has one or more indicators of criminality, those displays need checking, lest the infliction metastasize, within the youth and across the encountered population.[42] The first formal crime prevention division was formed in 1925, in Berkeley, California, as a crime prevention/juvenile unit. Crime prevention advocates believed in the idea of crime waves, acting in cycles and washing over populations, especially susceptible youth. By the 1950s, a concentrated focus on children in preventing homosexual activity would echo these measures, offering intimidating speakers and public service announcements geared at preventing school-age kids from same-sex experimentation—and marking careful or delicate dress habits as a suggested warning sign in boys.[43] As of yet, no comprehensive historical research connects crime prevention theories of the 1930s to later homophobic subjugation based on appearances, but correlation is apparent.

Whether disingenuously or not, Commissioner Mulrooney linked the gang violence at Club Abbey's to the popular "pansy" performances there, in a vice-begets-vice attitude. "Professional pansy" Jean (Gene) Malin served as Club Abbey's flamboyant host of events, performing a humorous stereotype of a homosexual man, following his earlier popularity as a female impersonator in a number of Manhattan venues, which had gained him marked notoriety—enough that, when Club Abbey closed a few days following the gang-related violence, Malin left New York City altogether to continue his career in Hollywood.[44] In a period when the newest theories about criminality focused on preventing crime, a varied host of supposedly deviant attributes signified a broader criminal nature. A perception of all "degeneracy" as mutually supportive helped the commissioner casually link aberrant dress to the violence disrupting nighttime order, even as gang-led commercial management expanded exactly because of the laws regarding such appearances.

Through the 1920s, national mass media culture as well as transportation innovation meant that more Americans than ever, and especially more New Yorkers, encountered sexually expressive entertainment. In bohemian Greenwich Village, Harlem, and eventually, established Midtown clubs, well-to-do "slummers" with Model Ts could participate in previously off-limits entertainment—whether paying for women's attention through taxi dances or dallying with "lady lovers" while openly queer blues musician Gladys Bentley performed in a tux.[45] This expansion of exposure to "vice" across class and race lines bolstered arguments about moral decay, sparking reaction from various levels. Proximity and interaction mattered, and as the line between spectacle and participation seemed to blur, moralists fine-tuned reform approaches and sought to redraw parameters of acceptable sexual representation, often relying on visual cues. Harlem Renaissance poet Langston Hughes called the Hamilton Club Lodge's annual drag ball, popular throughout much of the 1920s, a "spectacle in color." Known as "the Faggot's Ball," this event was the largest annual gathering of lesbians and gay men in Harlem, the city, and maybe the United States. As Hughes pointed out, it was only by a distant consuming gaze that the Hamilton Lodge's queens appear "authentic." "From the boxes these men look for all the world like very pretty chorus girls parading across the raised platform in the center of the floor. But close up, most them look as if they need a shave, and some of their evening gowns, cut too low, show hair on the chest."[46] Distance between performers and viewers was necessary in order to maintain the illusion of femininity, as well as acceptably chaste voyeurism. Increasingly, intimate New York City cabarets closed the gap, raising vice squad alarms.

The 1926 Cabaret Law prohibited, among other things, direct interactions between performers and patrons. In 1931, Commissioner Mulrooney further emphasized boundaries of spectacle first by limiting performers' actions to those that maintained illusion (disallowing rouged men to "lift their skirts") and six months later by specifying the prohibition of certain queer appearances. Additionally, Mulrooney declared "no more entertainers mingling with patrons at night clubs," a step intended to limit same-sex interactions and forestall opportunities for prostitution's assignations. Also intended to slow trade in prostitution, there were to be "no more taxi dance halls with men only allowed," as those infamous pay-by-the-dance events were viewed by some as nothing less or more than negotiating grounds for sex trade.[47] A similar problem focused the rationale of the Hays Code (as published March 31, 1930), which blamed the advent of technologies allowing for synchronized sound in movies. "Sound unlocked a vast amount of dramatic material which for the first time could be effectively presented on the screen."[48] In other words, talkies brought a new level of perceived intimacy between actors and public, elevating accusations of undue influence. Reformers argued cabaret-style encounters had similar effects.

In 1932, Mayor Jimmy Walker's administration launched a much-publicized campaign against body-baring burlesque, detailing prohibited appearances. Burlesque entertainment had, over the course of the century, evolved to be a sort of sexualized satire of feminine (and sometimes feminist) notions and appearances. By 1931, burlesque's geographical center was darkened, Depression-cheapened Broadway haunts, peppered with large, lurid electric-light signs summoning patrons with near-nude forms and declarations such as "Bigby Hind from Peoria."[49] Mayor Walker used the by-then-established means of dance-hall licensing to call major burlesque establishments to the carpet. In order to prove substantive difference from the nearly naked chorus lines of the more acceptable and more profitable Ziegfeld Follies and other popular revues, the commissions focused on specific sorts of ultra-revealing dress in a bid to protect established Broadway merchants by detailing burlesque-specific tropes, raising the question of whether fleshly exposure was really the ultimate target. As historian Robert Allen notes, "the real issues in the burlesque licensing issue were economic and political, not moral." As the *New York Times* acknowledged, the crudeness of the burlesque displays was "exceeded by their external frowsiness."[50] The material aspects of establishments in their entirety influenced the actionability of the dress or undress of their employees.

Tussling over burlesque establishments' licensing continued throughout much of the 1930s, ending in multiple prosecutions. The essential death of Broadway burlesque by 1939 amid the persistence of also-lurid, but-more-polished revues illustrated the selectivity of laws concerning dress and appearance, even as such laws multiplied. After the end of Prohibition, city officials eager for renewed liquor revenues sought to portray night life as ever exciting but newly restrained. As the *New York Times* claimed two months after legal liquor reemerged, New York had found "its old gayety and a new decorum in drinking."[51] In many ways, selective restrictions were only new in detail, not in kind, and represented ongoing debates over the rights and privileges of urban public spaces, as well as acceptable boundaries of spectacle and entertainment. In 1845, a law criminalized appearing "disguised" in public places (following a masked shooting at an Old Park Theater ball).[52] Private events were unaffected; if anything, the illegality of public masquerade added cultural cachet to the privately held but heavily publicized fancy-dress balls later in the century, such as the Vanderbilt Ball of 1883 and the Bradley-Martin Ball of 1897.[53] The ability to masquerade, to dress in departure from one's socially determined economic, racial, or gender status, and present that image to others, was deemed a formal privilege. In 1876, the law was revised to allow "masquerade of fancy dress ball[s]" with special licensing or police permission—allowing, for example, the Bradley-Martin Ball's location at the Waldorf Hotel, or the annual Patriarch's Ball at Delmonico's. As early as 1890, police applied the masquerade law to cross-dressers; in 1935, Mayor La Guardia demanded its enforcement to clear gender nonconformists from midtown Manhattan.[54] In 1938, the State Liquor Authority (SLA) forbade homosexual-themed bars and threatened "tolerant establishments with closure," ushering in an era of illicit, mob-controlled gay nightlife. In the two and a half decades that followed, the SLA, in coordination with other agencies, closed hundreds of bars that welcomed, tolerated, or even merely failed to observe the inclusion of gay men and lesbians.[55]

In this same period, vicarious and nonphysical spectacle was monitored and censored by the Hays Code, passed in 1930 and fully enforced by 1934. In a 1933 summary of Broadway's dilapidated state, *New York Herald Tribune* editor Stanley Walker highlighted three central "hallmarks" of disrepute: "cheap dances, lewd burlesque, [and] filthy pictures."[56] Numerous parallels exist between the progression of strictures placed on New York nightclub attendees and Hollywood film during the same period. There are clear and direct connections, for example, via actor Mae West, whose plays featured cross-dressing and other targeted "nonstraight" representation (West scoured Greenwich dance halls for female impersonators). West's *The Drag* and *Sex* were both curtained by William Randolph Hearst's statewide stage censorship law in 1927. Also in 1927, internal Hollywood censors issued a pre–Production Code list of "Don'ts" and "Be Carefuls," many of which Mae West's early screen productions would also fall afoul of.[57]

By 1931, pansy performers such as Jean Malin felt unwelcome in New York, and some would try their luck in Hollywood, but the silver screen would not be a safe haven for cross-dressing. In 1930, the Hays Code formalized the "Don'ts" and "Be Carefuls." Race, dress, and sex were the most thoroughly addressed under "Particular Applications," where several categories of sexual representation were forbidden according to "costume," including "dancing costumes intended to permit undue exposure or indecent movements," demonstrating that municipal attention to burlesque popularity extended to films.[58] Other dress-related no-no's were simply lumped under a catchall category of sexual perversion, but Hollywood censors made it abundantly clear that the sort of sexual comedy recently imported onto the screen from vaudeville and burlesque, including gender role reversal, was not acceptable. A much-censored and explosively controversial film, *So This Is Africa* (1933), underscored the joint importance of cross-gender dress and hinted-at interracial sex in the subsequent stricter enforcement of the code beginning in 1934. The slapstick plot of *So This Is Africa* is instructive, involving as it does, white men adopting female personas to avoid sexual subjection under primitive matriarchal nonwhite rule. Instead, adapting too much to their female garb, they succumb to inverted (by American standards) gender and racial subjection.[59]

At the same time Hollywood obliged with codes that included clear directives about gender-adherent dress and appearance, hundreds of New York nightclub owners were given even clearer directives as to what kinds of dress to allow into clubs hoping to remain legally solvent. The idea that there was a Hays Code of daily life is vital in relation to the crafting of segregated—by race as well as sexuality and gender presentation—public spaces. Just as there were clear economic motives for the enforcement of the Hays Code, the shift from integrated public sites to sexually exclusive recreational spaces was a response as much to demands to maintain economic hierarchies as it was to moral backlash.[60] The repeal of prohibition, vital context here, was justified both for its business stimuli and prevention of criminal activity. In 1933, Mulrooney left his post as police commissioner for chairman of the SLA. On the first anniversary of the repeal, Mulrooney argued that the only thing more salutary "than the economic impetus of repeal has been the profound effect upon the social and moral life of the country."[61] Upwards of $10 million in liquor license fees were collected in the New York District in 1934.[62] Profit from liquor sales were the carrot, but the specific conditions required for nightclubs to sell liquor legally served as the stick and legitimated increased and more subjective consumer surveillance.

Much as it was not only Hollywood actors and films' written content but also producers and studios that the Hays Code sought to control, municipal restrictions as conditions for liquor licensing required increased surveillance of as well as by nightclub owners. Just as anti-Semitism informed aspects of the Hollywood Hays Code, hegemonic racial and gender control can be inferred from the depiction of the nightclub owners ordered to follow Mulrooney's new commandments; one report from the newspaper *Afro-American* claimed that "Chinese, Filipino and colored managers were in the majority."[63] A front-page *New York Times* report justified the skewed representation (and placed the percentage lower, at one-fourth nonwhite) by claiming that it is "among these" that the "closed" dance hall was reported to be most popular, indicating a regulatory targeting of nonwhite prostitution, even as high-profile, elite-catering white madams such as Polly Adler escaped conviction repeatedly. The same article also simply reflected, "there were many women."[64] Mulrooney's rules put nightclubs wholly under surveillance, ownership included. Owner, operator, and manager were required to have verified addresses on file, along with photographs and fingerprints. Correct names and addresses of all employees were also required. Newspapers throughout the 1930s repeated claims that these measures unevenly disadvantaged small businesses under nonwhite, nonmale ownership. The 1926 Cabaret Law remained on the books as well, demanding nightclubs close at 3 A.M., as a "detriment to the town"; white, male fraternal organizations such as the Elks or the Masons were exempt from the curfew, as they were "an ornament," according to Mayor Walker.[65]

Nightclub Spaces

Numerous material changes to nightclubs in the 1930s facilitated increased surveillance of patrons and employees. Between 1933 and 1938, midtown nightlife resurged, adapted for the tenuous fiscal milieu, and was both boosted and corralled by the end of Prohibition. Unlike Hollywood films, Manhattan's nightclubs were themselves physical, interactive spaces. Some of the changes in venue locations, building structures and capacity, and cost, predated the Great Depression. Gone were most high cover changes, and as of December 1933, illegal liquor, too. After 1930, in a move to attract larger numbers with shallower pockets and mimicking the new model, clubs streamlined high-end services requiring internal personnel such as head-waiters, but kept or increased the boundary surveyors such as doormen, sometimes called bouncers by this time, who became requisite components of nightlife under the constraints and shifted costs of Prohibition. In the 1930s, bouncers' jobs evolved to include barring gender- and sexuality-nonconforming patrons, with the imperative of conforming to the require-ments for liquor licensing, and, by 1938, in keeping with new ordinances entirely prohibiting gender "masquerade."[66]

While bouncers remained, key architectural elements of the most popu-lar Manhattan nightclubs in the 1930s diverged from those of the previous decade. The 1920s speakeasies, responding to the imperative of legal obscu-rity, often had no windows and poor lighting. Mulrooney, addressing the Bond Club in 1932, bemoaned the clandestine aspects of speakeasies by reminiscing: "The old licensed place was fairly well lighted; it was reason-ably clean." Misbehaving customers only needed to be eased out of the ground-level swinging door, he went on, conjuring images of Old West sa-loons. "Now they are in subcellars and as high up as the thirty-sixth floor."[67] Spy-holes, manned by doormen or bouncers to limit entrance to trustwor-thy patrons, were the only visage to outdoors, and along with conveniently located drains for quick disposal of liquor and false wall panels for storage, the overall aesthetic of speakeasies was dark, close, and secretive. Even "class clubs" striving to attract a higher-end clientele, often created literal space between themselves and authorities in the 1920s. Roof gardens were elegant and out in the open—but often with numerous doors and multiple entrances and exits to elude or stall authorities.[68] Several of the measures taken by Commissioner Mulrooney in July of 1931 addressed the physical layout and attributes of clubs. Accordingly, he forbade "doors with buzzers to warn of police approach" as well as "closed booths inside."[69]

In the late 1920s, Mayor Jimmy Walker himself ordered expensive alter-ations to his favored nightspot, the Central Park Casino, so that he could monitor arriving guests from the dining room's main entrance. In this case, Walker's demands were purportedly crafted around a desire to maintain a tally over who was observing him out and about with his mistress, actress Betty Compton.[70] Whatever the private and economic motivations behind the renovations to 1930s nightclubs, trends for large, open spaces with brightly lit windows enabled surveillance of nightclubs—or "bars," as they were increasingly called, adjunct to other material changes to the venues. Commissioner Mulrooney, as a condition of repeal, made nightclubs "table drinking only," and allowed only service bars, which became more physically central to establishments. By the late 1930s, regulations demanded the physical separation of dance floors from restaurant tables, too, usually effected by roped-off zones, in order to limit interactions between guests and employees serving food and drink and musicians and performers.[71]

Clothing played a central role in the enforcement of new "orderly" requirements for establishments with liquor licenses, as well as in the details of those requirements. Starting early in 1931, Commissioner Mulrooney posted plainclothes officers outside all nightclubs featuring performances of female impersonators, which was no new ploy. SLA investigators and policemen echoed the stealthy procedures enacted by 1920s authorities. Then, vice squad reporters dressed to blend in, and canvassed their beats with a note-taking thoroughness that has left invaluable record of Manhattan surveillance in the 1920s. For example, in 1926, two policewomen staked out Club 300 before a raid "dressed and acting as if they were visiting flappers seeking a thrill."[72] By the late 1930s, the SLA, with its exclusive authority to hand out and revoke licenses, had well established similar practices in assigning investigators to nightclub beats. In 1939, individual SLA staff claimed credit for "hundreds" of detailed investigations of nightclubs reported to tolerate homosexual patrons, all conducted in plain clothes. According to the new statutes, authorities no longer had to wait for arrestable actions, but could and did exact retribution on the nightclubs merely for patrons' appearances.[73] Under Fiorello La Guardia's mayoral tenure (1934–45), anti-homosexual nightlife reform accelerated, especially in anticipation of the New York World's Fair in 1939 and 1940. Strict policing was enacted, and the added focus on public appearances—essentially, the new specifics of sexual profiling—was rooted in Mulrooney's earlier regulatory design.

The new regulations on appearances at Midtown nightclubs were in part a reaction against the perceived excess and liberality of the 1920s, in the context of the Great Depression. However, several factors enabled and required a rerouting of regulatory focus, including the failure to control either alcohol consumption or prostitution, owing not only to the participating citizenry, but to federal and municipal corruption. In the 1930s, changes in *who* regulated nightlife mattered as much as changes in *what* was regulated. In 1933, both the Anti-Saloon League and the Committee of Fourteen disbanded, not long before the repeal of prohibition, and in the wake of reporting on Women's Court corruption and police prostitution graft. While the Committee of Fourteen did not have formal regulatory power, their surveillance and advisory oversight had shaped legislation and enforcement for decades. Their disappearance indicated the failure of foregoing efforts and signaled new imperatives for nightlife control. At the same time, the moral precedent of Prohibition, despite its compromises, emboldened subsequent regulators. Prohibition, arguably the broadest, most ambitious morally motivated legislation attempted in the United States, interpreted the Constitution in a way that limited, rather than protected, the personal liberties of individuals.[74] The issuing of dance licenses during the 1920s had already given the licensing department ample experience in policing nightlife. Adding liquor licenses as rewards for good behavior and acceptable appearances greatly enhanced the authority of licensing and created a sort of urban panopticon for nightlife participants by distributing enforcement responsibility to individual owners and managers.[75]

In some regards, the strictures on personal appearances made regulatory sense, following as they did alongside patterns of oversight designed to conform consumers to a top-down vision of wholesome nightlife, to be projected broadly in a bid for economic recovery. However, social, cultural, and even medical perceptions and expectations of dress and sexuality brought these regulatory aims into question by casting doubt on clear sartorial links to "abhorrent" behaviors such as homosexuality and prostitution. In an era when dress defined the sexual proclivities of the wearer less and less apparently, laws regarding apparel reflected expectations of sartorial conformity more than effective efforts to control sexual behavior, presaging or even shaping the gender-conforming dress and fashions of post–World War II America.

CHAPTER 7

High Priority

Business's War on Drugs and the Expansion of Surveillance in the United States

JEREMY MILLOY

It takes spies to win a war, and we're in a war.
—William Huston, security chief, Boise Cascade

It raises the specter of Big Brother and fosters an incredible snitch mentality. It's getting to the point where it's not "Just Say No" but "Just Say Who."
—Loren Siegel, American Civil Liberties Union attorney

Businesses and employers must make it clear that drug use and employment are incompatible.
—President George H. W. Bush

In 1987, Peyton Schur was in the private investigation business, and business was booming. "We used to spend half our time hustling business," he told the *Los Angeles Times*. "Now it's almost to the point we're beating them off with a stick." Schur's Confidential Management Services had just opened a third California office. Schur's new clients were not worried spouses or defense attorneys but businesses concerned their employees were getting high. Cal Flores, with Schur's competition at Kennedy Consulting Investigations, echoed his report of a banner business climate, saying "local businesses are developing an awareness for the first time of how bad the [drug] problem is in the workplace."[1]

The previous October, the cover of *Nation's Business*, the official magazine of the U.S. Chamber of Commerce, had announced "Business' War on Drugs." The headline was appropriate. While historians have revealed much about the war on drugs as a government intervention—supported by law enforcement and the media, targeting illicit drug users, especially users of color, and deeply intermeshed with American imperial foreign policy in drug-producing regions—both the government and business itself felt that the private sector also had a major role to play.[2] In 1986, the Reagan administration's Executive Order 12564—Drug-Free Federal Workplace—argued that the federal government, "as the largest employer in the Nation, can and should show the way towards achieving drug-free workplaces through a program designed to offer drug users a helping hand and, at the same time, demonstrating to drug users and potential drug users that drugs will not be tolerated in the Federal workplace."[3] To encourage others, President Reagan and Vice President George H. W. Bush both participated in urine testing. This touched off a testing mania in the 1986 midterm elections, when, in the words of Harry Levine and Craig Reinarman, "candidates challenged one another to urinate into specimen cups to prove their moral purity."[4]

American business largely endorsed this zero-tolerance approach. Many businesses believed that they bore much of the estimated $140 billion that drug and alcohol abuse cost the U.S. economy each year and that substance abuse among employees was causing absenteeism, lowered productivity, greater risks to themselves, their coworkers, and firms' security and profitability.[5] Businesses were also convinced that they were uniquely placed to spearhead the attack on substance abuse. As *Nation's Business* argued, "business has the potential for being more effective than any other force in turning back the drug invasion."[6] Experts in the recovery field and employers alike argued that addicts would put their addiction ahead of their friends, their partners, their children, but could be jolted out of denial by a threat to their employment. Despite the integral role played by business in the war on drugs, however, historians have largely ignored employer involvement and its impact.

This chapter historicizes business's war on drugs, placing in the context of the larger history of corporate, expert, union, and worker interventions to identify and treat workers with substance use disorders. In the 1980s and 1990s, these interventions were superseded by a punitive approach that focused on illicit substances above more commonly used and problematic legal ones: surveillance, exemplified by but not limited to drug testing

Figure 7.1. In the 1980s, American businesses increasingly placed surveillance at the center of their drug and alcohol policies. William Hoffer, "Business' War on Drugs," *Nation's Business*, October 1986, 18. Courtesy of the Hagley Museum and Library.

(Figure 7.1). This surveillance turn in workplace health touched off clashes in workplaces and courtrooms nationwide. It complemented and advanced neoliberal management innovations that individualized employees and prioritized the identification and elimination of future risks. By successfully establishing workplace drug testing as normative, employers won crucial cultural and legal battles that opened the field for greater biometric and digital employee surveillance. Business also established employee's bodies and social lives as lucrative sites of profit for a burgeoning new drug-testing industry.

Scholars have discussed earlier corporate intrusions into the off-hour activities of workers, including employee housing in company towns, the use of medical exams to evaluate worker health, welfare workers who sought to improve the lives of employees while being accountable to employers, and Henry Ford's peering into workers' homes through his Sociological Department.[7] Business's war on drugs was in this tradition but departed from these earlier initiatives in important ways. Whereas earlier incursions were primarily surveillance occurring as part of the administration of benefits to workers—higher wages, health care, company welfare programs, and workplace improvements—business's war on drugs created additional barriers to employment and offered the extension of no separate benefit, aside from some surveillance-linked employee assistance programs. The surveillance turn of the 1980s, exemplified by urinalysis, was generally more bodily invasive than earlier employer intrusions, affected a greater number of workers who lived much more greatly mixed into the general American population and focused more narrowly on drug and alcohol use—and often solely drugs. It also exposed workers to much greater risks of legal consequences. Therefore, while workplace surveillance, even over substance use, did not begin in the 1980s, the term "surveillance turn" is apt, considering the expansion of substance use surveillance in the era, the changing employee health emphasis from treatment to surveillance, and how the decade's normalization of drug-related surveillance anticipated the crucial role surveillance through wearable devices and smartphone applications now plays in employee health and wellness plans, as legal scholar Elizabeth A. Brown has explored.[8]

Recovering and understanding the nature, impact, and reach of employee assistance programs and drug testing presents challenges for the historian. While policies and proposals are fairly easy to find, confidentiality and stigmatization mean information about how programs actually worked is elusive. In order to obtain the widest possible sample of data on these programs and their impact, I have drawn opportunistically on contemporary media accounts, business reports, and academic studies; court records; and congressional hearings. This gave me a broad, wide-ranging set of data that allowed me to evaluate trends in the reasons for program adoption, the nature of surveillance instituted in the workplace, and the controversies and conflicts that arose from business's war on drugs nationally, across a variety of industries and workplace settings. As noted below, large companies were more likely to institute testing and to offer employee assistance programs. These large firms, however, are pivotal in influencing national workplace dynamics and management approaches.

This chapter aims to contribute a necessary historical dimension to scholarly understandings of surveillance. While this literature is of great theoretical vision, it often fails to locate surveillance, and resistance to it, in specific workplaces and contexts. Surveillance literature has taught us much about surveillance capacities and operations.[9] Historical work enhances surveillance knowledge by recovering what surveillance has actually done and how surveillance has been implemented and contested in the real world; how much it lives up to the totalizing potential with which it is billed; and what the impacts of surveillance have been on people and spaces.

This piece generates its insights into worker surveillance from an analysis of changes and continuities in workplace surveillance as actually practiced. I am thus operating in the tradition of surveillance scholars including Kirstie Ball, Karen Levy, and my collaborators on this volume, from who I have learned a great deal. Like Levy's work on truckers, this chapter reveals how generating data on previously invisible aspects of workers lives opens new frontiers of control for employers. Ball's work highlights surveillance's "transformative effects on . . . occupational experiences." It informs my interest in the normalization of surveillance through the workplace, as well as the possibilities and limitations of worker resistance to the employer and state gaze. Finally, the work of Shoshanna Zuboff, particularly her *In The Age of the Smart Machine*, a deep meditation on the impacts of computational technology on the lives and spirits of blue- and white-collar workers, shares my interest with how the introduction of information technology, in this case drug testing and surveillance, reshaped the experiences of American workers and American workplaces in the 1980s, and shows that, in this case, surveillance was not a revolution from above in search of social control;

it was implemented after the employee recovery work of many different parties, while largely humanistic in focus, nonetheless legitimized employer observation and intervention in worker substance use.

The surveillance turn was influenced by a number of factors: not simply government encouragement and a desire for social control but also economic incentives, including the perceived high cost of rehabilitation programs versus drug testing; the growth of a private drug testing industry with significant connections to key government drug warriors; a belief in the certainty and clarity of drug testing; and corporate cultures that increasingly focused on risk management and employee flexibility, which fostered a greater employee interest in monitoring employees' habits, encouraging them to monitor their own. This chapter grounds surveillance theory in the complexity of actualization, revealing the contingency, contestation, and partiality that shape how and why employers actually implement and conduct surveillance and how workers respond.[10]

This is particularly salient given Zuboff's observation that workplaces are "the gold standard of habituation contexts, where invasive technologies are normalized among captive populations of employees."[11] Business's expansion of surveillance clearly served the prerogatives of American capitalism, and in turn it is illustrative of the extent to which these prerogatives have influenced how substance use, and people who use substances, are understood, defined, and treated by employers, health providers, and the state. It also did significant work as part of the wider war on drugs. Through surveillance, employers established the workplace as a crucial arena for advancing the war on drugs, expanding the expectation of drug-related surveillance from marginalized, racialized, criminalized citizens to "straights" or "regular people" whose personal habits normally would not be the focus of surveillance; who enjoyed a greater expectation of privacy than street drug users and racialized communities who already lived under intense state scrutiny. The surveillance turn in workplace health was a crucial front in the war on drugs, influencing approaches to substance use and advancing corporate biometric and social surveillance as an acceptable phenomenon in American life. In turn, participation in a government-led war on drugs empowered businesses to more heavily surveil their employees. In the battles over business's war on drugs, employers won key legal and cultural victories that enabled their widespread use of digital and biometric surveillance to exploit and control workers in the years to come. Before there were Google

Glass and keystroke capture, in other words, there were "eyes on the bottle" urine testing and locker searches.

Addiction Treatment and Substance Surveillance in the Postwar Workplace: From Industrial Alcoholism to a "Broad Brush"

Despite the breathless proclamations of government, media, and CEOs in the 1980s about the new scourge of worker substance use, business had already dealt with a perceived epidemic of drug use and abuse among employees—in just the decade before, in fact. During the 1970s, employee drug use, connected to returning Vietnam veterans and the counterculture aging into regular employment, was identified by business, media, and experts as a serious, growing concern. A 1971 *New York Times* article warned that "secretaries and office boys report being approached by marijuana dealers in the New York Telephone Company; service employes sniff cocaine in some Miami hotels." The article's closing words belonged to Robert Wiencek, a General Motors plant medical director, who argued, "Eventually industry will have to rehabilitate the drug user. . . . The prevalence is increasing at a high rate among young people and they are the reservoir of the future work force."[12]

Concerns over employee drug use presented a challenge to the industrial alcoholism movement, which had grown rapidly after World War II, in concert with the growth of Alcoholics Anonymous. Here also, employers had been major players in the response to a perceived workplace addiction crisis, exemplified by the figure of R. Brinkley Smithers, a former IBM executive and recovered alcoholic who gave millions to fighting alcoholism and did more than perhaps any other American to popularize the disease concept for understanding and treating alcoholism.[13] Adding concerns about drug use to existing programs for employee alcohol abuse was an important factor influencing a major shift in workplace interventions, from industrial alcoholism to an employee assistance plan (EAP) or "broad-brush" model. EAPs sought to diminish possible stigmatization by removing explicit references to alcoholism in service provision, to capture alcoholics in denial by offering assistance for other personal problems that might have had alcoholism as a root cause, and to attract employees with other psychological and health problems, including debt, marital conflicts, and, of course, drug addiction.

A leading labor figure in the treatment of worker alcoholism lambasted this shift as a pernicious expansion of employer surveillance. Leo Perlis, director of community programs for the AFL-CIO, argued in a letter to union leaders and union community service providers that

we have avoided all current "catch all" phrases and programs such as Troubled Employee, Broad Brush, and Employee Assistance. These programs are designed to lump all job problems and behavioral elements into one basket. They include, among other things, a job performance surveillance system. This is coupled with a so-called "personal" record keeping, often on a daily basis, about an "employee's work performance or behavior." . . . It would seem that is a matter for normal collective bargaining and grievance procedures rather than for "Personal" record keeping by supervisors.[14]

However, no matter their name, both industrial alcoholism and broad-brush programs depended upon employer surveillance of employees. Constructive confrontation, the most influential approach, proceeded from the conviction that people with substance dependence lived in obstinate denial and that the job was a key pressure point to shatter that denial.[15] General Motors' 1972 Employe Alcoholism Recovery Program is a representative example of a program based on this approach. The approach held that worker alcoholism could and should be identified and addressed through supervisory observation of job performance. To effectively intervene without harassment or stigmatization, supervisors must focus on job performance, not the suspected underlying alcoholism. Early identification of a worker's alcoholism, which was critical to effective intervention, "should be based entirely on evidence of poor job performance and other related factors."[16]

Constructive confrontation attempted to surveil without being intrusive, resulting in a slippery indirectness. Presumably, employees failing to make the grade who were not suspected of alcoholism or drug abuse were not instructed to seek medical treatment, so how was it possible for constructive confrontation to rely solely on a supervisor's diagnosis of work-related metrics without diagnosing an underlying, substance-related cause? Perhaps this murkiness later made urinalysis more attractive to many employers. Certainly, its perceived clarity and scientific infallibility were factors influencing its growing adoption in the 1980s. Other crucial factors hampering EAPs by this point were growing concerns about poorly defined, inconsistently followed ethical standards in the addiction treatment field and skyrocketing treatment costs for private employers.[17]

Even during the 1970s, employers' concerns about drug use among workers prompted them to expand drug testing, years before testing became a national issue. Agis Salpukas's report on drug use in the *New York Times* noted that between 70 and 80 of the nation's Fortune 500 companies were "now testing most of their job applicants," according to the director of a testing laboratory performing "400 to 500 [tests] a day," up from 20 to 30 weekly a year earlier.[18] However, testing was just one response among many from the nation's businesses, not the central thrust, and as the decade wore on, appears to have waned in popularity. In 1974, a New York conference on drug abuse by workers, sponsored by the state government and attended by representatives of Citibank, Equitable Life, Con Edison, Chemical Bank, and Exxon, rejected approaches based on surveillance. Anthony Cagliostro, chairman of the New York State Drug Abuse Control Commission, remarked that "Initially, many sought to solve the problem, which was thought to be primarily heroin addiction, by seeking out and terminating employee drug abusers and introducing screening techniques to prevent the employment of current users. However, many employers are now adopting an approach in which drug dependency is viewed as a treatable condition. The increasing adoption of this non-punitive approach suggests that the formerly used prevention model 'Don't hire any more and discover and fire users' failed."[19]

The reports on the group discussions held at the conference reflect skepticism about drug testing: "Some participants characterized urinalysis as costly, time-consuming, not very reliable and, therefore, not very helpful. Instead, many companies were increasingly moving away from urinalysis and surveillance techniques and attempting to develop more constructive approaches to individuals with drug problems."[20]

These approaches were informed by a more holistic view of drug use that recognized, in Cagliostro's words, "some people use drugs to remain functional rather than become dysfunctional." With that in mind, group discussion concluded that companies needed to be increasingly sensitive to "the wide variety of drug use among workers, including experimental, recreational, and adaptive drug use, and assume a flexible approach,"[21] keeping in mind that large employers were inseparable from the communities in which they operated. Only a decade later, this thinking had largely disappeared from corporate, government, and media discourse. Surveillance became the centerpiece of mainstream approaches to employee substance use, and any use of illicit substances, whether occasional or chronic, work-related or recreational, was constructed as harmful and threatening. This drastic change was encouraged by government influence, economic incentives, and management prerogatives, far more than technological changes or best practices in the treatment of substance use disorder.

A key early government initiative that anticipated drug testing in the private sector was the United States Navy's response to the 1981 crash aboard the USS *Nimitz*, a navy aircraft carrier. Fourteen service members were killed in the crash and toxicology tests indicated the presence of illegal drugs in the bodies of some of the deceased. The following year, the navy instituted an antidrug program that included random urine testing, searches of personal property, drug dogs, and undercover operations, after vocal advocacy by Queens Democratic congressman and Appropriations Committee member Joseph Addabbo. In 1982, the navy credited the program with major declines in the number of those who tested positive for drugs. Criminologist Kenneth D. Tunnell notes that in the following two years Greyhound Bus Lines instituted a testing program, setting a standard for other transportation companies, while research groups issued several reports and studies claiming that drug abuse was a major problem for the American workplace. Combined with drug-related news stories that received extensive media coverage, such as the death of basketball star Len Bias and the introduction of drug testing at the Olympics and by major league baseball, business and the public were becoming increasingly exposed to hyperbolic concerns about the threat drug abuse posed to the nation's workers and economy.[22] That the drug studies estimating massive productivity losses due to employee drug use usually cited by those expressing concern fell far short of convincing evidence or proper scientific practice mattered not at all.[23]

As in the 1970s, voices from all corners agreed that business was uniquely positioned to intervene and get users back to the straight and narrow path. "No segment of American society can do a better job of curing the drug sickness than employers," according to *Nation's Business*. Addiction was a "disease of denial," it argued in 1986, that needed to be shattered by the prospect of termination.[24] "Drug abusers will give up their cars, their homes and their families, and risk jail, before they give up drugs," said workplace consultant Bruce Wilkinson, "but the threat of losing a job is usually the one thing that gets through to them."[25] *Washington Post* columnist Courtland

Milloy (no relation to the author) argued that testing was "the only way" to reach "a spoiled baby boomer generation."[26] Attorney General Ed Meese, speaking to the U.S. Chamber of Commerce, called on business to give financial bite to antidrug efforts by testing workers and disciplining users. Meese also exhorted management to "indicate its willingness to undertake surveillance of . . . locker rooms, parking lots, shipping and mailroom areas and nearby taverns if necessary" and "maintain a good working relationship with the local police." Meese's line on surveillance was based on a *Harvard Business Review* piece by former Drug Enforcement Agency head Peter Bensinger, who later in the decade moved into advising corporations on antidrug programs. This overlap between government drug warriors and business practice exemplified the surveillance turn.[27]

The 1980s: Business's War on Drugs

In contrast to the 1970s, when a different political context allowed for many more experimental approaches to be funded, during the 1980s the federal government pushed a much more consistent approach, founded on surveillance, prohibition, and abstinence—"Just Say No," in the words of First Lady Nancy Reagan's controversial campaign. Between 1981 and 2003, the War on Drugs spending grew 1,200 percent.[28] Republican politicians hyped drug use as a major threat to the nation's health and the nation's economy. In 1983, then-obscure Republican senator Dan Quayle cited "the devastating effect of alcoholism and drug abuse" as the culprit for American economic woes.[29] Government officials stoked these fears as major threats to the nation's employers. J. Michael Walsh, head of workplace initiatives at the National Institute on Drug Abuse (NIDA), argued that crack was turning functioning workers into nonfunctioning "addicts" within weeks: while it might require "10 to 12 years for an alcoholic to become totally dysfunctional . . . we are seeing people who have been using crack-cocaine for short periods of only six to eight weeks who are unable to get up and go to work."[30] Labor department assistant secretary for policy Roland Droitsch cautioned small businesses of a coming influx of drug-addicted workers, saying "the word is spreading that the larger firms do drug testing and if you have a problem, not to go to them."[31]

As Meese's comments suggest, as businesses moved to counteract this perceived crisis, government strongly encouraged a turn to surveillance, both biological and observational. The clearest message in support of testing came from the president himself, of course, through his executive order calling for testing of all federal workers in "sensitive positions." The states also provided economic incentives to employers offering workplace drug testing. Aside from government initiatives, employers also had strong risk-avoidance incentives to address substance use. As a 1986 report issued by the Cornell School of Industrial and Labor Relations argued, "rapid changes in tort liability and escalating costs of liability insurance" mandated employers do something "to eliminate the problems caused by employees working under the influence of illicit drugs as well as alcohol."[32]

Often, the government bureaucrats leading the federal drug strategy and the consultants selling companies on drug testing and punitive policies were the same people. Georgia Power's approach, an employer often cited as an exemplar of aggressive antidrug strategies, was developed by the aforementioned former DEA chief Peter Bensinger, who argued, "Industry has a problem with the recreational drug user, and that includes the recreational user of marijuana. The whole concept of drug use as recreational—even marijuana—flies in the face of medical reality." Georgia Power instituted an anonymous hotline that encouraged employees to call and inform on coworkers using drugs. Five employees disciplined after hotline allegations placed a complaint with the Department of Labor, alleging they were targeted for reporting plant safety issues to the Nuclear Regulatory Commission.[33] Their experience points to how drug-related surveillance measures could perhaps be used to serve other employer interests. Robert DuPont went from director of the National Institute on Drug Abuse to heading a company that consulted on matters concerning drugs at work. DuPont advocated testing based on his conception of drug use as a disease—a contagious one: "the person using drugs is not only a menace in terms of what he does to himself or herself, but they are also likely to spread drug-using behavior, and the associated negative values, to other people."[34] These kinds of links between government drug warriors and the private sector raised the hackles of Employee Assistance Professionals Association president Tom Delaney who wrote a letter to the *Albany Times Union* alleging a "revolving door between the White House Office of Drug Abuse Policy and the drug testing labs." Delaney alleged that the federal government would "rather browbeat industry into drug testing than address the real problems that cause drug use among our young people. It sure helps to get the next government contract if you can show you are a true believer in the "Just Say No" campaign whether there is a problem or not."[35]

Searching for Certainty: Risk Management, Drugs, and Surveillance

Another contextual factor influencing the rise of testing was the increasing concern of business about risk, and a related desire for certainty about its employees, on and off the job. As sociologists Luc Boltanski and Eve Chiapello demonstrated in their landmark *The New Spirit of Capitalism*, capital's post-1968 adoption of networked, project-based management, demanding increased autonomy and flexibility by professional and managerial employees. This incentivized being able to trust employees while simultaneously, as Steven Nock has shown, making that trust more elusive.[36]

This development was intensified by the growth in communications technology and a greater emphasis on individual expression and dedication by workers that blurred the previously solid separation between private and professional selves that had characterized mid-twentieth-century management arrangements. Ulrich Beck characterized the period as the dawning of a "risk society." Anthony Giddens helped mobilize this concept, arguing, "we increasingly live on a high technological frontier which absolutely no one completely understands and which generates a diversity of possible futures." Drug testing seemed to address multiple business risks: that one would hire a problem employee; that employees would sue for wrongful dismissal; that impaired performance would lead to losses and lawsuits. Employer drug testing is thus a signal example of how business's increased concern with risk identifications and mitigation "shift[s] the relation between collective and individual responsibility in many risk situations." The surveillance turn downloaded the risks of harmful substance abuse when possible onto individual workers, in contrast with the more holistic employee assistance approach of the 1970s.[37]

Surveillance directed at Wall Street stockbrokers, simultaneously being lionized as the decade's archetypal capitalists in films like *Wall Street*, is a revealing example of the relationship between trust, risk, and the surveillance turn among the professional-managerial class. Senator Joe Biden's 1987 congressional hearings on drug testing in the workplace heard testimony from Edward Weihenmayer at the Kidder, Peabody, & Co. brokerage that we did a series of undercover things and we found that at lunchtime a number of very, very expensively-clad Wall Street executives, women and men, were literally waiting in line at an apartment house, walking up, slipping their money through the door, and getting their coke. There was a line like going to a movie.

We just sat there and filmed it all, watched it all.

Spying on these particular employees was motivated by the risk concerns and certainty demands of financial sector employers. Weihenmayer justified Kidder, Peabody going beyond testing for cause to the widespread testing of current and prospective employees because "when people place their assets with us, their life savings, I think they have a right to expect that they are going to have trained, sober, and drug-free people managing and processing those assets."[38] Kidder, Peabody was no outlier. According to Weihenmayer, "almost every Wall Street firm tests for drug use on a pre-employment basis and many today are considering testing of current employees." Weihenmayer submitted to the committee a charter for a prospective organization called "Securities Firms for a Drug Free Workplace."[39]

As we will see, surveillance and testing in the 1980s did disproportionately target employees of lower status. However, its deployment in this context, applied to these high-status workers attests to the expansion of drug-focused employee surveillance in the 1980s and its connection with discourses of risk.[40] As we saw above, the risk of tort liability was also a factor. What urinalysis and undercover surveillance seemed to promise employers, rather than more holistic approaches, was certainty with respect to who was using drugs and the ability to screen them out of the workplace with the support of hard evidence that could shield them from another risk: a wrongful dismissal proceeding.[41]

The combination of government encouragement, economic incentives, and changing management priorities that emphasized risk management and personal integration between worker and company strongly incentivized businesses to adopt surveillance as their primary response to employee substance use in the 1980s. Most often, businesses tested for drugs and sometimes alcohol using urinalysis. As a method of surveillance, urinalysis could be intrusive and humiliating. A *Washington Post* editorial called the Department of Transportation's plans for drug testing "a staggering invasion of privacy . . . what does this do to the morale and dignity of these workers?"[42] A female Georgia Power employee's experience of drug testing, described in *Harper's* magazine: "Meant being forced by a nurse to drop her pants to her ankles, bend over at the waist with her knees slightly bent, hold her right arm in the air, and with her left hand angle a specimen bottle between her legs. She sobbed and shook, wet herself, and vomited. She was fired for insubordination: refusal to take another test."[43]

Testing advocates had to address concerns about this type of bodily invasion. Richard K. Willard, assistant attorney general at the Civil Division of the Department of Justice, argued that testing could be valuable even without eyes on the bottle, as the mere fact of a required test would still present a deterrent to drug use. By allowing for more privacy, he argued that urinalysis for drug use would be "no more intrusive . . . than an ordinary visit to the doctor."[44] Other testing advocates pushed the argument that testing was not invasive of privacy even further. A Long Island school board that wanted to test its employees argued, supported by a brief by the U.S. attorney general, that there was no expectation of privacy with regard to urine because it was a "waste product" that the employee was disposing. The court rejected the claim, presumably guided by the knowledge that most people go to the bathroom with the door closed and flush once they are finished.[45]

No matter how invasive the test, critics pointed out repeatedly that urinalysis would not measure current impairment, only past exposure. New York University pharmacology professor John Morgan argued at Biden's congressional hearings that

> the application of these tests in unimpaired people, in essence, constitutes surveillance. It means I am going to look at you and your past life to see if you may have committed a crime or consumed an illegal drug.
>
> Indeed, it may bring about some of the positive results that these gentlemen have talked about, but it strikes me that it is as justified for a company to do this to its workers as it would be for the workers to send around operatives to management homes to look for evidence of insider trading or expense account fiddling.
>
> In conclusion, George Bernard Shaw said to every difficult and complex problem, there is a simple answer and it is wrong, and that is what urine testing of unimpaired workers represents in the United States today.[46]

One management veteran of substance abuse policy also expressed doubts about the adoption of testing as a panacea. General Motors health and safety director Robert Wiencek, interviewed by the *Washington Post* during the first worker drug scare in 1986, called it "a knee-jerk reaction . . . the problem has not been cured in the past by the screening of people. I don't think it's going to do much in the future unless a fuller approach to the drug problem is used. There is a need in all of these systems to offer the person using drugs or dependent on drugs a helping hand."[47]

Urinalysis did not actually provide the certainty that many employers had hoped for. Testing received an embarrassing black eye in 1987, when Delbert Lacefield, director of a lab that did testing for the Federal Railroad Administration, admitted in court to faking lab reports of railroad crews who were tested after accidents. Lacefield "conceded he had neither the knowledge nor the equipment to test blood plasma for alcohol or narcotics use," according to an Associated Press report.[48] As early as 1986, the *Los Angeles Times* reported that "soaring demand" was overwhelming the capacity of testing laboratories to conduct tests with efficiency and accuracy. Former NIDA research director Robert E. Willette estimated that up to 30 percent of drug testing labs "are not doing good work, and their results are open to question."[49] The rise of testing stimulated the rise of a shadow industry devoted to helping workers foil testing, as detailed by Kenneth D. Tunnell in *Pissing on Demand*.[50] Testers were confronted with the choice of allowing tested employees more privacy, and risking urine substitution or other methods of subverting the tests, or greater scrutiny of the testee, and thus greater intrusiveness and controversy.

While urinalysis was the most prevalent method of surveillance adopted in this era, and the most highly publicized, the surveillance turn also featured employers adopting elaborate, expensive undercover sting operations directed at their workers. New Mexico newspaper publisher Thompson Hughes Lang led a surprise assault on his workplace, aimed at ferreting out drug-using employees. Lang "watched from a glass-enclosed catwalk above the production floor as the dogs sniffed around a mailroom conveyer belt and security guards led employees suspected of drug activity to restrooms for testing. Refusal, the employees were told, was cause for firing." Crucially, Lang was emboldened and empowered in such tactics by the relative lack of constitutional protections employees of a private business had against such surveillance. Lang originally thought about having the police involved in such an investigation but that "meant we would have problems with the

Fourth Amendment. . . . We didn't want to be involved with that. If you have police, immediately you have to have different standards. And those aren't the standards that a private employer wants to have to follow." "'What Mr. Lang did, if it were a police activity, would have violated the Constitution,' said Deputy Chief Elton Hodgson of the Albuquerque Police Department. 'You can't just violate a person's privacy that way. . . . At least, we can't.'"[51]

While his tactics were extreme, Lang was certainly not the only boss launching undercover investigations. In at least one California case, a local police department recommended a private investigation to an employer who contacted them concerned about drugs.[52] In fact, a number of high-profile Southern California employers hired private firms to conduct investigations. A 1990 *Los Angeles Times* piece named General Motors, Universal Studios, Allied Signal Aerospace, and the Times itself as employers that did undercover investigations of their workers. Again, the federal government played a major role in encouraging such an approach. The piece quoted an executive of a business employing thousands locally who cited the Drug-Free Workplace Act as a key reason for the growing popularity of employee investigations: "Our customer is the government, and we do what we have to do." According to a union lawyer, such practices "breed incredible mistrust among workers," while an area unionist called it a "throwback to the days when companies hired detectives to spy on labor organizers." Indeed, Pinkerton, the iconic private detective of early twentieth-century capitalists, was also involved in the surveillance turn, admitting the agency had private investigators in at least ten companies.[53] Another Los Angeles entertainment employer, ABC/Capital Cities, had a "varied program" of surveillance." According to an executive there, they valued the psychological jolt it provided: "Once in a while we might march a dog through. If the problem gets bad enough, we might have an undercover operation. . . . What we wanted to do was create a non-use atmosphere. . . . Hopefully we'll heighten the paranoia. Fear, from what we've learned, is the greatest deterrent."[54]

Some employers opted for technological surveillance. A San Diego trolley company deployed a machine that sought to measure impairment at the beginning of a shift, to detect "employees whose on-the-job performance might be impaired by drugs, alcohol, emotional stress, or other causes." Workers had to "play the machine" upon arriving at work, which allowed them to catch not just drug use but personal problems that would otherwise have passed unnoticed. In a telling example of how drug-related surveillance facilitated wider employer knowledge, the employer touted the machine's detection of upset in a worker who had broken up an engagement with his fiancée: "That incident was for me compelling because to have seen him, you never would have suspected anything was wrong," he said. "But the machine found out something was wrong."[55] Security cameras were another form of technological surveillance that business employed to screen out substance use.

Whether a business adopted drug testing or undercover busts, it likely had an increasingly free hand to heighten its surveillance of employees. During the 1980s, the employer backlash against organized labor and worker power was in ascendance, buoyed early in the decade by an economic context of recession and high unemployment. Civil libertarian Norma Rollins concluded that, "barring specific legislative enactments, more and more Americans can expect to be confronted by the demand to acquiesce to testing at the penalty of losing or not getting a job."[56] Even workers represented by a powerful union like the United Auto Workers (UAW) found it less likely to go to bat to fight drug and alcohol-related sanctions. An article by an auto industry publication stated: "None dispute that the UAW attitude towards workers with alcohol or drug problems has changed. Those who won't accept help can no longer expect automatic union backing, particularly when the issue is drugs," in a climate where autoworker substance use was "under a media and consumer microscope," and compared to autoworkers in competing vehicle plants. One UAW shop steward said of workers battling substance abuse, "we can't carry them like we used to, and my members want drugs out of the plant."[57] Indeed, many workers, perhaps influenced by the era's antidrug hysteria, were concerned about drug use among their coworkers. Overall, though, unions were almost unanimously opposed to random testing.[58]

Nevertheless, some workers did contest urinalysis and other forms of intrusive surveillance. These were generally workers in the public sector whose employer, being the government, was somewhat constrained by protections against search and seizure in the Constitution; and those employers represented by a union. During the mid to late 1980s, several public sector unions clashed with various government entities seeking to test workers for substance use, in both court hearings and arbitrations. Early on, rulings on testing varied. Over time, a judicial consensus emerged allowing testing of public sector employees for cause, the random testing of those in safety-sensitive positions, and post-accident testing.[59] John Gilliom and Kenneth

Tunnell have shown that the overall impact of court rulings on testing was the expansion and endorsement, not limitation, of surveillance.

High profile accidents, such as the 1987 Conrail crash that killed sixteen people and the 1989 *Exxon Valdez* disaster, influenced a greater acceptance of testing in the transportation sector. Risk was again an important element here—*Nimitz*, Conrail, and *Valdez* all showed that testing could support arguments that substance use helped cause an accident, which likely accelerated employer and union fears of liability. After a 1991 New York City subway accident in which the police alleged the driver was intoxicated and a crack vial was discovered inside the cab, Transit Workers Local 100 president Sonny Hall publicly abandoned his previous stance against random testing of his membership, to fight "the perception of substance abuse among transit workers."[60] Others in the transportation sector called for a greater understanding of the complex interrelationship of drug use and transport work. Victoria Frankovich, the president of the Independent Federation of Flight Attendants, called drug testing "technological surveillance" motivated by political pressure. She noted that pilots and attendants had to deal with multiple time zone crossings and interrupted sleep patterns, which encouraged the use of sleeping pills. Flight attendants, subject to weight standards, were incentivized by the employer to use diet pills or other drugs that suppressed appetite. Frankovich thus advocated for "a realistic look at what drugs may potentially cause impairment and what drugs can be used but not abused" and "a list of safe alternative medications that will not jeopardize the employers or the travelling public but realistically take into consideration the rigors of the job."[61] However, in the Just Say No era this type of holistic understanding of workplace-related substance use was largely ignored in the rush to ensure that drug users would be kept out of the workplace.

Standard Procedure: Business's War on Drugs and the Normalization and Extension of Surveillance

By the time the dust settled in the early 1990s, American business had widely established drug testing as a normative, expected procedure in American work contexts. Thirty years on from the surveillance turn in business substance use policy, it is time to begin investigating the historic consequences of this shift. Despite the rhetoric about white-collar drug abuse, it appears that the burden of surveillance fell mostly on working-class employees. Data published in 1997 estimated that "social class and income are inversely related to drug testing."[62] A *Washington Post* piece about the experience of Donal Kelley, a man whose career was derailed by a positive test for marijuana, noted that blue-collar workers were "more likely to be tested than those in the front office."[63] Similarly, a personnel official at an auto parts plant remarked that "salaried is 'assumed' not to have a problem," indicating that policies were primarily interested in surveilling hourly workers.[64] However, how categories of class, race, gender, and ability have intersected with drug testing and other forms of employer surveillance requires more investigation. The effect of corporate substance-related surveillance, treatment, and sanctions on the lives of workers is another field that demands attention. So too do the connections between American business and the carceral state since the acceleration of mass incarceration in the 1970s. While this research points to the interweaving of public and private punitive policy as part of the war on drugs, other ways employers may have bolstered, shaped, profited from, or even resisted the carceral turn, especially in the nonimprisoned workforce, require study. Certainly, it has proven to be lucrative: one market research firm estimated that the U.S. drug testing industry was worth $2.2 billion in 2017.[65]

Critics of the surveillance turn argued that it was a move directed more at disciplining and controlling employees than fighting substance use. Abbie Hoffman, the sixties radical who made the fight against testing the last campaign of his life, wrote in his book *Steal This Urine Test* that "pulling workers' pants down lets 'em know who's boss. It threatens their jobs and dignity."[66] Similarly, Steven Nock has characterized drug testing as an "ordeal" that employers used to manage questions of trust in societies with weaker affective ties. Placing employer substance surveillance in historical context shows that employers were active in desiring to treat greater numbers of employers as strangers, to enable greater flexibility in their deployment or disposal; surveillance was one method used in this effort.[67] My own contention is that the government's push for testing, along with employers desire to minimize employee risk and present or future liabilities were the primary motivators for the surveillance turn, although state and employer desire to subjugate and control workers was an aspect, and likely the key one at some firms.[68] Beyond causes, further research is needed on the effects of urine testing on class consciousness, workplace cultures, and class conflict.

What was the impact of the turn to testing for EAPs? One union assistance director warned in 1986 that drug testing "could kill your EAP" by destroying the trust employees needed to have in the intentions of the caregivers, with employers now "assum[ing] a dual role of policeman as well as rehabilitation."[69] EAP leader Tom Delaney also fretted about "pressures on EAP to assume a more critical and adversarial role to labor and management."[70] While Harrison Trice's erstwhile collaborator Paul Roman was more optimistic about the response of EAPs to the surveillance turn, arguing that EAPs "have been strengthened by the campaign for a drug-free workplace," even he admitted that the campaign had taken time away from responding to the much more common issue of alcohol abuse.[71] The overall trend in employee assistance provision between the 1970s and the 2000s was toward third-party, short-term managed care. While the surveillance turn certainly seems to have played an important part in this shift, its exact impact and the consequences of this shift for business, workers, and people with substance abuse disorder need more investigation.[72]

Certainly, concern about an opioid epidemic in the 2010s highlighted that drug use among workers remained a problem. This indicated that employer surveillance largely failed to deter societal use and mitigate substance-related harms. At the time of writing, drug use among workers is yet again being presented as a major concern, and yet again major media outlets like Salon are claiming that business is turning a "blind eye" to the problem, noting that fatal overdoses at work rose by almost one-third from 2015 to 2016. However, over the past thirty years, business's drug-fueled gaze, the technological and biometric surveillance of workers, has continued to enlarge. Workers' computer keystrokes, social media posts, and company-issued smartphones are regularly scrutinized by employers, often resulting in discipline and firing. This type of surveillance further blurs the separation between professional behavior deemed deserving of scrutiny and off-hours behavior belonging solely to the workers' personal, nonwork reputation. As law professor Elizabeth A. Brown, who has studied the surveillance of workers' biometric health data, notes, this surveillance "presents a substantial benefit to employers and substantial risks to employees."[73] Employee rights and privacy concerning the collection and use of this data are as yet largely unprotected by federal law.

This piece presents evidence that this far-reaching, yet seemingly unremarkable, employer surveillance of American workers can be traced to business's successful expansion of surveillance aimed at the substance use and personal lives of its employees. While major controversies surrounding this work erupted in the 1980s, as businesses changed the focus of substance use efforts toward surveillance of their employees, and were largely resolved by the 1990s, it must be remembered that the identification of worker substance use as a legitimate area of inquiry was hastened by businesses, unions, workers, the state, and substance abuse professionals working together in the 1950s, 1960s, and 1970s. These actors expanded industrial alcoholism programs into a "broad-brush" employee assistance model that empowered management to further investigate and intervene in employees' use of alcohol and drugs on the job or off. Their expansion of employee substance use as a legitimate area of concern and observation helped create the conditions for business to play a major role in the more punitive war on drugs of the 1980s. Business was a crucial soldier in this war, legitimating drug abuse as a perceived epidemic problem in American society and extending surveillance to millions of mainstream, "respectable" Americans who may otherwise have remained outside the ambit of state surveillance. Business's surveillance turn was a key component of the war on drugs and the ascendance of neoliberal workplace policies. Employers largely won the battles over drug testing that resulted, paving the way for current practices of technological and biometric employer surveillance. However, history also reminds us that surveillance, past and present, has always been partial, incomplete, and contested.

CHAPTER 8

_____

Why Did Uptown Go Down in Flames?

Uptown Cigarettes and the Targeted Marketing Crisis

DAN GUADAGNOLO

Throughout the month of April 1990, after each of his Sunday sermons, the Reverend Calvin Butts led his congregation out of Abyssinian Baptist Church in Harlem, New York, carrying buckets of white paint and long-handled roller brushes. The congregation would set themselves up at busy street corners and proceed to paint over the many billboards featuring tobacco and alcohol advertisements that had multiplied throughout Harlem over the past few years. On these newly blank canvases, the congregation painted works of art recognizing members of their community. Where a massive billboard at 138th Street and Lenox Avenue had once advertised Salem cigarettes, it now offered a happy eighty-fifth birthday to Clara Hale, the founder of Hale House, a respite home for precariously housed youth living with addiction or HIV.[1]

The congregation's protest action garnered media coverage across the United States. As photographs of Harlem seniors and young children carrying roller brushes made their way into the national press, the Association of National Advertisers pressed New York City mayor David Dinkins to arrest the parishioners for vandalism. There was little Dinkins could do, however. In New York, a misdemeanor arrest required a complaint, and no billboard owner or advertiser had filed one. No firms were willing to risk the damage to their public image. Instead, billboard, alcohol, and tobacco companies conceded to the community. Billboard companies quickly offered their signage as community public service announcement spaces instead. Sale Point Posters, which had 23 of its 250 billboards in Harlem painted over, refunded

$2,500 in advertising dollars to clients and lost $86,000 in contracts canceled. One liquor importer, Schieffelin & Somerset, whose ads were also whitewashed in the action, announced that it would no longer advertise on billboards in any low-income neighborhoods.[2]

Reverend Butts, having only recently assumed his position as the pastor of Abyssinian, used the pulpit to critique the oversaturation of billboard advertising in Harlem.[3] The action was a direct response to a recent line of menthol cigarette developed by RJR Nabisco, the snack and tobacco conglomerate responsible for Chips Ahoy! cookies and Newport, Camel, and Pall Mall cigarettes. Six months earlier in December 1989, RJR Nabisco had announced Uptown cigarettes, a sleek new menthol brand designed for African American consumers. Uptown would be introduced in a six-month trial market run in downtown Philadelphia the following February. Protesters and advertising critics alike condemned the brand, arguing that the Uptown was both racist and exploitive as the brand was built to aggressively target addictive tobacco products at black youth. Community organizations across Philadelphia banded together to form the Coalition Against Uptown Cigarettes, countering the tobacco corporation's public relations machine and spurring Health and Human Services secretary Louis Sullivan to pen a public letter condemning the brand. Within weeks of the protests, community organizers saw their goal realized. RJR Nabisco canceled the Uptown test market and shelved the brand. In the months that followed, however, Uptown's dramatic failure became a catalyst for a new, very public conversation over the uneven stakes of market segmentation in the early 1990s as protest actions drew what had once been obscure marketing strategy out of corporate boardrooms and into public life.

This chapter examines the creation of the Uptown cigarette brand, its failure, and the debates over target marketing that followed. In doing so, it animates how corporate actors like RJR Nabisco put race to work in their market research and consumer composite construction.[4] All market research constructs a consumer type with which a merchandiser believes its product belongs. RJR Nabisco's consumer profile for Uptown was a market fantasy of blackness rooted in specific ideas about black youths' economic precarity, their social alienation, and intense dedication to brands that communicated ideas about success. As one executive charged with developing Uptown put it, referring to the commercial viability of new cigarette lines targeting young people with poor economic outlooks: such consumers were "like an annuity, paying dividends far into the future due to brand loyalty."[5]

The addictive nature of tobacco and the well-known ways in which it exacerbated health inequities between the general population and African Americans enabled community activists to frame Uptown and market segmentation as a form of "target marketing" designed to amplify these inequalities. This shift in language to "targeting" laid bare how segmentation unevenly distributed the benefits of a consumer society. What's more, it forced marketers, advertisers, and merchandisers alike to openly discuss the techniques they used to construct markets for their products.

The Uptown controversy raged in different ways on Manhattan's Madison Avenue and Harlem's Lenox Avenue. Where Butts and the Uptown Coalition argued for community control over the advertising images that entered their neighborhoods, the African American advertiser and market researcher Caroline Jones argued instead that target marketing was not the problem. Rather, in pieces for *Penthouse*, in *Adweek*, and elsewhere, Jones suggested that Uptown failed because African American communities had become frustrated by the lack of advertisements for everyday goods outside the realm of alcohol or tobacco. Her own market research indicated that even when merchandisers had a strong share of black consumers for a specific product, they sought white consumers instead. Jones's argument was self-serving, but it was also correct: while market segmentation had created new formulations of consumer citizenship for African Americans since the 1960s, by the late twentieth century many major merchandisers simply ignored consumers of color.

Uptown and the target marketing crisis that followed are a striking, early example of popular resistance to data-driven marketing and the entanglements of racial formation and surveillance capitalism in our own moment. For white consumers, market segmentation in the 1980s promised endless junk mail and unwanted preapproved credit cards, a story told as early as 1964 in Vance Packard's *The Naked Society*.[6] For African American consumers, however, marketing looked decidedly different: an overabundance of tobacco and alcohol products defined the commercial media they encountered in the 1980s and early 1990s.

Advertising Tobacco to the Black Consumer

It was only in the years after the Second World War that African Americans workers were recognized as a viable consumer market for tobacco in the United States. During the war, the R. J. Reynolds Tobacco Company became the first tobacco firm to advertise in the black press, breaking a long-held agreement between major U.S. tobacco corporations to not spend ad dollars on African American media.[7] This decision was spurred by a number of factors, including a growing number of marketers who had begun to pitch black consumers to American merchandisers. The African American marketer David J. Sullivan was one of the first to forward studies that emphasized the consuming power of African Americans in the United States. Sullivan's work aimed to upset the marketing assumptions held by white merchandisers about the nature of black consumers: "it is the general opinion of advertisers and marketers that a majority of Negroes live on the other side of the railroad tracks, or resemble something closely akin to a sharecropper," he suggested in 1945. Rather, the reality in the immediate postwar years was that of an industrial working-class defined by relatively high wages, growing buying power, and constrained consumer options thanks to Jim Crow.[8]

In 1969, R. J. Reynolds conducted its first study of ethnic markets, which it defined as African Americans, Jewish people, and "Spanish-Language" consumers. The company argued that such data would enable marketing managers to measure the viability of extending tobacco brands into such markets.[9] The study drew upon work from a number of market research and advertising agencies that specialized in these segments, including the African American advertising firm D. Parke Gibson and Associates and the Jewish marketing and advertising consultancy Joseph Jacobs Associates.[10] In an admission of the slippery nature of marketing data deployed to construct consumer types, in his forward report author Gehrmann Holland noted that "quantitatively, this presentation is not intended to represent the actual situation. The accuracy of available standardized data on these groups is hampered by the shortcomings of both research availability and measurement methodology, as well as by obsolescence."[11] As with all marketing, such reports would gain value when they were put to work to construct a consumer type.

The Holland market research study examined how ethnic communities navigated a media economy defined by a deep investment in whiteness. It argued that advertising images and campaigns developed by Reynolds for racialized communities would have to be tailored to media that spoke to these communities in some substantive, meaningful way. In an admission of the race logic that shaped the mass market, the author argued that "most media basically reflect the interests, desires, and aspirations of their majority audience, which is largely middle-class white. Classification of these media as 'white-oriented' would be far more accurate and functional than their more frequent classification as 'general media.'"[12] Such an interpretation placed the idea of race difference outside of the ostensibly white general market.

Indeed, to get the most bang for its buck out of ethnic consumer markets, the study argued that Reynolds ought to advertise in media that allowed ethnic consumers and consumers of color to identify in the same manner as white consumers did with the mass market. "The consensus of opinion today is that if brand awareness is the primary advertising objective," the report argued, "then national advertising does generally *reach* this audience in proportion to their place in the total population. . . . However, if the key objective is to *sell* more of Product A to more negroes, *then they must be communicated with, not merely reached.*"[13] For black consumers across the United States, the study insisted that magazine and radio markets would be the ideal media for speaking meaningfully to such consumers.

The conclusions of the ethnic market study dovetailed with a legislative push to curtail tobacco advertising in the United States, including a series of decisions that would see Big Tobacco funnel ad dollars into the black press and other highly segmented media. In the same year that Reynolds produced its internal study of ethnic markets, the federal government had begun taking active steps to regulate tobacco advertising on television. In 1967 a Federal Communications Commission ruling known as the "fairness doctrine" determined that for every three advertisements that a tobacco firm produced, the firm would have to produce an anti-smoking public service announcement. As critiques of tobacco advertising mounted, Joseph F. Cullman III, then president of Philip Morris and the chairman of the coordinated lobbyist group the Tobacco Institute, committed to Congress that his firm would exit television and radio advertising by 1971. In doing so, the tobacco industry gave up television, but also successfully ended the production of PSAs. With the passage of the Public Health Cigarette Smoking Act in 1970, tobacco advertising was effectively banned on television one day into the new year, on January 2, 1971, ending a long and profitable relationship between the three major broadcasters and tobacco corporations.[14]

With television out of the picture, tobacco advertising dollars began flowing into other media. One *Newsweek* report on the ban suggested magazines would be the beneficiaries of industry spending, though many different publishers remained "wary about provoking health-warning requirements for cigarette ads—a possibility that has been threatened by the Federal Trade Commission."[15] Indeed, the *New York Times* had estimated an annual loss of $500,000 in tobacco ad revenues for 1970 alone when they began requiring cigarette ads to display the same warnings that had been legally mandated to appear on the product cartons. Well aware of public opinion shifting against them, Philip Morris magazine director Jack Landry attempted to massage the narrative in favor of a restrained approach: "Any huge increase there [in magazine tobacco advertising] would lead to drowning the magazines in cigarette advertising," suggesting this was an outcome he and the firm did not want. Following suit, his counterpart at R. J. Reynolds agreed: "the magazines don't want that and it just wouldn't make good marketing sense."[16] The statements from the Philip Morris and Reynolds representatives were a deep contrast with what the journalist Thomas Whiteside would later reveal was the intense push to court magazine publishers in the first months of 1971.[17] A March profile by Whiteside in the *New Republic* found that within the first few weeks of that year, tobacco advertisers had poured millions into the magazine market.[18]

Big tobacco found a powerful vehicle for commercial marketing in black periodicals like *Ebony, Jet, Our World,* and *Tan.*[19] By the mid-1960s, all six large tobacco firms in the United States were advertising in *Ebony,* with cigarette advertisements in *Ebony* greatly outstripping the number that appeared in *Life.* By the mid-1980s, cigarette advertising alone would constitute nearly 12 percent of *Essence*'s total advertising income and nearly $3 million in yearly ad revenue for *Ebony.*[20] Partly this was a product of scale. African American magazines had a much smaller circulation compared to large, national "mass market" magazines like *Life* and therefore had a more difficult time either giving up or reducing their tobacco advertising revenue.

By the 1980s, the sheer scale of tobacco spending in advertising writ large gave tobacco firms enormous power in American media markets. In 1985, when R. J. Reynolds merged with Nabisco (formerly the National Biscuit Company), the new RJR Nabisco conglomerate became the fourth largest advertiser in the United States.[21] Three years later in 1988, the conglomerate flexed its newfound influence when it fired and blacklisted one of the largest advertising agencies in the United States, Saatchi & Saatchi. The agency had produced a nine-week TV commercial for Northwest Airlines in which passengers applauded the airline's in-flight smoking ban. Since

Saatchi & Saatchi did not represent any of RJR Nabisco's tobacco brands, the conglomerate punished the ad agency by instead canceling $80 million worth of Nabisco-related snack accounts held by Saatchi & Saatchi and banning the agency from future work for any of RJR Nabisco's other brands, including Oreo's, Chips Ahoy!, Bubble Yum, CareFree gum, and Life Savers. The move sent shockwaves through the industry, securing front-page headlines in *Advertising Age*. It is illustrative of the enormous sway Big Tobacco held over the cultural and corporate intermediaries that shaped modern American commercial culture. The needs of firms like RJR Nabisco informed the work marketing professionals did to construct highly racialized and gendered consumer market segments and types.[22]

Constructing the Uptown Consumer

RJR Nabisco's targeting of African American consumers with Uptown was not a particularly new phenomenon, nor was it out of line with the strategic, brand-based marketing approach cigarette corporations had run with in the African American market for nearly thirty years. By the 1980s, the vast majority of Big Tobacco's promotional and special market spending went to African American community associations and legislative organizations at the state and federal level.[23] What was unique at the end of the twentieth century, however, was the growing anti-tobacco sentiment among African American community associations in the United States alongside what one tobacco company called an "emerging temperance movement" that touched upon not only cigarettes but drunk driving and other forms of substance abuse as well.

In response, the tobacco industry pivoted to new arguments in order to justify the introduction of brands like Uptown. Firms such as RJR Nabisco emphasized the sheer number of tobacco brands, line extensions, and sub-brands on the market by 1989—nearly 350—to argue that new brands were designed not to attract new smokers but instead to claw away "market share" lost to competitors. These claims made it into countless news items regarding the announcement of new cigarette lines, often with the claim that in a shrinking cigarette market with hundreds of brands, a 1 percent market share equated to roughly $358 million.[24] With such arguments, Big Tobacco looked to obfuscate their primary interest in growing the total number of smokers. Indeed, the internal market research used to develop Uptown suggests the brand was built on the explicit assumption that it would garner a specific kind of new smoker: black downwardly mobile young men.

In his July 1988 remarks regarding the first steps toward creating a new youth-oriented brand, John T. Winebrenner, senior vice president for marketing at R. J. Reynolds, parroted the typical narrative of postwar market segmentation. "Until the mid-1950s," he argued, "smokers were a fairly homogeneous group, with a handful of cigarette brands and styles satisfying the vast majority of smokers."[25] In the ensuing forty years, many more brands had been introduced, "catering to a wide variety of consumer subgroups with unique product desires and perceptions."[26] Turning on the intersection of brand and identity, Winebrenner and his research team argued that "definite differences in the product preferences and purchasing patterns of various subgroups of smokers" were increasingly central to consumer choice.[27] In his remarks, Winebrenner summarized decades of research on the low-income black consumer as a particularly promising consumer market for Big Tobacco. "Experience," he argued, "has shown that tailoring our advertising and promotional efforts to specifically meet these consumer preferences gives us our best possible chance for success."[28] Reynolds's marketing department noted that these consumers were relatively concentrated in urban enclaves in states like California, Texas, Florida, Illinois, and New York. Reynolds's top brass argued that African Americans and Hispanics were "growth sectors in the U.S. market," with various experts debating multiple strategies for capturing these highly urban, localized communities.[29]

Reynolds sought new lines for the black youth market because its own menthol brand, Salem, had suffered a significant loss in market share over the 1980s. Philip Morris's more popular Newport cigarette had come to hold nearly 40 percent of the market during that period, with growth largely attributed to "its popularity among younger adult Black smokers."[30] In response to these losses, Reynolds developed a number of tracking studies to be launched in April 1989 in Chicago, Memphis, and Cleveland.[31] These studies followed the purchases of Newport smokers in order to construct their habits and lifestyle preferences. This was done to better understand the ways in which smoking fit into their lives and what might justify or compel a potential brand switch. This data would form the basis of personality profiles that animated tastes and preferences for the imagined Uptown consumer. Research summaries prepared for their studies made clear the blue-collar orientation of the youth they counted as potential consumers for the new brand: "It is important to differentiate young adult smokers from young adults in general. Preppy, 'good,' conservative young adults do not smoke and are not our target. Our target is rebellious, lives on the edge, is today rather than future oriented," reported the study. "Our target is composed of nonconformists who are suspicious of anything vaguely phony."[32]

In 1988, Reynolds developed a research task force, "Project Delta," to examine the commercial viability of young "rebellious" adult smokers as a long-term investment vehicle. The task force would set up an exploratory series of focus group and in-depth interviews to better understand the values and interests of young adult smokers, or what they called the "YAS" market.[33] They would then use the findings from these discussions to develop a list of potential new tobacco brands. Yet the Delta research proposal constructed its ideal smoker before any research had been completed. "Younger adult smoker exploratories will reveal important information concerning their lifestyles, motivations, and product wants," noted one set of study suggestions. "In general, more younger adults tend to have low income and are not attending college." Another set of notes from the study went onto suggest that such consumers were "often motivated by their peers to go along with the crowd. This is witnessed by the fact that younger adult smokers tend to smoke the same product as their friends."[34] Crucially, these young consumers were "starting to smoke @ 10–14 y o." Most lived at home with parents and grandparents, were decidedly blue collar, and often worked two jobs.[35] They did not attend college, and they quickly "increase[d] in [cigarette] usage from ½ pack to 3 packs/day."[36] One draft sketch argued that 42 percent of young people who took up smoking never changed brands, meaning these consumers generated long-term returns.[37] Over six months, the Delta findings resulted in four potential premium brands targeting the youth market, with Reynolds leadership concluding that the premium brand for the black young adult market, Uptown, was the firm's best bet. Following Uptown was Dakota, a brand for young midwestern white women, which was also green-lit, as well as two brands targeting young white men, Prime and Jolt, both of which the company wanted to examine further before a decision was made.[38]

In 1988, Reynolds had also hired the African American market researcher Kelvin Wall as a consultant to advise on positioning the company's brands against others on the market.[39] Wall, who had worked with African American advertising and marketing firms, offered up a first-person narrative composite for Reynolds to work from. While the composite was developed to explain the appeal of Salem, another Reynolds brand, it nonetheless offers insights into the construction of the black consumer that RJR Nabisco was operating upon in its Uptown strategy: a specific vision of low-income blackness as precarious but profitable. "I am twenty years old and live in Harlem. Like many of my friends school did not work out for me, so I dropped out," began the profile. "Now work is not working. I cannot get a job that makes me feel good about myself. Downtown doors of success are closed to me."[40] Wall's composite was unable to find either social or economic security through school or work and so he looked to consumption to satisfy these needs and his sense of self: "My special way to getting over is carefully picking the things people will notice about me. My clothes, my gym shoes, their lacings, my haircut or style, my brand of cigarette or jewelry all say something about me. . . . Off the street, I relax by listening to my favorite radio station or records. During basketball season, when I am not playing, I watch it on TV. I'm as good under the basket as on the disco floor."[41] Whether or not Wall's composite bore any resemblance to the young men who R. J. Reynolds sought out ("disco floor" suggests Wall's insights were perhaps dated by 1988, when the document was submitted to the tobacco giant), it nonetheless turned on a number of the same signifiers that would be built into the Uptown brand. With this data, Reynolds concluded that middle-class brands built on respectability did not speak to the young, economically precarious, and inner-city consumer that the company imagined, such as the composite Wall put forward.

Design and branding choices reflected the needs of the consumer that Reynolds had conjured up. First, the name Uptown was chosen because it rendered the brand "local in scope" while insuring it had the "ability to translate nationally" across the urban centers its demographic occupied. Second, in terms of product design, the packaging departed from the classic teals and greens that had signaled menthol cigarettes for much of the mid-twentieth century. Instead, Reynolds used black and gold to construct what it called an "ownable" look, banking on "nightlife" and "entertainment" as key signifiers. This color scheme signaled the premium position of the brand, signposting that Uptown was a menthol for a very specific, younger generation of black men. To deal with the premium price point—central to the economic fulfillment its imagined consumer was hungry for—Reynolds sold the cigarette in half packs, reducing the cost per unit and rendering it accessible to a youth market with little to no access to income.[42]

Taken together, the branding strategy was designed to articulate a sense of place accessible through the cigarette. Branded with the tagline "The Place, the Taste," Reynolds developed campaign visuals that positioned "UT [Uptown] as a 'classy,' 'quality' product which is an integral part of the targets' perception of an ideal 'fantasy world.'" Campaign photographs featured "target users in an elevated mood en route to a place of entertainment." They offered a "sharp focus on couples suggesting that they are celebrities" often shot against an urban background using a "paparazzi technique." These couples, photographed "dusk to dark," communicated an "urban, mystical, exciting, vibrant" party atmosphere that all contributed to framing Uptown itself "as a place" to which target consumers could come.[43] Mock-up advertisements were planned for billboards, magazines, and popular forms of early 1990s mobile retail, such as party vans that would distribute samples of the cigarette as they drove through club districts.

Reynolds also undertook a careful community relations strategy to soften the arrival of a new tobacco product on the market, managing both consumers' response and that of public health actors, scholars, and activists. It maintained a trove of data on what they called tobacco "zealots," which included those who might slander the industry and the brand in Philadelphia. Since the 1960s, tobacco corporations had used strategic giving in order to use African American figures as a frontline force in defense of the industry. For Uptown in particular, Reynolds recognized that some would object to a cigarette designed to appeal to young black men. The "introduction of the brand," the company warned, "carries with it the potential for a great deal of controversy. Black leaders may object to a cigarette designed to appeal solely to younger blacks. Anti-tobacco groups can be expected to portray the [Philadelphia-area] market test as a racial/health issue. The use of a ten-pack may lead to public health debate over whether the product is designed to appeal to underage smokers who frequently lack the funds to purchase a full pack."[44] A sensible concern—since it was.

To manage community responses in Philadelphia, Reynolds sought to minimize criticism of Uptown from either community or government officials by providing what it called an "environment of acceptance by black leaders of UT and RJR's marketing program."[45] This began by hiring Lynn M. Fields of Commonwealth Consultants, who would advise Uptown on the Philadelphia black community, identifying community leaders, city council members, and administrative personnel in the city who could be recruited to endorse, or, at minimum, strategically ignore, the brand. Under the heading "Tactics—Media Activities," Reynolds explored restoring advertising in key black publications to previous levels and developing a series of meetings with publishers and editors; donating billboard space and other advertising materials to local black community organizations in the test market; and possibly donating $250,000 to the United Negro College Fund (UNCF) during the UNCF's annual national telethon in December. On this last point, Reynolds's external relations also sought to tie the grant into letters "to black opinion leaders, enclosing a copy of the release on UNCF contribution, stressing RJRN's [RJR Nabisco's] continuing commitment to minority support."[46] The telethon promised a second potential tie-in as well, with Reynolds purchasing local commercial airtime to donate to local black organizations.[47] Finally, for the actual distribution of the cigarette, the firm adopted retail incentives for local distributors and the use of local African American marketing managers who could claim membership in communities even as they represented the interests of RJR Nabsico.

How Uptown Went Down in Flames

RJR Nabisco publicly announced Uptown in December 1989 through a press release carried in the *Philadelphia Daily News*, Philadelphia's African American newspaper, with its multimillion-dollar test market ready to begin on February 5, 1990.[48] The press release made no mention that Uptown was explicitly designed to target young adults, even as the branding and merchandising strategy skewed much younger by departing from the more traditional aesthetic used to advertise menthols. "We expect Uptown to appeal most strongly to black smokers," announced Lynn Beasley, vice president of strategic marketing for Reynolds. "Our research leads us to believe that Uptown's blend . . . will be an appealing alternative to smokers currently choosing a competitive brand. We have developed a product based on research that shows that a significant percentage of black smokers are currently choosing a brand that offers a lighter menthol flavor than our major menthol brand, Salem."[49] Reynolds's public announcements noted that Philadelphia, with its 40 percent black population, would serve as Uptown's test market for six months and emphasized that advertising funds would be funneled into black newspapers and magazines, such as the *Philadelphia New Observer*, the *Tribune*, *Ebony*, and *Jet*.

The response from African American community groups in the Philadelphia area was immediate. Members of over thirty organizations began to put together a rally to protest Uptown's downtown test market, citing not only the firm's blatant targeting of black consumers but the sheer saturation of tobacco advertisements already plastering African American neighborhoods in the city.[50] These community organizations quickly came together to form the Uptown Coalition. According to the journalist and public relations expert Charyn Sutton, who served as an Uptown Coalition organizer and spokesperson, the coalition's speedy emergence was the result of Philadelphia's large network of black churches and their decades-long history with community action. With the support of the pulpit, the coalition used Sunday sermons as a communication vehicle instead of relying on the press to organize a potential boycott or rallies. "We'll rely on the community organizations and the preachers to ring out from the pulpits not to buy or accept as a gift Uptown cigarettes," argued one coalition leader, the Reverend Jesse Brown, in a statement to the *Philadelphia Daily News*.[51] Sutton connected this strategy to a longer history of urban organizing in Philadelphia, including the Reverend Leon H. Sullivan, who as pastor of Zion Baptist in 1963, had led a collective community action called "400 Colored Preachers" wherein he used the pulpit to identify and shame companies with weak black employment records.[52] In addition to Philadelphia's network of black churches, coalition organizers also came from the ranks of the American Cancer Society, the American Lung Association, the Fox Chase Cancer Center, and the Graduate Hospital in Philadelphia. These organizations had spent years developing coordinated anti-smoking outreach programs designed to bring local voices into their anti-tobacco messaging at both the local and national level, electing African American community members to executive leadership positions within regional and city chapters. In this way, critiques of the new brand would come from the community itself, rather than a broad network of national organizations that were often heavily under the surveillance of industry-funded organizations like the Tobacco Institute.[53]

Thanks to these relationships, the Uptown Coalition was able to present a coordinated and rapid response to the new brand. In mid-January, the coalition called for Reynolds to cancel its test market and pull the brand. "We want to halt it before Feb. 5th," said Patti LePera, vice president of marketing and communications for the Philadelphia branch of the American Cancer

Society. "We want R. J. Reynolds to know we don't want it here." The president of the North Carolina branch of the National Association for the Advancement of Colored People (NAACP) argued that Uptown would only further exacerbate health disparities between African Americans and other communities: "With the poor health among black folks today, we do not need anything else to cause even more health problems. R. J. Reynolds's targeting of blacks is unethical."[54] Robert Robinson, president of the National Black Leadership Initiative on Cancer in Philadelphia followed suit: "The African American community is already suffering the highest rate of cancer in the country. They develop more cancer and die from cancer more than anyone else, especially from smoking-related cancers."[55]

RJR Nabisco attempted to manage the negative response by deploying a number of different PR strategies, all of which circulated widely in the national press. As the *New York Times* reported in early January 1990, RJR Nabisco argued that it was not targeting black consumers necessarily, but rather Uptown was "a cigarette for the entire market but which is likely to attract a disproportionate number of black smokers."[56] David N. Iauco, senior vice president for marketing at Reynolds, offered a similar refrain in an interview with the *New York Times*: "Everything we do is going to be assaulted and picked at by the anti-smokers. . . . But taking away business from our competitors is the only thing that Uptown is about."[57] When this argument failed to quell calls to shelve the brand, the company shifted to freedom of choice, arguing that black smokers had the right to buy products that fit their preferences and that the introduction of a new brand would not encourage people to smoke.

The Uptown Coalition responded to these arguments using a variety of strategies, many of which were drawn from a longer history of Black Power and calls for community control. Connecting Uptown to concerns over the self-determination of urban communities, coalition members argued that "the Uptown struggle was one of 'taking back' the issue of choice and redefining it in a larger, community context." No one "in the community asked for this new cigarette," or the "excessive billboard advertising in African-American communities" that pushed tobacco products. Instead of continuing to endure a barrage of tobacco advertising, they argued, communities should "have the right to choose what products enter their neighborhoods" in the form of advertising campaigns. When Reynolds representatives sought to argue that they were uninterested in growing the total number of smokers in the United States, the coalition turned marketing statistics back on them, arguing that so few brand switches happened that this made little sense from a commercial perspective. Since publicly available data suggested that "most smokers begin when they are less than 19 years old, marketing fundamentals would dictate that marketers attempt to reach potential smokers during their teenage years," argued the coalition.[58]

The coalition helped make Uptown into a national news story. After their call for Reynolds to pull the brand, two national broadcast network news teams and a national news magazine came to Philadelphia to cover the story and the community response. As the coalition planned to hold its first major news conference on January 29, their actions led Dr. Louis W. Sullivan, secretary of Health and Human Services under President George H. W. Bush and president of Morehouse School of Medicine, to lend them his support. He condemned the Uptown test market decision in a public letter that described the new cigarette as purposeful targeting. "The brand," he argued, "is cynically and deliberately targeted toward black Americans at a time when our people desperately need the message of health promotion. Uptown's message is more disease, more suffering and more death for a group already bearing more than its share of smoking-related illness and mortality." Sullivan said he had written to Reynolds, "expressing my grave concern and urging them to cancel their plans to market this brand." The secretary went on: "A marketing strategy such as the one apparently planned for Uptown would severely undermine the kinds of health promoting attitudes that Americans, especially Black Americans, today need to understand."[59] As two public health scholars have noted, even more direct than Sullivan was the comedian Jay Leno, who suggested that R. J. Reynolds selected Uptown not for its Harlem connotations, but "because the word 'Genocide' was already taken."[60] On January 20, a month after the announcement of the Uptown test market, the coalition saw its goals realized when Reynolds announced the cancellation of the test market in Philadelphia and the permanent shelving of the brand.

As a community organization, the Uptown Coalition was the result of the confluence of a growing anti-tobacco movement and Philadelphia's history of local black activism. Their campaigns challenged the racist tropes that Reynolds's market research was built upon. They called for community control over the kinds of advertising images that filled their neighborhoods. And what's more, they succeeded in shifting the language of market segmentation. In doing so, they set off a troubling conversation for the marketing profession, one that centered on the ethics of market segmentation and the inequitable nature of "target marketing" in the 1990s.

"After Uptown, Are Some Niches Out?": The Target Marketing Crisis

As Reverend Butts began his billboard campaign in April 1990, coverage of the now failed Uptown brand ignited the "crisis" of target marketing. Some marketing professionals suggested that Reynolds had functionally compromised the very nature of marketing by drawing into public discourse how corporations used aggregate consumer data to construct specific consumer types: "After Uptown," they asked, "are some niches out?"[61] "Suddenly everywhere," wrote another critic in *Adweek*, "advertising is under the gun. After eight years of the Reagan administration's hands-off attitude that insulated marketers from regulation, anti-advertising legislation is popping up in Congress again." James E. Miller, former chairman of the Federal Trade Commission (FTC) under Reagan, suggested that thanks to Uptown, tobacco companies ought to fear "a lower threshold for [federal] intervention" for the 1990s. "The fact that the White House let Secretary Lou Sullivan say what he did is a signal of encouragement for the FTC."[62] Activist actions and a flurry of headlines drew segmentation into public conversation, shifting the language of marketing from segmentation and to "targeting" and presenting it as a form of pernicious exploitation.

In April 1990, the House Subcommittee on Transportation and Hazardous Material argued about the risks of target advertising, especially when it came to using data to target specific demographic niches. "At stake," suggested Howard Schlossberg of *Marketing News*, was "much of the future course of targeted marketing and advertising."[63] The tobacco industry and the Association of National Advertisers (ANA), the latter of which counted among its membership nearly 80 percent of all national merchandisers in the United States, attacked the committee's interest in targeting at all, arguing that attempts to regulate marketing to consumers of color was "bordering on racism, let alone censorship," with ANA executive vice president of government relations Dan Jaffe going as far as to argue that constraining consumer choice was an attack on the fundamental liberty of the buyer as a citizen: "to suggest that adult black women can't discern about cigarettes is saying they can't decide on a congressman either."[64] John O'Toole, president of the American Association of Advertising Agencies, followed this argument in his own remarks regarding the hearing, publicly acknowledging the way race was put to work in market research: "As long as the product is legally sold, advertisers will continue to target the most prolific segments. Blacks smoke three times as many menthol [cigarettes] as whites, so who do you think they are going to target? People who don't want the product?"[65] Such commentary coming from some of the most important marketing and advertising executives in the United States was in effect an admission of the racial logic that the activists had so deplored.

RJR Nabisco competitors followed Uptown and the target marketing crisis closely. In 1990, the Philip Morris tobacco company issued an internal report on how the crisis had unfolded and its impact on the company's own marketing strategies. Titled "Anatomy of a Failure," the report cited a number of different professional and magazine reviews where journalists and marketers alike had attempted to understand where Uptown had gone wrong. "RJR was foolish to announce it was targeting blacks," suggested the report. "Uptown isn't the first cigarette directly or even indirectly to target minorities. Name brands like Virginia Slims, More, Rio, Dorado, Salem, and Newport are heavily marketed in the inner city. Most are supported by advertising as well as billboards and promotions." The study went on to note that "in recent years, a number of new generic and sub-generic brands have been introduced. The makers of these cigarettes have never said they were targeting minorities. But their critics have said these very low-priced cigarettes are an effort to bring in or keep in the market, blacks, Hispanics, and children. Unlike Uptown, however, the introduction of generics and subgenerics did not prompt a public backlash."[66]

Perhaps most pressing, however, was how the activists had succeeded in pulling marketing into public life and, in the process, transformed the language of segmentation. "In reality, 'segmented marketing,' as it's called, is an accepted and normally uncontroversial method of selling products," noted the report. "You could argue that the cigarette companies would be foolish to spend their advertising dollars across the board when only selected groups continue to smoke in increasing numbers. So the RJR strategy makes sense from a marketing point of view, but as it discovered, little sense from a political point of view."[67] Philip Morris attributed this paradox to the success of the Uptown Coalition. The firm argued, "There are issues that have become touchstones for public outrage in the black community: advertising of smoking and liquor products targeted to the inner city, particularly to teenagers," was now considered a risk. Moving forward, tobacco corporations were now forced to reckon with "the concept of stewardship" that had increasingly become organized around community engagement. "Respected leaders like the Rev. Calvin Butts in Harlem have fought against the use of billboards in their communities to advertising smoking and liquor products. There is much more sensitivity to issue."[68] The coalition, then, had not only forced a public conversation on targeting but shifted the discourse within tobacco corporations themselves.

In an *Adweek* article regarding the soon-to-arrive 1990 census, Peter Francese, president and publisher of the marketing periodical *American Demographics*, worried over the ethics of target marketing in public life. The 1990 census was to be the "motherlode of all databases, the benchmark of all consumer databases and research." Yet Uptown raised questions about the ethics of constructing consumer categories. Francese believed that even if marketers claimed they were simply satisfying demands that their research showed already existed in a population, the very accuracy of new marketing techniques used by companies like RJR Nabisco exacerbated these potential weaknesses. What's more, headlines condemning such practices further cast marketers and advertisers as a gang of hidden persuaders. This deep suspicion over the kinds of information held on ordinary people fueled demands for regulation, while the uneven effects of that data when deployed complicated merchandisers' relationships with minority communities. "If I choose to market to [specific communities], am I just being a good target marketer—or am I exploiting that population?" For Francese, the idiom "information is power" defined the dangers that lay waiting. In his estimation, marketing experts would have to reckon with this concern as data continued to become more granular and particular.[69]

The failure of Uptown dragged into public life the many different strategies that merchandisers used to sell their products to particular communities. In the process, the Uptown Coalition succeeded in transforming both the public discourse around market segmentation and internal marketing discussions as well. The coalition's actions revealed how marketing did not distribute the benefits of a consumer society evenly. They forced marketing professionals themselves to think through the impact of their work, leading some to wonder over the ethics of new information resources like the coming census. As Philip Morris's internal review of the Uptown brand suggested, these contestations limited the immediate movements of merchandisers looking to capitalize upon young, black urban consumers.

"Target Marketing: Racist or Right?"

In the year following Uptown and the target marketing crisis, the New York City Department of Consumer Affairs published a report on representation in the American mass market. Titled *Invisible People*, the report documented what appeared to be the disappearance of models of color from major American periodicals. "The slippage in black representation in magazine advertising lends support to a theory heretofore cautiously advanced by marketing experts," suggested a review. "Marketers' improving ability to reach specific consumer targets in specialized media is leading to the disappearance of minority images in many media with broader appeal."[70] *Invisible People* had found that the proportion of black models had declined since the activist push of the 1960s and early 1970s. By 1991, most depictions of African Americans were as athletes, musicians, or the subjects of philanthropy. Executives at major advertising agencies stressed that the situation was not the result of an antiblack bent, but the outcome of new forms of advance market segmentation and narrowcasting. They tied the whiteness of the general market to commercial marketing techniques that had screened race difference out of these spaces.

The black advertising and marketing executive Caroline Jones contested this argument. She critiqued both merchandisers and ad agencies alike for their treatment of black consumers. Since 1986, when Jones had opened Caroline Jones Advertising, her firm had amassed a wealth of market research data on African American, Latinx, and Asian American consumer market preferences. "The argument is always on the side of going with the white images in the white media," remarked Jones in a *New York Times* report on *Invisible People*. "People want to talk to the consumers they want rather than the consumers they have or the consumers they could have. . . . And the consumers they want are 'people like me.'"[71] Indeed, even as popular cultural aesthetics increasingly turned to the urban, *Invisible People* suggested market segmentation retained the notion that the mass market itself was a coherent marketing construct defined by whiteness.

Jones had followed Uptown and the target marketing crisis closely, using her firm's market research as well as her own experience in the industry to develop a set of arguments that shamed advertisers and merchandisers while maintaining market segmentation and targeting as a technique. In this way, her arguments offered one solution to the tensions that both *Invisible People* and the target marketing crisis had pointed to. In an essay titled "Target Marketing: Racist or Right?," Jones resisted the claim that targeting ought to be dismissed, as had been argued by both Reverend Butts and the Uptown Coalition. She argued instead that target marketing was not the issue at hand. Rather, it was that most major merchandisers simply chose to ignore evidence that suggested their products were well used by people of color. "What looks like a *concentration* of cigarette and liquor advertising," argued Jones, "is due to the *lack* of other kinds of messages. Where are the stereos, perfumes, jewelry, clothes, baby food?"[72] By Jones's estimation, the real issue was a lack of robust and engaged advertising toward black consumers writ large.

In her commentary on Uptown, Jones cautioned activist rejections of targeting altogether. "The recent uproar about cigarette and alcoholic beverages billboard advertising is one indication that normally complacent Black consumers are waking up. And yet," Jones signaled to her potential clients, "I would caution advertisers and their advertising agencies to understand one thing: Just because some Blacks say, 'do not target us for cigarettes,' does not mean 'do not target us period.'"[73] Framing Butts and his ilk as a marginal group within a larger African American consumer market, Jones's narrative worked to suggest that African American buyers wanted more advertising, not less. She argued that "Rev. Butts should be fighting to get a more diverse group of advertisers marketing their goods on Harlem's billboards. . . . Rev. Butts shouldn't be fighting against target marketing . . . because there's nothing wrong with target marketing."[74] In this way, her critique stood in tension with the demands made by communities that felt they were under siege by billboard advertisements for tobacco.

Jones developed a report to build out her argument that black consumers were a significant market that merchandisers chose to ignore. She examined the lack of advertising to black consumers across a number of product categories. She had found that African American families "spend more on food, recreation, clothing, household furniture, personal care products, automobiles, audio-visual equipment, alcoholic beverages and a host of other products," yet advertisers ignored them.[75] It was not that cigarette and alcohol advertisers focused on black consumers with any zeal, Jones concluded, but rather the bulk of American marketing and advertising firms took little

note of black consumers even when they had them. Indeed, Jones claimed
that products like Uptown were so alienating because it was white merchandisers, white advertisers, white creatives, and white consultants who produced campaigns, generated research, and developed creative strategies for
black consumer markets. Without engagement with ethnic media outlets or
experts of color with in-group community knowledge, advertisers would
find themselves increasingly alienated from consumers of color and their
growing market share. As much as segmentation was shrouded in the language of an ever-expanding consumer market, Jones's critique pointed to
the ways in which segmentation had in fact whitewashed the general or average consumer. Market segmentation might have created visibility, but this
visibility meant little if African American media outlets stood in an anxious
relationship to the general market, capitalized upon by only a handful of
merchandisers.

Jones's critique both preserved targeting and simultaneously condemned
the agencies and merchandisers that willingly ignored black consumers. She
called for a form of market segmentation that tapped into the resources and
knowledge of firms owned and operated by African Americans, arguing
that these organizations could help merchandisers develop advertising campaigns that spoke to African American communities through their own
lived experience. Jones saw targeting as an opportunity to garner consumer
attention for black consumers: a space wherein the recognition of African
American consumers as a distinct and profitable market would bring with it
civil, social, and political legitimacy. Yet Jones's vision of the African American consumer market was cast on terms amiable to herself, her firm, and to
her merchandiser clients as well. It minimized activists' calls for community control, casting Reverend Butts and the Uptown Coalition as a critical
fringe of the monolithic black community that she packaged, promoted,
and sold.

Conclusion

In 1998, the Uptown Coalition joined the National Association of African
Americans for Positive Imagery (NAAAPI) in a civil rights lawsuit against
tobacco companies that manufactured mentholated tobacco products. The
class action lawsuit, with the Reverend Jesse W. Brown, Jr., acting as plaintiff
on behalf of the Uptown Coalition, was filed in Federal District Court in

Philadelphia on October 19, 1998.[76] While the Uptown Coalition had successfully forced RJR Nabisco to withdraw its Uptown brand, Reynolds itself sought new avenues and strategies in marketing to African American consumers. As late as 1994, Reynolds's "Menthol Initiative Program" (known internally as MIP) sought to address the emergent "nuances" of the African American consumer market, to turn away from an emphasis on young adult smokers, and to double down on "a highly visible commitment to social responsibility," which they argued had become "fundamental to ethnic marketing."[77]

The popular press of the early 1990s had been full of refrains of "how did they get my name?" as white Americans commented upon the growing mass of commercial media that wound up in their mailboxes. Uptown and the target marketing crisis made clear the uneven effects of marketing across lines of race difference. In the 1960s and 1970s, market segmentation brought with it the promise of widespread commercial transformation in America. Many marketers argued that through segmentation consumers of color could perhaps flourish under American capitalism. But in the 1990s, the techniques that provided commercial promise to white suburbanites were the very same ones that sapped wealth out of black urban communities, going as far as to name, in plain language, young black men as perpetually renewing investments for Big Tobacco.

By the early 2000s, technological shifts would obscure the power of target marketing. While alcohol and tobacco advertising would be constrained through policy decisions at the level of the state, the arrival of digital social media platforms and the enclosure of the internet would transform the marketing profession. The billboards painted over by Reverend Butts and his congregation would be replaced by digital advertisements that continued to capitalize upon demographic vectors like race, gender, and class, but obscured the targeting of specific groups through the language of the "personalized" advertising experience. In recent years, scholars have pointed to the ways these digital regimes perform their social sorting and typing.[78] This scholarship has powerfully documented how social media platforms' appeals to quantification obscure the work they do with race. As this chapter has illustrated, marginalized communities have contested these kinds of data-driven typologies since well before the digital age.

Contemporary personalization emerges out of the very same typologies that firms like RJR Nabisco used to develop Uptown: the construction of highly racialized and gendered consumer categories in market research.

Even today, such categories remain socially and politically powerful constructions that operate well beyond their marketing utility. They shape how both merchandisers and ordinary people alike navigate and understand the world. These categories give marketers inordinate power. And yet, as Uptown reminds us, these categories are never wholly or uncritically encountered by their intended audiences. The Uptown brand was both an exercise in market segmentation as well as the construction of a specific kind of consumer market, one based on a vision of precarious black life upon which RJR Nabisco's marketing team believed they could draw enduring, long-term profits. In this way, the Uptown Coalition's rejection of the brand was also a rejection of the reductive vision of black life that it represented.

CHAPTER 9

Surveillance Capitalism Online

Cookies, Notice and Choice, and Web Privacy

MEG LETA JONES

Cookies are perhaps the most recognizable and widespread technical tool feeding digital surveillance capitalism today. Online users accumulate cookies stored on their computers and are presented cookie notifications repeatedly as they interact with various sites and services. Both cookies and their attendant notification systems are products of the early web, but also even earlier exceptionalism of marketing in privacy protections and the rhetorical tie between marketing and communication infrastructures. As the web was made into a commercial enterprise, it took on attributes of older regimes and utilized tools from older privacy debates. This chapter retells the origin story of surveillance capitalism on the web by focusing on cookies and those who wielded and debated them from developer message boards to industry groups and enforcement agencies. Through analysis of www-talk archives, Internet Engineering Task Force (IETF) working group archives, previous browser versions and settings, trade literature, and interviews, as well as government reports, case law, congressional hearings, and legislative history, the chapter details how over a short period users became consumers, notice and choice became privacy, and cookies became mechanisms of entrenchment for surveillance capitalism.

Pioneers

The origins of surveillance capitalism, according to Shoshana Zuboff who popularized the term, are in 2000 at Google, where ads were initially set up and managed by the search company on behalf of subscription-paying clients before it importantly moved to a self-service program called AdWords.[1] Google is a powerful figure and certainly a pioneer in the story of surveillance capitalism, but Google picked up and refined existing practices among an industry that emerged hungry and consolidated after the dot-com crash in 2000. Beyond noting Google's seventh employee Amit Patel's discovery of "[Google's] accidental data caches," as Zuboff does, we should also question the creation and design of those logs. After all, raw data is an oxymoron.[2] Search logs, like cookies, are part of what Josh Lauer calls the "evidential paradigm" in communication technologies. They are new media that produce new evidence, "each with its own material form and truth claims."[3] The "gold dust"[4] of Google's surveillance capitalism is not a natural substance discovered by corporate explorers; it is also part of the logic, technology, and rhetoric of surveillance capital.

Others have written earlier works pointing to the origins of surveillance capitalism, by different names and approaches, and situating it within advertising, personalization, or Silicon Valley economics. For instance, in an April 2019 *New York Times* opinion, Tim Wu writes, "We have witnessed the rise of what I call 'attention merchants' and what the sociologist Shoshana Zuboff calls 'surveillance capitalism'—the commodification of our personal data by tech giants like Facebook and their imitators in telecommunications, electronics, and other industries,"[5] but Wu's book *The Attention Merchants* traces the long history of advertisers, propagandists, and publishers that have cashed in on "selling eyeballs."[6] Joseph Turow has detailed the contemporary advertising landscape, its power arrangements between companies and consumers.[7] Since the release of Zuboff's *The Age of Surveillance Capitalism*, other parallel projects have also contributed new insights. Julie Cohen's *Between Truth and Power* describes the co-construction of law and the informational economy, focusing on the way law has helped produce the shift and also shifted in fundamental ways.[8] In *The Costs of Connection*, Nick Couldry and Ulises Mejias ask global questions of surveillance capitalism and argue that the logic should be recognized through the lens of colonialism.[9]

This chapter will trace another tributary that led to surveillance capitalism. Though powerful tools for surveillance capitalism, cookies were not always about surveillance. In fact, cookies were originally about privacy and decentralized power. By focusing on the early technical tools upon which surveillance capitalism operates today—cookies and interfaces of notice and choice—the chapter argues that between 1994 and 1997 these mechanisms, proffered directly by the direct marketing industry, became entrenched. Mechanisms of entrenchment, according to Paul Starr, are those that provide "strong inertial forces."[10] He explains, "Things that work satisfactorily come to be thought of as right: laws, methods, and systems that appear to be successful become the basis of standards, often gradually appearing to be natural and inevitable, as if they could be no other way."[11]

Here the mechanisms of entrenchment are the idea that better advertising can serve as an infrastructure for communications and the notification systems that inform individuals on how to prevent advertisements as a form of privacy. In an attempt to create a new and exciting future on and out of the web, the technologists that designed and implemented cookies utilize these mechanisms of entrenchment, as do the commercial players that sought to make the web a profitable place. Although early commercial web developers came to find notice an important aspect of deploying cookies, industry groups were able to quickly rely on a long-standing opt-out practice that had satisfied investigations into privacy concerns for decades. What makes surveillance capitalism so powerful is not its novelty but its long-entrenched tools, rhetoric, and everyday practices. Properly understanding mechanisms of entrenchment in surveillance capitalism offers alternative moments and avenues for intervention.

State

In April 1995, Brian Behlendorf, lead engineer on HotWired.com[12] and co-founder of the Organic, Inc.,[13] wanted to talk about how users navigated websites. He articulated the problem: "There are a couple systems starting to be deployed now that attempt to gain information about 'clickstreams.' 'Clickstreams' are the paths people take when they traverse your site—many content providers would find it useful to be able to detect common patterns or the effectiveness of various user interfaces. The problem is, of course, that HTTP [hypertext transfer protocol] is stateless, and beyond the hostname offers very little in the way of identification of unique 'trips' through the content site." He sent the message to the www-talk mailing list, maintained

by Tim Berners-Lee's World Wide Web Consortium (W3C), wanting to discuss creating a new HTTP header called "session-ID."[14] HotWired had been
using access controls like HTTP basic authentication or the HTTP "From"
header, which requested an email address in response. Behlendorf included
in his initial prompt that "any proposed solution *must* protect the anonymity of the user, for it's not really necessary to lose that when all that's
cared about is unique sessions."[15]

Lou Montulli, who is considered the inventor of the now-universal
web cookie, replied, explaining he had been doing "work along these
lines" at Netscape. He detailed the set-cookie HTTP header and how it
worked.[16]

>   Syntax of the Set-Cookie HTTP Response Header:
>   Set-Cookie: NAME=OPAQUE_STRING \
>   [; expires=] \
>   [; path=] \
>   [; domain=] \
>   [; secure]
>
>   Syntax of the Cookie HTTP Request Header:
>   Cookie: NAME=OPAQUE_STRING *[; NAME=OPAQUE_STRING]

Montulli, a University of Kansas computer science graduate, created cookies in order to provide a division at Netscape the shopping cart they had
asked for. While a student, Montulli began working on a project called Lynx
that merged hypertext and Gopher as the network protocol until he began
integrating Berners-Lee's web protocols a year later. Designed for mainframe terminals with limited functionality, the web was initially within
reach to academic and scientific communities. When Marc Andreesen and
fellow students and employees of the National Center for Supercomputing
Applications at the University of Illinois built Mosaic as one of the early
browsers meant for a broader audience, it was still designed for a Unix X
Windows System. Berners-Lee envisioned the web to be stateless by design—
to retrieve a document and disconnect in order for the web server to be free
to respond to other users.

This retrieval system became understood as a "memory" problem.[17]
Montulli joined Andreesen in California to start a technology company
that focused on the web browser and would solve the memory problem in

a particular way for particular reasons creating a particular type of evidence accessible to particular parties. The X Windows System used a "magic cookie" generated by the server and transferred to the client for a specific user logged in on a particular display to be retrieved later.[18] Montulli utilized the concept in the first version of Netscape Mosaic in September 1994.

Behlendorf responded to Montulli's cookie header, "A very mature proposal—now we need some test implementations :) Any volunteers? The browser should allow the user to NULL their session ID at any time (or turn off the functionality, even if by default it is on)."[19] While anonymous, the memory system devised through cookie protocols is not visible to the user but can be controlled by the user. The 1988 X Windows System manual states, "The magic cookie defined in a user's .Xauthority file is basically a secret code shared by the server and a particular user logged in on a particular display. . . . Basically, under the magic cookie authorization scheme, a display becomes user-controlled."[20] Web cookies operate similarly with the same characteristics. When a client (i.e., user) requests an HTTP object (i.e., goes to a website), a server can send a piece of state information with the returned HTTP object (i.e., the site can send a cookie with a webpage). A cookie is simply a string of text that is placed into the memory of the browser stored on a user's hard drive and associated with a value in a database available to the web server. Future HTTP requests made by the client to the server will include the most recent value of the cookie pulled from the client's browser storage and sent back to the server. It is called an "opaque" memory, meaning it is "opaque to the user agent and may be anything the origin server chooses to send, possibly in a server-selected printable ASCII encoding. 'Opaque' implies that the content is of interest and relevance only to the origin server."[21]

The visibility is, of course, an important component to control. In his message arguing to keep the discussion alive, Marc Hedlund, working as director of engineering at Organic, wrote, "A while back someone asked what was wrong with the Netscape Cookie proposal. A long delayed response: it doesn't tell the user what it's doing."[22] Koen Holtman, one of the few Europeans engaged on the list, was interested in "stateful dialogs," not improving site statistics for marketing, but suggested a browser interface that might provide user control[23] inspired by the selections users made to download images, which on early networks could take a significant amount of time.[24]

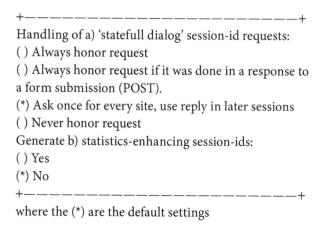

```
+———————————————————————————+
Handling of a) 'statefull dialog' session-id requests:
( ) Always honor request
( ) Always honor request if it was done in a response to
a form submission (POST).
(*) Ask once for every site, use reply in later sessions
( ) Never honor request
Generate b) statistics-enhancing session-ids:
( ) Yes
(*) No
+———————————————————————————+
```

where the (*) are the default settings

The debates were also reminders of the reality of "the market" as both an inevitable force pushing for metrics and functionality as well as a way to get privacy on the web right. One effort attempted to analogize the conversation to caller ID, explaining that the problem of various desires for identifying a caller and being identified when calling were met by developing protocols that allow callers to block sending their information and recipients to block calls without caller ID and then relying on the market to sort out the rest. The poster goes on to argue:

> Technical solutions that are based on social judgements have problems, the biggest of which is their lack of generality. . . . Computer systems that seek large market share should not attempt to behave in a paternalistic manner, deciding for users what their legitimate needs are and meeting those needs (and only those needs). Systems that are paternalistic . . . are not likely to gain large market share and may indeed lose market share over time to systems that allow the user to do what he wants without requiring him to do it only that way.. Market pressures demand session-IDs, both for maintaining states and for user tracking. Either session-ID capability will be implemented sensibly or it won't, but in no case will its emergence be prevented.[25]

Behlendorf's initial message explained that he had people asking for clickstream data and statistics, and a theme of marketing demands comes in and out of threads. Wrapping up his final call for consensus or an end to the discussion, Behlendorf wrote, "Anyways, at this point I'm ready to throw in the towel and just go back and tell the people screaming for this kind of functionality and go 'look, without intrusive measures like password protection or broken mechanisms like session-ID-URL-munging or heuristics which work one day and not the next, I just can't get that info for you with any reasonable accuracy.' And then we'll see which path they choose."[26]

Infrastructure

Even with the popularity of Netscape Navigator, it was not clear how the company would make money. Netscape eventually brought money in from enterprise software sales that included server packages, browser, email, and custom software, and annual support contracts, as well as ad revenue derived from traffic on the portal and distributor bundle packages on operating systems. A great number of revenue sources were being pursued on the internet by 1994, including utility charges for connectivity, access to the web, and email, subscriptions, and premium fees for specialized information and entertainment, licensing schemes for browsers, search tools, and software libraries, and advertising.

Kevin O'Connor and Dwight Merriman considered profits the primary problem the web needed to have solved, as recounted on Brian McCullough's *Internet History Podcast*.[27] How would people make money on the web? As they brainstormed a new venture in Atlanta, the two asked what would be the plumbing and the electricity of the web.[28] They continued to come back to the inevitability of advertising and started the Internet Advertising Federation in 1995 and set out to contribute to the "infrastructure" of the decentralized network of the future that would take on the walled gardens of online service providers, namely AOL, CompuServe, and Prodigy. Both men were trained engineers, O'Connor with a degree in electrical engineering from the University of Michigan and Merriman with a degree in computer science from Miami University of Ohio, but O'Connor took up learning the business of advertising and headed to the library to check out Ed Nash's *Direct Marketing*.[29] O'Connor was quickly convinced that the web could provide the measurements, tracking, and targeting at the core of advertising, and Merriman worked to deliver on the technical side. As O'Connor worked to understand contemporary advertising, reading marketing news at the library and looking for potential competition, he came across an announcement for DoubleClick out of Poppe Tyson—a new division designed to sell advertisements on clients' websites. It turned out the advertising firm was in need of Merriman's technology, and the two companies combined forces under the name DoubleClick. O'Connor and Merriman moved to New York to plant a flag in what would become Silicon Alley.

Although the engineers saw a new kind of potential for advertising on the web, selling the internet and online advertising to traditional advertising players, who were comfortable with the metrics of radio, television, and print, was the vital job of Wenda Harris Millard, a founding member of DoubleClick's executive team.[30] There's a saying in advertising: "If you don't know Wenda Harris Millard, you're not in marketing."[31] After twenty years in traditional media, Millard knew everyone and legitimized the company to Madison Avenue early, putting the services in terms the industry used and educating traditional groups. DoubleClick came to be known as the most dominant player in the online advertising and its sales force.[32] A small group of like-minded companies were founded at the same time, but none would dethrone DoubleClick.

These early internet advertising companies came to the same realization from different perspectives,[33] like Real Media[34] at the beginning of 1996 started by Gil Beyda (a California developer who started his first tech company in high school called Mind Games while working at a local computer store called Computers Are Fun) and Dave Morgan (who had worked as an attorney for a newspaper trade association that had a commercial arm selling ads to its members).[35] Or Engage cofounded by Daniel Jaye (who was trained in astrophysics and computing for scientific projects at Bell Labs and later managed databases across Fidelity Management and Research) in late 1995 as part of College Marketing Group Information Services' (later CMGI's) push to cultivate the internet.[36] These companies sought to provide advertising to support independent sites on the new decentralized web through a centralized network of advertisers. The companies drew distinctions between themselves to some extent. RealMedia was initially designed to similarly provide ads to small news sites. Jaye ("credited with inventing online behavioral advertising and pioneering internet privacy standards")[37] at Engage came straight out of direct marketing. All have claims to the origins of targeted behavioral advertising, but when the dot-com crash ripped through the industry, what emerged was a handful of consolidated companies that would "target users not pages,"[38] meaning users would be tracked across sites and content providers/publishers/websites would sell access to their "unused inventory"—user data.

Traditional advertising and marketing had ventured into computing technologies of the time and generated minor privacy scandals. In 1983, Martin Nisenholtz founded the Interactive Marketing Group (IMG) at advertising agency Ogilvy & Mather Worldwide, where he worked on teletext as a form of interactive consumer media in analog broadcast television spectrum (and later cable), as well as videotex to bridge the telephone with the television using a decoder box.[39] Direct marketing had moved quickly into computing; in fact, its growth is tied to computing and printing technologies.[40] The "consumer-database" industry of the 1980s and 1990s confronted the privacy issues of the decade prior and those to come. A *Wall Street Journal* article from 1991 asked:

> Want to send junk mail to short fat guys with glasses? The consumer-database industry has the service for you. In their eternal search for intimate data about Americans, a few firms are buying state driver's license records to get such data as consumers' height, weight and use of "corrective lenses." Even in the omnivorous mailing-list industry, the use of height and weight data is controversial. Most drivers who register for a license have no idea their personal information finds its way into the hands of marketers. Two of the biggest consumer-database companies . . . don't sell height and weight data because it's too personal.[41]

In the late-1980s, privacy concerns about "computer matching" were spread across private and public sectors but minimized as consumer friendly and cost reducing.[42] When Lotus Development Corporation revealed its newest product—the Lotus MarketPlace—at the MacWorld computer expo in 1990, the target was small businesses and the goal was to increase sales through direct market mailing lists that could be run on a personal computer desktop. But, the goal was never realized, because the product was shelved in response to public outcry over privacy concerns.[43]

Still, the web provoked new possibilities for advertising. A 1996 *Wired* article explained the "webonomics," stating, "Not someday, today—advertising on the Web makes economic sense. You just have to forget everything you ever learned about the business."[44] Advertising on predecessor networks like Usenet was controversial[45] because the nature of the network is "mutualized" and operated as a commons, but the web was delivered to users by a commercial service provider and presented through the package of a corporate homepage and conceived by those working on it as a place for media consumption just like any publishing enterprise that placed advertising next to content.[46] In an attempt to provide guide rails to this practice on a new medium, Nisenholtz wrote for *Advertising Age* (covered by the *New York Times*) in 1994: "Radio, telephone, and TV networks were all born primarily as commercial services. . . . If you were to advance the theory (in, say, one of the alt.newsgroups) that the purpose of the Internet was to make money, you would probably get flamed. . . . No one owns the Internet. There is no single governing body that controls it. . . . Everyone would probably like to see the Internet become a financial self-sufficient entity. The question is how."[47] In calling for consensus around a set of guidelines, Nisenholtz proposed six: (1) intrusive email is not welcome, (2) internet consumer data is not for resale without the express permission of the user, (3) advertising is allowed only in designated newsgroups and list servers, (4) promotions and direct selling are allowed but only under full disclosure (consistent with the rules developed by the Direct Marketing Association for "analog merchants"), (5) consumer research is allowed only with the consumer's "full consent" (which meant "ready and easy access to information outlining the uses and implications" of participation), and (6) internet communications software must never hide concealed functions.[48] In what may represent the first web privacy policies,[49] these tenets speak to a moments of internet culture when users spent time in newsgroups, were exposed to spam, and the default would keep data with the content creator but also hints at the flimsy state of the concept of consent and the shift away from "user data" to "consumer data."

Defaults

The British *Financial Times* article by Tim Jackson, future founder of the UK-based auction site QXL.com and later tech venture capitalist, brought cookies as a privacy issue to the public for the first time in February 1996. The story explained, "Most extraordinary of all, this information can be stored on customers' own PCs without their knowledge. It can be kept in a form so that only the company that collected the information can benefit from it. . . . Moreover there appears to be only one way to disable the facility: by manually amending or deleting the COOKIE.TXT file containing all the cookies."[50] Jackson further, and incorrectly, explained, "They do not allow one company to snoop on another, and they gather only information about consumers' behaviour at a single company's Web site, or information that customers themselves volunteer."[51]

It is not surprising that in February 1996 Jackson did not know about DoubleClick's growing advertising network and cross-site tracking. Back in April 1995, when Montulli was explaining cookies on the www-talk list, he stated, "Only hosts in the specified domain can set cookies for a domain. Therefore it is not possible to set a cookie for the B domain unless you are in the B domain."[52] By 1997 the conversation (and participants) had changed and the issue was whether third-party cookies deriving from companies (like those in the advertising business) should be prohibited, allowed but only when the user accepts, or the default but possible to change.

In December 1995, a state management subgroup was created within the HTTP Working Group, led by Dave Kristol and included Montulli, Amazon's first employee Shel Kaphan, a couple of engineers at the W3C, Eric Sink at competitor browser Spyglass Mosaic, and a small group of other developers. The group consulted over email and adopted Netscape's mechanism as a starting point for generating more precise specifications.[53] After the initial Internet-Draft (a draft version of the document made available through the IETF directory for informal comment) was published beginning with version 2.3 in February 1996,[54] "unverified transactions" (later known as third party cookies) were identified as a significant privacy issue, and the specification outright prohibited them or allowed them if the user could control them through a browser with a default set to reject them.[55] More changes and Internet-Drafts followed, and the working group had Last Call (notification triggering a period for final comments) in June and steering group Last Call in August, but in October suggested that the specification was too lenient on distinguishing between verified and unverified transactions. After some final adjustments, the specification was documented as RFC (Request for Comment) 2109 in February 1997. RFC 2109 detailed a Proposed Standard (the first in three levels of internet standards maturity) called HTTP State Management Mechanism, coauthored by Kristol and Montulli.

As the debate took off in March 1997 on the www-talk and HTTP-WG (HTTP Working Group) lists, Ted Hardie, who was working at NASA Science Internet Project after earning a doctorate from Stanford and who today is a senior member of the Internet Evangelism team at Google Research, wrote:

There is nothing in the spec which forces you back to a "login" method to track unique users. The spec requires that you make sure that the same cookies are not used across domains; it allows you to do what you want *within a domain*. If you want to make sure that a dejanews user sees an advert three times and then gets moved to a different ad, you are welcome to use cookies to do so. If you wish to use cookies to make sure that a user sees an advert three times *at any site* before moving on to a different ad, sorry. Because the use of the same cookie across sites allows for the creation of very invasive clicktrail analysis, that has been ruled out. There is something which says that if you are using cookies, you need to manage them within your domain.[56]

While the working group set out to resolve some outstanding technical is-sues, two other new voices joined this debate and brought public attention to the normally insular world of IETF standards: DoubleClick and the pri-vacy organization EPIC (Electronic Privacy Information Center).[57] In March 1997, Dwight Merriman argued from DoubleClick for modifications to the 2109 specification:

In its current form, this section of the spec has potentially huge ram-ifications for Internet advertising networks and remote ad delivery services. Ad networks and remote delivery services use cookies for at least three functions: 1) measuring reach, 2) frequency stop target-ing, and 3) user interest targeting. If the new RFC is adopted, these capabilities will be lost for networks, but still available and effective for the largest individual sites which accept advertising. I am unsure if ad networks, which provide an important economic model for smaller web sites, will be able to compete effectively in the long term if this happens.[58]

In April 1997, EPIC sent (and posted) a letter to the IETF, cc'ing Microsoft's president Bill Gates and chief technology officer Nathan Myhrvold and Netscape's president Jim Barksdale and CTO Marc Andreesen.[59] The letter of support for 2109 concludes by stating, "We believe that 'transparency'—the ability of users to see and exercise control over the disclosure of person-ally identifiable information—is a critical guideline for the development of sensible privacy practices on the Internet. The alternative would be the surreptitious collection of data without the ability to exercise any control."[60]

The advertising industry also made public appeals. ADSmart's Sue Doyle explained, "What concerns us is the tone of the proposal, which is that advertising is not good for us, so we want to avoid it. That begs the question, how is the Web going to be funded?"[61] Microsoft and Netscape were also courted directly.[62] The tangle of technical and social issues resulted in delays, and Kristol decided to find consensus on the technical part, which he did in February 1998, and to reintroduce the "unverified transaction" language later,[63] which he did without response, but the steering group composition had changed in the three years it had taken to move 2109 along and now wanted more privacy and security.[64]

In the end Montulli decided not to follow the standard he coauthored[65] and apparently the drafting committee had gone against his wishes.[66] Both Microsoft and Netscape provided users the ability to change their preferences to alert them before a cookie was placed by each web server and to reject it—the default was to accept all cookies,[67] which went against the 2109 standard but not against the law. Montulli, like Behlendorf and others, did not see third-party tracking coming before it happened but, when it occurred, assumed that other social forces like laws or government regulation would then step in:

> Any company that had the ability to track users across a large section of the web would need to be a large publicly visible company. Cookies could be seen by users so a tracking company can't hide from the public. In this way the public has a natural feedback mechanism to constrain those that would seek to track them. . . . Governments have an ability to regulate the collection of data by large visible companies and [have]shown a willingness to do so. The public has a responsibility to keep pressure on both the companies that have the ability to track users and governments to enact reasonable privacy regulations and enforce them.[68]

He insisted that cookies are the most privacy-protective technique available because they provide anonymity and control, and the other options for tracking, which would inevitably remain, were harder to observe and disable. He reasoned, "The nature of the advertising business is to collect as much information as it possibly can, so the public needs to push back when it goes too far."[69]

Choice

While the Clinton administration touted an explicit self-regulatory strategy for the internet, it pushed the commercialization of the internet into the hands of new, powerful, commercial-consumer-focused institutions. Margaret O'Mara describes the important relationship, as part of a legacy of important relationships between Silicon Valley and Washington, between the computer industry and the Clinton administration,[70] and Meghan Grosse details the strong self-regulatory policy and the important move to the Department of Commerce and Federal Trade Commission in a global context.[71] The "constitutive choice" (that includes the legal and normative rules, the specific design of communication, network, and organizations, and institutions related to the media)[72] of the Clinton administration was vital to transforming users into consumers, and over the course of the late 1990s, internet privacy became consumer privacy. Consumer privacy revolves around choice, and on the internet (and in Zuboff's surveillance capitalism), choice is an opt-out system.

The legacy of opt-out begins in 1971[73] with the Direct Mail Marketing Association's flagship program: the Mail Preference Service.[74] The service was established after bills restricting direct mail lists were introduced in 1969 and 1970. In a hearing dedicated to H.R. 2730 and related bills introduced by the Ninety-First Congress, testimony from New Jersey representative Cornelius Gallagher reads:

> Nothing more clearly illustrates this [danger to privacy and the Bill of Rights] than a recent event in Chicago which is directly relevant to these hearings. A suit has been filed by Encyclopedia Britannica against three former employees charging that they copied computer tapes. These tapes contained the names and addresses of 2 million Encyclopedia Britannica customers and were sold to mailing list brokers. One broker, who had received the stolen property, then sold a list containing 800,000 of those names to Curtis Books, Inc., a competitor of Encyclopedia Britannica. I believe this shocking example typifies the necessity for the Congress of the United States to begin to understand

how vulnerable to abuse the computer is, and how its willing tool, the junk mail industry, welcomes and actually encourages such abuse. At least, it has no scruples about buying any collection of names, and the humans to whom those names refer have utterly no control.[75]

Gallagher told another story about how a woman's pregnancy was revealed to her family when diaper coupons were mailed to her home after a lab sold her information, and he insisted that direct mailers know far too much about Americans, while little was known about the industry. Also included was a *New Yorker* article explaining how list brokers sold information to target addresses from census data: "As it turns out, one of the minor disadvantages of being a Negro slum dweller in the United States is being deprived of a fair shore of orange-juice coupons."[76] Data breaches, sexual privacy, informational asymmetries, and racial bias were issues with direct marketing expressed by members of Congress in 1970.

In response, representatives of the Direct Mail Advertising Association (DMAA, established in 1917; its name was later changed to Direct Mail Marketing Association [DMMA] and then Direct Marketing Association [DMA]), argued that direct mail was an important form of advertising, that it had no real harm, and that it was in favor of limiting the distribution of pornographic mail, but did not mention mechanisms of control in 1970. While bills to ban pornographic mail floated around Congress, the DMAA presented its program to the House Appropriations Committee in 1971:

We recognize that in this uptight world there's a percentage of people who don't like *anything*. Since a key characteristic of our medium is selectivity. DMAA is pioneering a forward-thinking program to help consumers. We call it the Mail Preference Service (MPS), whereby we ask our cooperating members to remove from their mailing lists the names of those who seriously object to *all* advertising. Curious point: despite the alleged hue and cry that this mail is unwanted— when given the opportunity pilot tests confirm what has been indicated all along: *most people prefer to receive advertising mail.* They want to make the individual choice each time whether they are interested in a particular sales offer.[77]

The organization described its test launch and publicity in newspapers, which got very few inquiries in response and less than fifty forms returned with a preference to be placed on the "off" list and so concluded that people want to get advertising mailed to them.

In 1973, the internationally influential Health, Education, and Welfare Department's Records, Computers and the Rights of Citizens report ("HEW Report"), which included principles[78] later to form the basis of almost all privacy legislation around the world and led by renowned computer security engineer Willis Ware, directly addressed mailing lists, giving them their own appendix.[79] At the time, computer equipment was large, cumbersome, and labor intensive, so maintaining detailed addresses and data for individuals was not worth it except for very large direct mail marketers (mostly successful national magazines). The committee found no evidence that direct mail advertising was "anything more than an annoyance to a small part of the population"[80] and that their principles did not seem applicable. Noting that "an underlying function of the Advisory Committee's recommended safeguards is to provide effective feedback mechanisms that will help to make automated personal data systems more responsive to the interests of individuals," the committee agreed that the direct marketers already "concentrate almost obsessively on methods for maximizing response and minimizing complaints."[81] They argued the DMAA's Mail Preference Service should be publicized more prominently but also suggested that, if mailing lists become a problem, a check box could be provided on forms like applications or purchases that would allow the recipient to grant consent for secondary use, in line with the HEW Report principles.

When the Privacy Protection Study Commission (PPSC), put in place by the 1974 Privacy Act, began holding hearings in 1975, it sought to "answer the question raised by the [act] . . . 'whether a person engaged in interstate commerce who maintains a mailing list should be required to remove an individual's name and address from such a list upon the request of that individual.'"[82] Largely a response to the Watergate scandal, the Privacy Act is considered one of few broad privacy laws in America, though it only applies to personal information held by federal agencies and has many exceptions. The PPSC dedicated three days of hearings to rights related to mailing lists. More so than the HEW committee, the PPSC discusses the postal service's economics and its reliance on direct mail. When justifying its recommendation to *not* legally enforce an individual's request to be removed from a mailing list, the Commission explained the historical importance of mail to the freedom of expression, charity, and elections and the reliance mail has on direct marketing. It further explained that direct mail was important to the national economy and that the economics of putting a removal system in place would increase the costs of operating the mail and drive advertisers to the telephone.[83]

In the end, privacy in terms of mailing lists was considered sufficiently protected by the "negative check off systems" implemented by single entities like American Express and *Computerworld* managing their own mailing lists and the organized "delisting" put in place by the industry group DMMA.[84] Organizations that made personal information available to third parties were to provide detailed notice and implement removal processes with their partners, and such organizations were not to make personal information available to third parties beyond the context of the original purpose unless "customers" are informed and given an opportunity to indicate that they do not want their name used for such secondary purposes. The PPSC did not recommend any legal measures, instead recognized the "difficulty and the undesirability of forcing record keepers to assume that responsibility," and explained that "because so many appear to be willing to assume it voluntarily, the Commission believes that voluntary implementation is likely to be a successful as well as adequate solution to the problem."[85]

A number of reports were issued by government agencies in the late 1990s that further pushed the rhetoric of consumer privacy and opt-out choice as a governance tool. A 1998 National Telecommunications and Information Administration (within the Department of Commerce) discussion draft titled "Elements of Effective Self-Regulation for Protection of Privacy" suggested using the principles in the HEW Report, but focused on consumer transparency, education, and choice.[86] The Federal Trade Commission (FTC) issued a 1998 report to Congress called *Privacy Online*, which also interprets the HEW Report to suit self-regulation, emphasizing consumer notice, choice, access, security, and redress.[87] Further, the agency explained: "In the online environment, choice easily can be exercised by simply clicking a box on the computer screen that indicates a user's decision with respect to the use and/ or dissemination of the information being collected. The online environment also presents new possibilities to move beyond the opt-in/opt-out paradigm. For example, consumers could be required to specify their preferences regarding information use before entering a Web site, thus effectively eliminating any need for default rules."[88] The 1998 report found that self-regulation had not become effective on the web and sought to more strenuously encourage its development to protect consumer privacy online.

Also issued in 1998 was the Department of Energy's Computer Incident Advisory Capability information bulletin on internet cookies, which refers to "users" and never mentions the term "consumer." Nonetheless, the bulletin found concerns about cookies unwarranted: "No files are destroyed or compromised by cookies, but if you are concerned about being identified or about having your web browsing traced through the use of a cookie, set your browser to not accept cookies or use one of the new cookie blocking packages."[89]

In 1999, DoubleClick acquired NetGravity, which maintained ad display software for sites and was an example of the consolidation that occurred regularly and quickly in the industry. DoubleClick also announced plans to merge with Abacus Direct, which triggered a number of legal proceedings. Abacus marketed consumer-purchasing data to catalog firms engaged in direct marketing and planned to expand to e-commerce retailers. The direct marketing data company earned $11.4 million on revenue of $47 million while the internet advertising firm lost $18.1 million on revenue of $80 million in 1998.[90]

The FTC responded to EPIC's 1999 complaint about the merger by investigating, which prompted DoubleClick to voluntarily put a number of mechanisms in place to promote user choice and privacy education.[91] These voluntary measures were developed by and shared among members of the Network Advertising Initiative (NAI)—established in 2000 by DoubleClick, Engage, 24/7 Media, and the few other web advertising networks operating at the time[92] The NAI, inspired by the Direct Mail Association's opt-out system,[93] developed a "set of self-regulatory standards governing Interest-Based Advertising [and] also pioneered the creation of the industry choice page for consumers."[94] The FTC unanimously applauded the NAI for developing the self-regulatory system.[95]

Additionally, ten state attorneys general—led by New York attorney general Eliot Spitzer—began investigating the company in 2000. The thirty-month-long investigation resulted in a settlement that involved websites that partnered with DoubleClick to disclose activities in their sites' privacy policy and 100 million banner ads that directed users to DoubleClick's privacy education campaign and opt-out page,[96] which the company was already proactively doing under the foresight and guidance of in-house counsel Elizabeth Wang, the NAI, and a strong united front of industry associations.[97]

While enforcement agencies investigated, a number of class-action lawsuits were filed and consolidated in January 2000 against DoubleClick for its use of cookies. This charge was led by another high-profile figure: Bill Lerach. One of America's most famous attorneys of the twentieth century, Lerach, also called "the most feared man in Silicon Valley,"[98] helped take down Enron and later was sentenced to two years in prison and disbarred.[99] The claim against DoubleClick alleged that the company had violated the Electronic Communications Privacy Act, the Computer Fraud and Abuse Act, and the Wiretap Act, as well as other state laws.[100] The federal claims were dismissed because the court determined that DoubleClick was authorized to collect user data through the company's affiliation with the sites visited. The parties settled in 2002. DoubleClick agreed to extensive notice practices, a consumer education effort involving 300 million banner ads, and $1.8 million in costs and legal fees. EPIC objected to the settlement, because it did not require the company to do anything it was not already doing.[101] In fact, none of the investigations, lawsuits, or settlements required DoubleClick to do anything beyond what Wang and her team had put in place: an aggressive public education campaign that directed users to information about data use and provided a means for exercising tracking preferences across the advertising network.

The secondary commercial collection of data—the basis of surveillance capitalism—has proliferated under a transparency policy established to empower consumers and support important infrastructure. Matthew Crain points out that this transparency (1) is ineffective because it occurs within a privacy asymmetrical relationship wherein people are increasingly monitored while those monitoring are increasingly hidden from view and (2) serves as regulatory deflection.[102] These were precisely the concerns of the HEW committee and PPSC, but the committees—the most powerful privacy advocates of a pivotal moment—exempted direct market mailing lists from regulatory attention by relying on (1) advertising sustaining communication and (2) an opt-out mechanism of choice to protect. As the economics of delivering ads changed with communication and computer industries, user data was collected at every opportunity and repackaged as consumer data that could be opted out of. All data became consumer data, and all of it was swept up into the rhetoric of infrastructure and choice set aside by committees trying to protect privacy in the mainframe era, long before Google.

Conclusion

Google bought DoubleClick for $3.1 billion in 2007. The same year AOL bought Dave Morgan's later venture Tacoda, Yahoo! bought Right Media for $680 million, the British WPP bought 24/7 Real Media for $649 million, and Microsoft bought aQuantive for $6 billion. In an interview with *EconTalk*'s

Russ Roberts, Zuboff responds to Roberts's suggestion that data-driven or interest-based advertising is not new by stating the analogy to prior practices "is just silly" and insists we must recognize historical discontinuity when it is real.[103] Zuboff wants us to recognize "the unprecedented"[104] because unprecedentedness provides a powerful moment of distinction that may lead to attention and action. However, resistance to surveillance capitalism has failed not because of its novelty but because of its long history and relationships to powerfully entrenched structures, ideas, and mechanisms. Marketing has been repeatedly carved out as an exception to strong privacy protection and the early commercialization of the web has resulted in more consumer rhetoric, debate, and laws—all of which serve a surveillance capitalism. Cookies and notice-choice systems remain in place twenty-five years after their introduction online. These mechanisms of entrenchment from the 1970s helped take the early web from one of users to one full of consumers, conditions under which surveillance capitalism and Google could flourish.

AFTERWORD

SARAH E. IGO

What does yesterday's junk mail—or its cigarette campaigns or urine tests—have to do with American capitalism in the present? Far more than we might have imagined, the splendid essays in this volume suggest. Each transports us to a specific site, spanning the 1780s Caribbean to the mid-1990s World Wide Web. And each reveals the centrality of surveillance to business practices and economic life in the United States. The informant networks mobilized by both plantations and Pinkertons, the watchful practices of long-gone nightclubs and hotels, and the customer data captured by the earliest feedback surveys and digital cookies all pay dividends here.

History often humbles claims of the unprecedented. This collection testifies once again to the importance of historical work in clarifying our present. "Surveillance capitalism," as a term of both analysis and approbation, has captured the contemporary imagination. Coined as recently as 2014, it responds to the seemingly sudden dominance of an economic model based on expropriating personal data. Yet its logics can be spied in the eighteenth-century monitoring of enslaved people by watchmen and in the Gilded Age trade in personal names and addresses. To these examples we can add multifarious attempts before and since by owners, employers, businesspeople, entrepreneurs, inventors, and corporations to profit by channeling and commoditizing human behavior. It means that those who would pronounce surveillance capitalism a fresh force in the world have some explaining to do.

The claim to the new is nonetheless understandable. The pace of technological change, the incentives for commercial interests to pursue and harvest personal data, and the seeming inability of U.S. political and regulatory systems to meaningfully intervene have ensured that what goes under the banner of "surveillance capitalism" compels our attention right now. Even as Americans weigh the promise of digital tracing by giant tech corporations like Google and Apple in the midst of the COVID-19 pandemic, we fret over data mining, social media profiling, targeted advertising, prediction markets, behavioral "nudging," and algorithmic bias. Digital-age citizens are just beginning to reckon with the implications for individual privacy, social justice, and democratic life.

What *is* relatively new is the public focus on the threat such commercial practices pose. Recognition of the extent to which private companies have been in the business of monitoring individual behavior and data has arrived rather late in the United States—especially when compared to long-standing concerns about government surveillance. (The fact that the state and private companies have regularly worked hand in hand to do such watching is yet another relatively recent realization.) As we grasp for a characterization of our lives as twenty-first-century economic subjects, the experience of being watched and manipulated by commercial interests seems freshly ubiquitous and more deeply invasive than we imagine it ever could have been in the past.

To those who proclaim that our tracked, targeted, and tailored existence is a recently accomplished fact or even a new stage of capitalism, these essays may surprise. For what we discover by looking backward is a much-expanded timeline, an unyielding quest for more data, a steady intensification of surveilling practices—and a rather less breathless perspective on present predicaments. Whether the focus is on workers or customers, managers or market share, it seems, watching has *always* been the business of business.

We learn, for instance, that racial profiling by online retailers and the algorithms they employ have a prehistory in the "ethnic markets"—the Jewish, African American, and Hispanic customers—that tobacco companies sought to tap starting in 1969. The systems of rating and "nudging" employees that we have become habituated to as Lyft or Uber riders (or drivers) echo the surveys invented by service industries in the 1910s to keep tabs on workers' appearance, manner, and friendliness. Contemporary biometric monitoring in the workplace rests on the pivot to drug testing in 1980, which itself built on midcentury employee assistance programs, not to mention the older use of labor spies. Today's packaging of surveillance in the name of customers' security and comfort, whether in the form of doorbell cameras or in-home sensors, would be recognizable to interwar hotel managers. The selling of personal data for direct marketing was not, it turns out, our century's—nor even last century's—innovation; magazine publishers had developed a robust traffic in names and addresses by the 1880s.

These essays reinforce familiar patterns of recent history, too. Take the porousness of state and commercial surveillance, brought home most dramatically in recent years by collaborations between big tech and the National Security Agency to track private communications. No neat public-private divide was to be found in the policing of sexuality in Manhattan's nightclubs in the 1930s either, as club owners—private actors—were conscripted into the state's regulatory ambitions.

Or consider today's intensive monitoring of every facet of employees' interaction with customers. More than a century ago, a network of "mystery shoppers" and outside consultants was employed to ascertain, and ensure, that "the public be pleased." Or think of the multivalent use of surveillance tools in the present, employed not just hierarchically—by managers over workers or by marketers over potential purchasers—but horizontally on business rivals. The case of the competing Pinkertons extends that practice back into the nineteenth century. Mine the past and you find still more lines of connection. The gaps and failures of even the most advanced of today's surveillance systems have precedents in subversive watchmen and unreliable drug tests. These systems' tendency to engender countersurveillance has analogues in the speakeasy peepholes of the Prohibition era and, of course, in criminals' working knowledge of security routines in just about any era.

But the work of deciphering something as complex, layered, and multifaceted as "surveillance capitalism" only begins by naming these precedents and echoes. After all, today's commercial monitoring systems do not simply *resonate* with, but are *outgrowths* of previous ones. What these histories track, as Josh Lauer and Ken Lipartito observe in their wide-ranging introduction, are the grooves carved by past technologies, policies, laws, and norms, which over time deepened into durable infrastructures. Contributors to this volume peel back the contemporary order of things to reconstruct how, why, and when specific surveillant practices became lodged in the U.S. economy.

This dialogue between past and present corrects one of the biggest errors in contemporary reportage, which is to treat our present, datafied moment as without parallel—indeed, without history. It foregrounds instead the cumulative effect of economic practices that have assumed many different forms over time and have only recently been grouped together under the banner of "surveillance." As the origin story of the cookie makes evident, the fact that in 2021 we conduct life online, and trade our personal data away in the process, is the intricate product of prior debates and decisions, with consequences that would only become clear in hindsight. Our economic present is a product of many such stories, fashioned at the confluence of powerful forces like profit and countless local contingencies.

More significantly still, historians are framing new questions about the past and our categories for apprehending it. The essays in this volume unearth dense linkages between mechanisms of profit and accumulation, on the one hand, and strategies of tracking and monitoring on the other. In other words, they refocus us on the foundational knowledge practices of American capitalism. Such practices, from patrols to paperwork, were perhaps always critical. But they became increasingly visible in the transition from rural and familiar landscapes to anonymous and price-driven markets in the nineteenth century, much as they have again in the twenty-first century courtesy of the new business models of digital platforms.

The United States, from this angle, has long been an "information society" or "knowledge economy." And data has always been a valuable commodity, critical to managing—if never quite taming—a chaotic and risky world of labor, prices, production, and credit. The systematic gathering of information by private companies (often, we should note, by trading on public tools and data infrastructures) powered profits. But, these essays show, it served other ends as well, from the strengthening of workplace control to the skirting of regulations and risks. Consider the prolific rationales voiced on behalf of commercial surveillance, or—to put it in less charged terms—on behalf of better, deeper, and more useful information. Capitalists of all stripes and at many different moments in American history have concurred that data, properly mobilized, would keep the market efficient, the consumer happy, the manager equipped, the worker productive, the economy humming.

Making human behavior as predictable and profitable as possible thus seems the essence of capitalist activity. But this insight troubles the assumption that there is something singular about U.S. surveillance capitalism in the present—and that it has superseded an earlier, presumably less vigilantly watchful, mode of organizing economic activity. Is there, we might ask, any form of capitalism (or any other economic program) that has not sought to surveil? Might the very terminology of "surveillance capitalism" be redundant?

These questions clarify the leading role that novel technologies, from keystroke monitoring to facial recognition software, have played in crafting a diagnosis of the new. But how, in fact, does the technology of surveillance matter? A focus on technology alone, no matter how "smart" and personalized, perhaps distracts us from what begins to look like the relentless aspiration of capitalists to *know*, and to act on that knowledge. At the very least, we need to precisely identify what it is about today's commercial surveillance practices—their capacity? their extensiveness? their efficacy? their durability? their potency?—that make them uniquely worthy of the modifier.

Alternatively, if capitalism has indeed always had surveillance at its core, perhaps what is truly called for is a charting of the visibility of these practices in American society. Rather than ask whether we have reached a new stage of capitalism, we could inquire: Under what circumstances have the techniques of commercial monitoring registered as such? When has the private apparatus of surveillance—because new, or offensive, or cumbersome—revealed itself for what it was? And how, in turn, have such systems of watching been naturalized, slipping from view and public debate? This history would also account for how new infrastructures of surveillance get built atop the rubble of the old, learning from earlier outrages and failures.

But perhaps there is a different kind of value to pairing capitalism and surveillance, one more rhetorical than categorical. By describing corporations as agents of surveillance, after all, we associate them with well-established critiques of state power and with a set of counterclaims to privacy, autonomy, and individual rights.

Indeed, much has been revealed about the path of capitalism in the United States as a result of the deliberate application of the concept of surveillance to business since the 1960s. Why have companies been granted the latitude to enact wide-scale monitoring of customers, for example—and to avoid such monitoring themselves by regulatory bodies? How have tactics, which would have been understood and protested as surveillance had they been conducted by a government agency, passed muster—or evaded notice—when undertaken by private actors? How, until relatively recently, have corporations managed to sidestep what now seems an obvious characterization?

To join "capitalism" and "surveillance," that is, may be an act of critical intervention as much as an empirical description, meant to bring to light analogous practices of watching in the public and private sectors. It is a step toward parsing how and why American corporations for so long flew under the radar of public condemnation or regulatory suspicion for tactics that included alarming invasions of privacy. And it exposes how the vocabulary of commerce—the language of efficiency, convenience, and gain—worked to stave off parallels to improper, state-like power. One beneficent product of the naming of "surveillance capitalism," then, has been the translation of long-standing commercial practices into an already-existing political framework.

But let the buyer beware! Scholars should make certain, even as we excavate the long, data-hungry history of capitalism, that we remain attentive to the varieties and valences of its expression. The essays in this volume encourage us to recognize strong continuities in the ambition to know and shape human behavior in the pursuit of profit. But they might push us at the same time to disaggregate capitalist surveillance. What were its distinct manifestations over time and space? And how was its presence felt in the lives of the full range of historical actors?

Since the first characterization of the United States as a "surveillance society" in the 1970s, the term has migrated from the realm of the state and military to that of commercial life and social relations. This volume is a product of that intellectual turn. But it is worth reflecting on how we wield the concept of "surveillance," and what reign we ought to give it over new territory.

That territory, just now, is vast—covering the act of being directly monitored on a plantation or a factory floor and also that of being silently tracked by a credit card or a cookie. Historians of capitalism could and should call for more precision as they consider the wealth of surveillance infrastructures and assemblages the past offers up as well as the always-evolving sensibilities of economic subjects.

How, whether past or present, did one's sense of being watched differ if the watcher was the national government versus a global media corporation? A police officer or a species of artificial intelligence? If the monitoring occurred in real time instead of intermittently or continuously? If the object of surveillance was a physical body or a body of records? We can ask too whether the harms of being targeted by an advertisement or a raid, or being tracked via a click or a fingerprint, shifted over the course of time; and how universally or particularly those harms were experienced.

These are distinctions that the field of surveillance studies has begun to take up. But they will lack for richness, texture, and specificity if historians of capitalism do not join the fray. Surveillance capitalism without history foreshortens our view of the patterned, yet never predictable, shape that economic life has taken in the United States. Without the vantage point of the past, we are cast adrift in the world capitalism has made: an unmoored, if ceaselessly tracked and monitored, present.

Whether in the end we judge "surveillance capitalism" to be old or new, the descriptor we need right now or a formulation too burdened by caveats, it is no small thing for a collection of essays to limber up our understandings of capitalism and surveillance alike. That is the bounty of this new volume—and a sure sign that this is a field to watch.

NOTES

Introduction

1. By most accounts, the term "surveillance capitalism" was coined by John Bellamy Foster and Robert W. McChesney, "Surveillance Capitalism: Monopoly-Finance Capital, the Military-Industrial Complex, and the Digital Age," *Monthly Review* 66, no. 3 (2014): 1–31. Vincent Mosco also used the term in *To the Cloud: Big Data in a Turbulent World* (Boulder, CO: Paradigm Publishers, 2014), 10. It gained broad scholarly currency, however, through Shoshana Zuboff's "Big Other: Surveillance Capitalism and the Prospects of an Information Civilization," *Journal of Information Technology* 30 (April 2015): 75–89, and subsequent book, *The Age of Surveillance Capitalism: The Fight for a Human Future at the New Frontier of Power* (New York: PublicAffairs, 2019). The reframing of information as a defining feature of late twentieth-century capitalism, the prerequisite of surveillance capitalism, can be traced to Fritz Machlup's *The Production and Distribution of Knowledge in the United States* (Princeton, NJ: Princeton University Press, 1962); Daniel Bell's *The Coming of the Post-Industrial Society: A Venture in Social Forecasting* (New York: Basic Books, 1973); and Marc Porat's *The Information Economy: Definition and Measurement* (Washington, DC: Department of Commerce, May 1977). Related variants of surveillance capitalism include information capitalism (Manuel Castells, *The Rise of the Network Society* [Oxford, UK: Blackwell, 1996]), digital capitalism (Dan Schiller, *Digital Capitalism: Networking the Global Market System* [Cambridge, MA: MIT Press, 1999]), platform capitalism (Nick Srnicek, *Platform Capitalism* [Cambridge: Polity, 2017]), and data capitalism (Sarah Myers West, "Data Capitalism: Redefining the Logics of Surveillance and Privacy," *Business & Society* 58 [2019]: 20–41). See also Jathan Sadowski, "When Data Is Capital: Datafication, Accumulation, and Extraction," *Big Data & Society* 6 (2019), https://doi.org/10.1177%2F2053951718820549.

2. Nick Couldry and Ulises A. Mejias, *The Costs of Connection: How Data Is Colonizing Human Life and Appropriating It for Capitalism* (Stanford, CA: Stanford University Press, 2019).

3. John Naughton, "'The Goal Is to Automate Us': Welcome to the Age of Surveillance Capitalism," *Observer*, January 20, 2019, https://www.theguardian.com/technology/2019/jan/20/shoshana-zuboff-age-of-surveillance-capitalism-google-facebook.

4. The volume and range of surveillance studies scholarship defies easy summary. Key early works related to automated surveillance include James B. Rule, *Private Lives and Public Surveillance* (London: Allen Lane, 1973); Shoshana Zuboff, *In the Age of the Smart Machine: The Future of Work and Power* (New York: Basic Books, 1988); Mark Poster, *The Mode of Information: Poststructuralism and Social Context* (Chicago: University of Chicago Press, 1990);

Oscar H. Gandy, Jr., *The Panoptic Sort: A Political Economy of Personal Information* (Boulder, CO: Westview, 1993); and David Lyon, *The Electronic Eye: The Rise of Surveillance Society* (Minneapolis: University of Minnesota Press, 1994). For overviews and collections, see David Lyon, *Surveillance Studies: An Overview* (Cambridge, UK: Polity, 2007); Kirstie Ball, Kevin Haggerty, and David Lyon, *The Routledge Handbook of Surveillance Studies* (New York: Routledge, 2012); and Torin Monahan and David Murakami Wood, *Surveillance Studies: A Reader* (New York: Oxford University Press, 2018).

5. See, for example, Alan F. Westin, *Privacy and Freedom* (New York: Atheneum, 1967); Arthur Miller, *The Assault on Privacy: Computers, Data Banks, and Dossiers* (Ann Arbor: University of Michigan Press, 1971); and Alan F. Westin and Michael A. Baker, *Databanks in a Free Society: Computers, Recordkeeping, and Privacy* (New York: Quadrangle Books, 1972).

6. Michel Foucault, *Discipline and Punish: The Birth of the Prison*, trans. Alan Sheridan, 2nd ed. (New York: Vintage, 1995); Gilles Deleuze, "Postscript on the Societies of Control," *October* 59 (1992): 3-7; Kevin Haggerty and Richard V. Ericson, "The Surveillant Assemblage," *British Journal of Sociology* 51, no. 4 (2000): 605–22.

7. For key studies of state surveillance, see Christopher Dandeker, *Surveillance, Power, and Modernity: Bureaucracy and Discipline from 1700 to the Present Day* (New York: St. Martin's Press, 1990); Jane Caplan and John Torpey, eds., *Documenting Individual Identity: The Development of State Practices in the Modern World* (Princeton, NJ: Princeton University Press, 2001); Simon Cole, *Suspect Identities: A History of Fingerprinting and Criminal Identification* (Cambridge, MA: Harvard University Press, 2001); Edward Higgs, *The Information State in England: The Central Collection of Information on Citizens Since 1500* (New York: Palgrave Macmillan, 2004); Craig Robertson, *The Passport in America: The History of a Document* (New York: Oxford University Press, 2010); Keith Breckinridge and Simon Szreter, eds., *Registration and Recognition: Documenting the Person in World History* (London: Oxford University Press, 2012); and Dan Bouk, "The National Data Center and the Rise of the Data Double," *Historical Studies in the Natural Sciences* 48, no. 5 (2018): 627–36.

8. See Max Weber, *Economy and Society: An Outline of Interpretive Sociology*, ed. Guenther Roth and Claus Wittich, 2 vols. (Berkeley: University of California Press, 1978); Anthony Giddens, *A Contemporary Critique of Historical Materialism*, 2nd ed. (Stanford, CA: Stanford University Press, 1995); and Giddens, *The Nation-State and Violence: Volume Two of a Contemporary Critique of Historical Materialism* (Berkeley, CA: University of California Press, 1985). For critique of these perspectives, see Josh Lauer, "Surveillance History and the History of New Media: An Evidential Paradigm," *New Media & Society* 14, no. 4 (2011): 566–82.

9. See, for example, Rowena Olegario, *A Culture of Credit: Trust and Transparency in American Business* (Cambridge, MA: Harvard University Press, 2006); Scott Sandage, *Born Losers: A History of Failure in America* (Cambridge, MA: Harvard University Press, 2005); Dan Bouk, *How Our Days Became Numbered: Risk and the Rise of the Statistical Individual* (Chicago: University of Chicago Press, 2015); Josh Lauer, *Creditworthy: A History of Consumer Surveillance and Financial Identity in America* (New York: Columbia University Press, 2017); Lauer, "Plastic Surveillance: Payment Cards and the History of Transactional Data, 1888 to Present," *Big Data & Society* (2020); Kenneth Lipartito, "Mediating Reputation: Credit Reporting Systems in American History," *Business History Review* 87 (2013): 655–766; and Martha Poon, "What Lenders See: A History of the Fair Isaac Scorecard" (Ph.D. diss., University of California, San Diego, 2012).

10. See, for example, William J. Novak, "The Myth of the 'Weak' American State," *American Historical Review* 113 (2008): 752–72; Novak, "Institutional Economics and the Progressive Movement for Social Control of American Business," *Business History Review* 93, no. 4 (Winter 2019): 665–96; Richard R. John, *Spreading the News: The American Postal System from Franklin to Morse* (Cambridge, MA: Harvard University Press, 1995); Theda Skocpol, *Protecting Soldiers and Mothers: The Political Origins of Social Policy in the United States* (Cambridge, MA: Harvard University Press, 1992); Frank Dobbin and John R. Sutton, "The Strength of the Weak State: The Employment Rights Revolution and the Rise of Human Resource Management Divisions," *American Journal of Sociology* 104 (1998): 441–76; Stefan Link and Noam Maggor, "The United States as a Developing Nation: Revisiting the Peculiarities of American History," *Past & Present* 246, no. 1 (February 2020): 269–306. See also Pamela Sankar, "State Power and Record-Keeping: The History of Individualized Surveillance in the United States, 1790–1935" (Ph.D. diss., University of Pennsylvania, 1992).

11. The concept of modernity is contested among scholars. We use the term "modern" here as a convenient chronological backstop, meaning post-1800 generally. From a contemporary vantage, what could be described as commercial surveillance existed in premodern and precapitalist Western societies. For example, on ancient writing and recordkeeping, see Jack Goody, *The Logic of Writing and the Organization of Society* (New York: Cambridge University Press, 1986); Giddens, *Contemporary Critique of Historical Materialism*; and Giddens, *The Nation-State and Violence*; on accounting, see Keith W. Hoskin and Richard H. Macve, "Accounting and the Examination: A Genealogy of Disciplinary Power," *Accounting, Organizations, and Society* 11, no. 2 (1986): 105–36; on identity and social networks, see Valentin Groebner, *Who Are You? Identification, Deception, and Surveillance in Early Modern Europe*, trans. Mark Kyburz and John Peck (New York: Zone Books, 2007); and Laurence Fontaine, *History of Peddlers in Europe*, trans. Vicki Whittaker (Durham, NC: Duke University Press, 1996).

12. It entered English as well at the end of the eighteenth century. Josh Lauer, "Surveilling," in *Information: A Historical Companion*, ed. Ann Blair, Paul Duguid, Anja-Silvia Goeing, and Anthony Grafton (Princeton, NJ: Princeton University Press, 2021), 790–795.

13. Karl Marx, *Capital: A Critical Analysis of Capitalist Production*, vol. 1, trans. Samuel Moore and Edward Aveling (New York: International, 1992), 231. See also Christian Fuchs, "Political Economy and Surveillance Theory," *Critical Sociology* 39, no. 5 (2012): 671–87.

14. E. P. Thompson, "Time, Work-Discipline, and Industrial Capitalism," *Past & Present* 38 (1967): 56–97.

15. Caitlin Rosenthal, *Accounting for Slavery: Master and Management* (Cambridge, MA: Harvard University Press, 2018); Sven Beckert, *Empire of Cotton: A Global History* (New York: Knopf, 2014); Edward Baptist, *The Half Has Never Been Told: Slavery and the Making of American Capitalism* (New York: Basic Books, 2014); James Oakes, "Capitalism and Slavery and the Civil War," *International Labor and Working-Class History* 89 (2016): 195–220; Eric Hilt, "Economic History, Historical Analysis, and the 'New History of Capitalism,'" *Journal of Economic History* 77, no. 2 (2017): 511–36.

16. Frederick W. Taylor, *The Principles of Scientific Management* (Mineola, NY: Dover, 1998), 15.

17. William H. Whyte, *The Organization Man* (New York: Simon & Schuster, 1956).

18. Priscilla M. Regan, *Legislating Privacy: Technology, Social Values, and Public Policy* (Chapel Hill: University of North Carolina Press, 1995), 13.

19. Sarah E. Igo, *The Known Citizen: A History of Privacy in Modern America* (Cambridge, MA: Harvard University Press, 2018).

20. Paul N. Edwards, "Infrastructure and Modernity: Force, Time, and Social Organization in the History of Sociotechnical Systems," in *Modernity and Technology*, ed. Thomas J. Misa, Philip Brey, and Andrew Feenberg (Cambridge, MA: MIT Press, 2002), 185–225; Thomas Hughes, *Networks of Power: Electrification in Western Society, 1880–1930* (Baltimore: Johns Hopkins University Press, 1983); Harold Innis, *The Bias of Communication* (Toronto: University of Toronto Press, 1951).

21. Geoffrey C. Bowker and Susan Leigh Star, *Sorting Things Out: Classification and Its Consequences* (Cambridge, MA: MIT Press, 1999). The internet, in this way, is an infrastructure that consists not only of servers, satellites, and undersea cables, but also codes, protocols, corporate actors, regulatory bodies, and the professional norms of engineers, investors, and entrepreneurs. Christian Sandvig, "The Internet as Infrastructure," in *The Oxford Handbook of Internet Studies*, ed. William Dutton (Oxford: Oxford University Press, 2013), 86–108.

22. Susan Leigh Star, "The Ethnography of Infrastructure," *American Behavioral Scientist* 43 (1999): 377–91.

23. See, for example, Frank Pasquale, *The Black Box Society: The Secret Algorithms That Control Money and Information* (Cambridge, MA: Harvard University Press, 2015); Cathy O'Neil, *Weapons of Math Destruction: How Big Data Increases Inequality and Threatens Democracy* (New York: Crown, 2016); Virginia Eubanks, *Automating Inequality: How High-Tech Tools Profile, Police, and Punish the Poor* (New York: St. Martin's Press, 2017); Sofia Umoja Noble, *Algorithms of Oppression: How Search Engines Reinforce Racism* (New York: New York University Press, 2018); John Cheney-Lippold, *We Are Data: Algorithms and the Making of Our Digital Selves* (New York: New York University Press, 2017); and Tarleton Gillespie, "The Relevance of Algorithms," in *Media Technologies: Essays on Communication, Materiality, and Society*, ed. Tarleton Gillespie, Pablo Boczkowski, and Kirsten Foot (Cambridge, MA: MIT Press, 2014), 67–194.

24. Foucault, *Discipline and Punish*, 192.

25. James C. Scott. *Seeing Like a State: How Certain Schemes to Improve the Human Condition Have Failed* (New Haven, CT: Yale University Press, 1998).

26. Federal Trade Commission, *Data Brokers: A Call for Transparency and Accountability*, May 2014, available at https://www.ftc.gov/system/files/documents/reports/data-brokers -call-transparency-accountability-report-federal-trade-commission-may-2014/140527data brokerreport.pdf; Matthew Crain, "The Limits of Transparency: Data Brokers and Commodification," *New Media & Society* 20 (2018): 88–104.

27. Given the dispersed, variegated flows of information that feed surveillance capitalism, its infrastructure can also be understood as a surveillant assemblage. The concept of assemblage, as Haggerty and Ericson explain, accounts for the heterodox sources of personal data, including state and commercial institutions, and its multipurpose use as a system of control. Haggerty and Ericson, "The Surveillant Assemblage."

28. See Michael Zakim and Gary J. Kornblith, eds., *Capitalism Takes Command: The Social Transformation of Nineteenth-Century America* (Chicago: University of Chicago Press, 2012); and John Lauritz Larson, *The Market Revolution in America: Liberty, Ambition, and the Eclipse of the Common Good* (New York: Cambridge University Press, 2010).

29. On the fundamental relationship between surveillance and inscription, see Foucault, *Discipline and Punish*; and Giddens, *The Nation-State and Violence*. Relatedly, on inscription

and scientific objectivity, see Bruno Latour, "Drawing Things Together," in *Representation in Scientific Practice*, ed. Michael Lynch and Steve Woolgar (Cambridge, MA: MIT Press, 1990), 19–68.

30. Alfred D. Chandler, Jr., *The Visible Hand: The Managerial Revolution in American Business* (Cambridge, MA: Harvard University Pres, 1977); see also James Beniger, *The Control Revolution: The Technological and Economic Origins of the Information Society* (Cambridge, MA: Harvard University Press, 1986).

31. Joanne Yates, *Control Through Communication: The Rise of System in American Management* (Baltimore: Johns Hopkins University Press, 1989); Craig Robertson, *The Filing Cabinet: A Vertical History of Information* (Minneapolis: University of Minnesota Press, 2021); and Cornelia Vismann, *Files: Law and Media Technology*, trans. Geoffrey Winthrop-Young (Stanford, CA: Stanford University Press, 2008).

32. Bouk, *How Our Days Became Numbered*; Lauer, *Creditworthy*.

33. Rand Kardex Bureau, "The Age of Vision in Business Affairs," *Boston Globe*, June 4, 1926, A7.

34. Ian Hacking, "Biopower and the Avalanche of Printed Numbers," *Humanities in Society* 5 (1982): 280. See also Ian Hacking, *The Taming of Chance* (Cambridge: Cambridge University Press, 1990); Theodore M. Porter, *Trust in Numbers: The Pursuit of Objectivity in Science and Public Life* (Princeton, NJ: Princeton University Press, 1995); William Alonso and Paul Starr, eds., *The Politics of Numbers* (New York: Russell Sage, 1987); and Patricia Cohen Cline, *A Calculating People: The Spread of Numeracy in America* (Chicago: University of Chicago Press, 1982).

35. Bouk, *How Our Days Became Numbered*; Jonathan Levy, *Freaks of Fortune: The Emerging World of Capitalism and Risk in America* (Princeton, NJ: Princeton University Press, 2012); Sharon Ann Murphy, *Investing in Life: Insurance in Antebellum America* (Baltimore: Johns Hopkins University, 2010); Viviana Zelizer, *Morals and Markets: The Development of Life Insurance in the United States* (New York: Columbia University Press, 1979); see also François Ewald, "Insurance and Risk," in *The Foucault Effect: Studies in Governmentality*, ed. Colin Gordon and Peter Miller (Chicago: University of Chicago Press, 1991), 197–210.

36. Sarah E. Igo, *The Averaged American: Surveys, Citizens, and the Making of a Mass Public* (Cambridge, MA: Harvard University Press, 2007); Lizabeth Cohen, *A Consumers' Republic: The Politics of Mass Consumption in Postwar America* (New York: Vintage, 2004); Joseph Turow, *Breaking Up America: Advertisers and the New Media World* (Chicago: University of Chicago Press, 1997).

37. Dan Bouk, "The History and Political Economy of Personal Data over the Last Two Centuries in Three Acts," *Osiris* 32 (2017): 85–106. See also Colin Koopman, *How We Became Our Data: A Genealogy of the Informational Person* (Chicago: University of Chicago Press, 2019).

38. See David E. Nye, *American Technological Sublime* (Cambridge, MA: MIT Press, 1994); Leo Marx, *The Machine in the Garden: Technology and the Pastoral Ideal in America* (New York: Oxford University Press, 1964) and "Technology: The Emergence of a Hazardous Concept," *Social Research* 64, no. 3 (1997): 965–988.

39. See Langdon Winner, "Sow's Ears from Silk Purses: The Strange Alchemy of Technological Visionaries," in *Technological Visions: The Hopes and Fears that Shape New Technologies*, ed. Marita Sturken, Douglas Thomas, and Sandra Ball-Rokeach (Philadelphia: Temple

University Press, 2004), 34–47; and Evgeny Morozov, *To Save Everything, Click Here: The Folly of Technological Solutionism* (New York: PublicAffairs, 2013).

40. Hughes, *Networks of Power*; Renate Mayntz and Thomas Hughes, eds., *The Development of Large Technical Systems* (Frankfurt am Main: Campus Verlag, 1988); Agatha C. Hughes and Thomas P. Hughes, *Systems, Experts, and Computers: The Systems Approach to Management and Engineering, World War II and After* (Cambridge MA: MIT Press, 2000).

41. On risk as a feature of modernity, see Ulrich Beck, *Risk Society: Towards a New Modernity*, trans. Mark Ritter (Thousand Oaks, CA: Sage, 1992); and Anthony Giddens, *The Consequences of Modernity* (Stanford, CA: Stanford University Press, 1990). On cultural manifestations, see Barry Glassner, *The Culture of Fear: Why Americans Are Afraid of the Wrong Things*, 2nd ed. (New York: Basic Books, 2018); and Frank Furedi, *Culture of Fear Revisited: Risk-Taking and the Morality of Low Expectation*, 4th ed. (New York: Continuum, 2006).

42. Michael Power, *The Audit Society: Rituals of Verification* (Oxford: Oxford University Press, 1997).

43. See, for example, Nora A. Draper, *The Identity Trade: Selling Privacy and Reputation Online* (New York: New York University Press, 2018).

44. Oscar H. Gandy, Jr., *Coming to Terms with Chance: Engaging Rational Discrimination and Cumulative Disadvantage* (Abingdon, UK: Ashgate, 2009).

45. Classic studies on worker resistance to control include David Montgomery, *Workers' Control in America: Studies in the History of Work, Technology, and Labor Struggles* (Cambridge: Cambridge University Press, 1979); David F. Nobel, *Forces of Production: A Social History of Industrial Automation* (Oxford: Oxford University Press, 1988); Harry Braverman, *Labor and Monopoly Capital: The Degradation of Work in the Twentieth Century* (New York: Monthly Review Press, 1974); and Michael Burawoy, *Manufacturing Consent: Changes in the Labor Process Under Monopoly Capitalism* (Chicago: University of Chicago Press, 1979). See also Kirstie Ball, "Workplace Surveillance: An Overview," *Labor History* 51 (2010): 87–106.

46. On retail surveillance, see Elanie S. Abelson, *When Women Go A-Thieving: Middle-Class Shoplifters in the Victorian Department Store* (Oxford: Oxford University Press, 1989). As in-store surveillance becomes more sophisticated, consumer monitoring systems and workplace surveillance have merged and inform one another. See Karen Levy and Solon Baracos, "Refractive Surveillance: Monitoring Consumers to Manage Employees," *International Journal of Communication* 12 (2018): 1166–1188.

47. Woodrow Hartzog, *Privacy's Blueprint: The Battle to Control the Design of New Technologies* (Cambridge, MA: Harvard University Press, 2018); and Darin Barney, Gabriella Coleman, Christine Ross, Jonathan Sterne, and Tara Tembreck, eds., *The Participatory Condition in the Digital Age* (Minneapolis: University of Minnesota Press, 2016).

48. This pattern is seen in the history of both lie detectors and fingerprinting. Ken Adler, *The Lie Detectors: The History of an American Obsession* (New York: Free Press, 2007); and Cole, *Suspect Identities*. See also Steven L. Nock, *The Costs of Privacy: Surveillance and Reputation in America* (New York: Walter de Gruyter, 1993).

49. Zuboff, *In the Age of Surveillance Capitalism*, 139.

50. Couldry and Mejias, *The Costs of Connection*.

51. Tung-Hui Hu, *A Prehistory of the Cloud* (Cambridge, MA: MIT Press, 2016).

52. Castells, *The Rise of the Network Society*.

53. Kenneth Lipartito and Lisa Jacobson, eds., *Capitalism's Hidden Worlds* (Philadelphia: University of Pennsylvania Press, 2019).

54. Yochai Benkler, *The Wealth of Networks: How Social Production Transforms Markets and Freedom* (New Haven, CT: Yale University Press, 2006); Dave Elder-Vass, *Profit and Gift in the Digital Economy* (Cambridge: Cambridge University Press, 2016); and Henry Jenkins, *Convergence Culture: When Old and New Media Collide* (New York: New York University Press, 2006). See also scholarship on "sousveillance," beginning with Steve Mann, Jason Nolan, and Barry Wellman, "Sousveillance: Inventing and Using Wearable Computing Data Collection in Surveillance Environments," *Surveillance & Society* 1 (2003): 331–55.

55. JoAnne Yates, *Structuring the Information Age: Life Insurance and Technology in the Twentieth Century* (Baltimore: Johns Hopkins University Press, 2009); Jeffrey Yost, *Making IT Work: A History of the Computer Services Industry* (Cambridge, MA: MIT Press, 2017); Nathan Ensmenger, *The Computer Boys Take Over: Computers, Programmers, and the Politics of Technical Expertise* (Cambridge, MA: MIT Press, 2010).

56. Louis Hyman, *Debtor Nation: The History of America in Red Ink* (Princeton, NJ: Princeton University Press, 2011); Jennifer Light, "Discriminating Appraisals: Cartography, Computation, and Access to Federal Mortgage Insurance in the 1930s," *Technology and Culture* 52 (2011): 485–522; Simone Browne, *Dark Matters: On the Surveillance of Blackness* (Durham, NC: Duke University Press, 2015); Ruha Benjamin, *Race After Technology: Abolitionist Tools for the New Jim Code* (Cambridge, UK: Polity, 2019).

57. Nora A. Draper and Joseph Turow, "The Corporate Cultivation of Digital Resignation," *New Media & Society* 21 (2019): 1824–39.

58. Karl Polanyi, *The Great Transformation: The Political and Economic Origins of Our Time* (Boston: Beacon, 1957).

59. Rogier Creemers, "China's Social Credit System: An Evolving Practice of Control," SSRN, May 9, 2018, https://ssrn.com/abstract=3175792; Genia Kostka, "China's Social Credit Systems and Public Opinion: Explaining High Levels of Approval," *New Media & Society* 21 (2019): 1565–93; and Simina Mistreanu, "Life Inside China's Social Credit Laboratory," *Foreign Policy*, April 3, 2018, https://foreignpolicy.com/2018/04/03/life-inside-chinas-social-credit-laboratory/.

60. Bani Sapra, "WeChat: Everything You Need to Know About China's Super-App," *Business Insider*, December 21, 2019, https://www.businessinsider.com/chinese-superapp-wechat-best-feature-walkthrough-2019-12.

61. See, for example, Stuart A. Thompson and Charlie Warzel, "Twelve Million Phones, One Dataset, Zero Privacy," *New York Times*, December 19, 2019, https://www.nytimes.com/interactive/2019/12/19/opinion/location-tracking-cell-phone.html.

62. Reed Albergotti, "Apple and Google Launch Coronavirus Exposure Software," *Washington Post*, May 20, 2020, https://www.washingtonpost.com/technology/2020/05/20/apple-google-api-launch/; Khadeeja Safdar and Kevin Poulsen, "Google, Apple Struggle to Regulate Covid-19 Tracing Apps," *Wall Street Journal*, June 5, 2020, https://www.wsj.com/articles/why-google-and-apple-stores-had-a-covid-19-app-with-ads-11591365499; and Mike Giglio, "Would You Sacrifice Your Privacy to Get Out of Quarantine?," *The Atlantic*, April 22, 2020, https://www.theatlantic.com/politics/archive/2020/04/coronavirus-pandemic-privacy-civil-liberties-911/609172/.

63. George Weisz, *Chronic Disease in the Twentieth Century: A History* (Baltimore: Johns Hopkins University Press, 2014), 17–36; in Elizabeth Fee and Daniel M. Fox., eds., *AIDS and*

the Burdens of History (Berkeley: University of California Press, 1988), see the contributions of Guenter Risse, "Epidemics and History: Ecological Perspective and Social Responses," 33–66; Dorothy Porter and Roy Porter, "The Enforcement of Health: The British Debate," 97–120; Elizabeth Fee, "Sin Versus Science: Venereal Disease in Twentieth-Century Baltimore," 121–46; and Allan M. Brandt, "AIDS: From Social History to Social Policy," 147–72; see also Amy Fairchild, Ronald Bayer, and James Colgrove, *Searching Eyes: Privacy, the State, and Disease Surveillance in America* (Berkeley: University of California Press, 2007).

Chapter 1

1. John J. McCusker and Russell R. Menard, *The Economy of British America, 1607–1789, with Supplementary Bibliography* (Chapel Hill: Published for the Institute of Early American History and Culture by University of North Carolina Press), 1991, 14.

2. Simone Browne, *Dark Matters: On the Surveillance of Blackness* (Durham, NC: Duke University Press, 2015).

3. Ibid., 53.

4. Across all of the properties, by far the largest classification of lives was field men (336) and women (405), followed by young children (222), invalids (180), and children of working age who labored in the grass gang (140). But after these large classifications, watchmen were the next largest category, with 100 across Dawkins's properties. Parnassus inventories in "Jamaica Account, 1779, providing a list of slaves, stock, cattle and horses on various plantations," box 13, item 2.1, Wilberforce House Museum, Adam Matthew Digital, Slavery, Abolition, and Social Justice.

5. Barry W. Higman, *Slave Populations of the British Caribbean, 1807–1834* (Baltimore: Johns Hopkins University Press, 1984).

6. *Abridgement of the Minutes of the Evidence Taken Before a Committee of the Whole House, to Whom It Was Referred to Consider of the Slave Trade, 1790* (London, 1790), 55–56, https://hdl.handle.net/2027/dul1.ark:/13960/t5w679c6h.

7. William Beckford, *A Descriptive Account of the Island of Jamaica* (London: T. and J. Agerton, 1790), 198–99.

8. Parnassus and Sutton's Estate inventories in "Jamaica Account, 1779."

9. Jamaican Slave Names Project, http://jamaicanslavenames.com/, drawn from Hope Plantation, 1788, Huntington Library, Stowe-Brydges Papers.

10. Ibid., drawn from York Plantation, 1778, University of Exeter, Gale-Morant Papers.

11. *Jamaica Watchman* (Kingston, Jamaica), April 30, 1831, p. 3, Readex: Caribbean Newspapers.

12. *Abridgement of the Minutes . . . 1790*, 128, 131.

13. Thomas Roughley, *The Jamaica Planter's Guide* (London: Longman, Hurst, Rees, Orme, and Brown, 1823), 89–90

14. *Abridgement of the Minutes . . . 1790*, 85, 89.

15. Beckford, *Descriptive Account*, 198–99.

16. Ibid., 55–56.

17. Sutton's Estate inventories in "Jamaica Account, 1779."

18. James M. Adair, *Unanswerable Arguments Against the Abolition of the Slave Trade, with a Defence of the Proprietors of the British Sugar Colonies* (London: J. P. Bateman, [1790]), 159.

19. Beckford, *Descriptive Account*, 199.

20. Benjamin Moseley, *A Treatise on Sugar* (London, 1799), 169.

21. Roughley, *Jamaica Planter's Guide*, 88.

22. Ibid.

23. Ibid., 89–90.

24. Adair, *Unanswerable Arguments*, 159.

25. *Report of the Trials of the Insurgent Negroes, Before a General Court-Martial, Held at Georgetown, Demerara* (Georgetown, Demerara: Printed by A. Stevenson, at the Guiana Chronicle Office, 1824), 29.

26. Adair, *Unanswerable Arguments*, 159.

27. Ibid., 158–60.

28. Roughley, *Jamaica Planter's Guide*, 90–91.

29. Ibid., 88.

30. *Royal Gazette* (Kingston, Jamaica), May 25, 1822, 16, Readex: Caribbean Newspapers.

31. R. C. Dallas, *The History of the Maroons . . .* , vol. 1 (London: Longman and Rees, 1803), 348–49.

32. *Barbados Mercury, and Bridge-Town Gazette* (Bridgetown), October 6, 1821, 2, Readex: Caribbean Newspapers.

33. John Williamson, *Medical and Miscellaneous Observations Relative to the West India Islands* (Edinburgh: Alex. Smellie, 1817).

34. Ibid., 362–64.

35. Ibid.

36. Ibid., 362.

37. Randy Browne, *Surviving Slavery in the British Caribbean* (Philadelphia: University of Pennsylvania Press, 2017), 72.

38. *The Laws of Jamaica: Comprehending All the Acts in Force . . .* , 2nd ed., vol. 5 (St. Jago de la Vega, Jamaica: A. Aikman, printer to the King's Most Excellent Majesty, 1824), 92.

39. Candace Ward, "'An Engine of Immense Power': *The Jamaica Watchman* and Crossings in Nineteenth-Century Colonial Print Culture," *Victorian Periodicals Review* 51, no. 3 (Fall 2018): 483–503, here 487–88.

40. Ibid., 484.

41. Ibid., 488.

42. Masthead, *Jamaica Watchman*, January 1, 1831.

43. As quoted in Ward, "'An Engine of Immense Power,'" 494.

44. *Jamaica Watchman*, December 8, 1830, 5.

45. Ibid.

46. Mary Turner, *Slaves and Missionaries: The Disintegration of Jamaican Slave Society, 1787–1834* (Urbana: University of Illinois Press, 1982); Mary Reckord, "The Jamaica Slave Rebellion of 1831," *Past & Present* 40, no. 1 (1968): 108–25.

47. *Jamaica Watchman*, May 16, 1832, 8.

48. Ibid., January 1, 1831, 3.

49. Ibid., January 7, 1832, 7.

50. Ibid.

51. Ibid., January 4, 1832, 6.

52. Ibid., January 7, 1832, 2.

53. Ibid., May 16, 1832, 6.

54. Ward, "'An Engine of Immense Power,'" 487–88, 494.

55. Masthead, *Jamaica Watchman*, June 20, 1832, 1.

56. Browne, *Dark Matters*, 78.

57. Ibid., 68.

58. *Slave Law of Jamaica: With Proceedings and Documents Relative Thereto* (London: J. Ridgway, 1828), 109 (clause 84).

59. Stanley L. Engerman, Richard Sutch, and Gavin Wright, "Slavery," in *Historical Statistics of the United States, Earliest Times to the Present: Millennial Edition*, ed. Susan B. Carter et al. (New York: Cambridge University Press, 2006), chap. Bb.

Chapter 2

1. "The Post Office in Augusta," *Pittsburgh Leader*, March 1887; "The Busy Capital City," *Industrial Journal* (Bangor, ME), undated clipping; "A Mammoth Enterprise," *Advertisers' Gazette*, July 1889, 106; *Kennebec Journal*, February 12, 1883. All in scrapbook O-1, E. C. Allen & Company Papers, Baker Library Historical Collections, Harvard Business School, Cambridge, MA (hereafter ECA); Clarence Stetson, "Augusta, Maine," *Puck*, May 22, 1889, 214.

2. Charles E. Clark, *Maine: A Bicentennial History* (New York: Norton, 1977), 41; Richard W. Judd, "Maine's Ice Industry," in *Maine: The Pine Tree State from Prehistory to the Present*, ed. Richard W. Judd, Edwin A. Churchill, and Joel W. Eastman (Orono: University of Maine Press, 1995), 282–83; James W. North, *The History of Augusta* (Augusta, ME: Clapp and North, 1870), 570–80, 598–600; Thomas Baldwin and J. Thomas, *A New and Complete Gazetteer of the United States* (Philadelphia: Lippincott, Grambo, 1854), 63.

3. North, *History of Augusta*, 638–40, 685–86, 777–82, 789–91; Charles Hoffmann and Tess Hoffmann, *Brotherly Love: Murder and the Politics of Prejudice in Nineteenth-Century Rhode Island* (Amherst: University of Massachusetts Press, 1993), 145–46, 172–73 n. 10.

4. Josh Lauer, *Creditworthy: A History of Consumer Surveillance and Financial Identity in America* (New York: Columbia University Press, 2017); Scott Sandage, *Born Losers: A History of Failure in America* (Cambridge, MA: Harvard University Press, 2005); Dan Bouk, *How Our Days Became Numbered: Risk and the Rise of the Statistical Individual* (Chicago: University of Chicago Press, 2015). On magazine publishers and market research, see Adam Arvidsson, "On the 'Pre-History of the Panoptic Sort': Mobility in Market Research," *Surveillance & Society* 1, no. 4 (2004): 456–74; Douglas B. Ward, *A New Brand of Business: Charles Coolidge Parlin, Curtis Publishing Company, and the Origins of Market Research* (Philadelphia: Temple University Press, 2009); Richard K. Popp, *The Holiday Makers: Magazines, Advertising, and Mass Tourism in Postwar America* (Baton Rouge: Louisiana State University Press, 2012); Shelley Nickles, "More Is Better: Mass Consumption, Gender, and Class Identity in Postwar America," *American Quarterly* 54, no. 4 (2002): 581–622. For an exception, which emphasizes the links between direct marketing and magazine publishing, see Andrew Case, "'The Solid Gold Mailbox': Direct Mail and the Changing Nature of Buying and Selling in the Postwar United States," *History of Retailing and Consumption* 1, no. 1 (2015): 28–46. On the not yet commodified nature of personal information in the nineteenth and early twentieth century, see Dan Bouk, "The History and Political Economy of Personal Data over the Last Two Centuries in Three Acts," *Osiris* 32 (2017): 89–98.

5. On the prehistory of database marketing, see Eleanor Novek, Nikhil Sinha, and Oscar Gandy, "The Value of Your Name," *Media, Culture and Society* 12 (1990): 525–43; Joseph

Turow, *Breaking Up America: Advertisers and the New Media World* (Chicago: University of Chicago Press, 1997); Turow, *Niche Envy: Marketing Discrimination in the Digital Age* (Cambridge, MA: MIT Press, 2006). For works that emphasize the importance of mass magazines for the middle class in the emergence of national marketing, see Richard Ohmann, *Selling Culture: Magazines, Markets, and Class at the Turn of the Century* (New York: Verso, 1996); Matthew Schneirov, *The Dream of a New Social Order: Popular Magazines in America, 1893–1914* (New York: Columbia University Press, 1994); Jennifer Scanlon, *Inarticulate Longings: The Ladies' Home Journal, Gender, and the Promises of Consumer Culture* (New York: Routledge, 1995); Ellen Gruber Garvey, *The Adman in the Parlor: Magazines and the Gendering of Consumer Culture, 1880s to 1910s* (New York: Oxford University Press, 1996); Susan Strasser, *Satisfaction Guaranteed: The Making of the American Mass Market* (New York: Pantheon, 1989); Jackson Lears, *Fables of Abundance: A Cultural History of Advertising in America* (New York: Basic Books, 1994); Pamela Walker Laird, *Advertising Progress: American Business and the Rise of Consumer Marketing* (Baltimore: Johns Hopkins University Press, 1998); Charles F. McGovern, *Sold American: Consumption and Citizenship, 1890–1945* (Chapel Hill: University of North Carolina Press, 2006). On directory houses and clipping bureaus that fed the mailing list trade, see Reuben S. Rose-Redwood, "Indexing the Great Ledger of the Community: Urban House Numbering, City Directories, and the Production of Spatial Legibility," *Journal of Historical Geography* 34 (2008): 286–310; Richard K. Popp, "Information, Industrialization, and the Business of Press Clippings, 1880–1925," *Journal of American History* 101, no. 2 (2014): 427–53.

6. Henry D. Kingsbury and Simeon L. Deyo, eds., *Illustrated History of Kennebec County, Maine* (New York: H. W. Blake, 1892), 452.

7. Frank Luther Mott, *A History of American Magazines*, vol. 3, *1865–1885* (1938; Cambridge, MA: Belknap Press of Harvard University Press, 1967), 37–38; "Death of E. C. Allen," *Profitable Advertising*, August 1891, 78; cashbook [late 1860s–early 1870s], unpaginated, CF-1, ECA.

8. George Presbury Rowell, *Forty Years an Advertising Agent, 1865–1905* (New York: Printers' Ink, 1906), 195; Wm. E. S. Whitman, *The Wealth and Industry of Maine for the Year 1873* (Augusta, ME: Sprague, Owen & Nash, 1873), 85. Circulation figures of roughly 1.5 million are cited in Joseph Griffin, *History of the Press of Maine* (Brunswick, ME: J. Griffin, 1872), 99.

9. "E. C. Allen," October 22, 1874, Maine, vol. 18, p. 88, R. G. Dun & Co. Credit Report Volumes, Baker Library, Harvard Business School, Cambridge, Massachusetts (hereafter RGD).

10. "True, Hallett & Co.," May 29, 1873, Maine, vol. 15, p. 558, RGD; "Geo. Stinson & Co.," November 8, 1877, Maine, vol. 15, p. 508, RGD.

11. George J. Varney, *A Gazetteer of the State of Maine* (Boston: B. B. Russell, 1881), 88; *Kennebec Journal*, February 12, 1883; "E. C. Allen," February 10, 1881, Maine, vol. 18, p. 153, RGD; titles and figures drawn from ledger K-1, pp.171, 107, ECA. On newspaper buildings, see Aurora Wallace, *Media Capital: Architecture and Communications in New York City* (Urbana, Ill., 2012). On the *Century* and *Munsey's*, see Schneirov, *Dream of a New Social Order*, 11.

12. Frank A. Munsey, *The Founding of the Munsey Publishing-House* (New York: De Vinne Press, 1907), 10; Varney, *Gazetteer of the State of Maine*, 91; George Britt, *Forty Years—Forty Millions: The Career of Frank A. Munsey* (New York: Farrar & Rinehart, 1935), 53–55.

13. "Peleg O. Vickery," in *Fortieth Annual Report of the Proceedings of the Maine Press Association* (Portland: Maine Coast Cottager Office, 1903), 45; "P. O. Vickery," September 22, 1871, March 20, 1874, August 9, 1878, October 9, 1879, June 10, 1881, November 22, 1883, Maine, vol. 18, pp. 41, 67, 128, 202, RGD.

14. "Mammoth Enterprise," 85; *Industrial Journal*, May 1889, clipping, p. 79, O-1, ECA; "Gannett & Morse," March 23, 1881, September 6, 1883, September 25, 1888, Maine, vol. 18, pp. 153, 247, RGD.

15. "In Memoriam of Edward Charles Allen," 1892, XC-1, ECA; "The Publishing Business in Maine," in *Eighth Annual Report of the Bureau of Industrial and Labor Statistics for the State of Maine, 1894* (Augusta, ME: Burleigh & Flint, 1895), 124–35.

16. Richard John, *Spreading the News: The American Postal System from Franklin to Morse* (Cambridge, MA: Harvard University Press, 1995); David Henkin, *The Postal Age: The Emergence of Modern Communications in Nineteenth-Century America* (Chicago: University of Chicago Press, 2006).

17. Richard Burket Kielbowicz, "Origins of the Second-Class Mail Category and the Business of Policy Making, 1863–1879," *Journalism Monographs* 96 (1986): 1–26; Wayne E. Fuller, *The American Mail: Enlarger of the Common Life* (Chicago: University of Chicago Press, 1972), 125–47, esp. 139.

18. Wendy A. Woloson, "Wishful Thinking: Retail Premiums in Mid-Nineteenth-Century America," *Enterprise & Society* 13, no. 4 (2012): 790–831. On caveat emptor, see Edward J. Balleisen, *Fraud: An American History from Barnum to Madoff* (Princeton, NJ: Princeton University Press, 2017), 43–104.

19. "U.S. vs. George Conant, Alias Hunt & Co.," February 28, 1883, box 3, Case Files of Investigations, 1838–1903 (hereafter CFI), Record Group 28, Records of the Post Office Department, 1773–1971, U.S. National Archives and Records Administration, Washington, DC (hereafter RPOD-NARA); "Elite Neckwear Co.," August 28, 1896, box 7, Fraud Order Case Files (hereafter FOCF), RPOD-NARA; "Weil & Bros.," October 18, 1895, box 5, FOCF, RPOD-NARA.

20. Marshall Cushing, *The Story of Our Post Office* (Boston: Thayer, 1893), 593; James Lee, *Twenty-Five Years in the Mail Order Business; or, The Experiences of a Mail Order Man* (Chicago: Arthur E. Swett, 1902), 119–21. On attempts to sell other goods, see "U.S. vs. Frank Coker, Alias the Gem Publishing Co.," August 8, 1883, box 6, CFI, RPOD-NARA.

21. Allen's place in rural consumerism is described in Hal S. Barron, *Mixed Harvest: The Second Great Transformation in the Rural North 1870–1930* (Chapel Hill: University of North Carolina Press, 1997), 161–63; Arthur E. Swett, "The Evolution of Advertising," *Mahin's Magazine*, December 11, 1903, 752; "From Shore to Shore," advertisement, in Phebe A. Hanaford, *The Life and Writings of Charles Dickens* (Augusta, ME: E. C. Allen, 1871).

22. *Our Fireside Journal*, May 13, 1876, XE-3, ECA.

23. Ibid., 8, 15, XE-3, ECA.

24. *True's Illustrated Magazine and Home Companion*, July 1882, 12–13, XE-2, ECA.

25. *Oxford English Dictionary*, 2nd ed. (1989), s.v. "outfit"; Richard White, *The Republic for Which It Stands: The United States During Reconstruction and the Gilded Age, 1865–1896* (New York: Oxford University Press, 2017), 407. On self-ownership, see Jonathan Levy, *Freaks of Fortune: The Emerging World of Capitalism and Risk in America* (Cambridge, MA: Harvard University Press, 2014). On sales work, see Walter A. Friedman, *Birth of a Salesman: The Transformation of Selling in America* (Cambridge, MA: Harvard University Press, 2004);

Timothy Spears, *100 Years on the Road: The Traveling Salesman in American Culture* (New Haven, CT: Yale University Press, 1997). On direct sales and self-transformation, see Nicole Woolsey Biggart, *Charismatic Capitalism: Direct Selling Organizations in America* (Chicago: University of Chicago Press, 1989); Jessica K. Burch, "'Soap and Hope': Direct Sales and the Culture of Work and Capitalism in Postwar America," *Enterprise & Society* 17, no. 4 (2016): 741–51.

26. "Find the Right Way; Then Push Onward" [1890], XC-3, Advertising Circulars, True & Co., ECA. A near identical brochure was distributed to Geo. Stinson & Co. agents. See *Profitable Work*, XC-3, Advertising Circulars, Stinson, ECA.

27. Description based on *General Direction and Instruction to Agents for the People's Illustrated Journal*, XC-3, ECA.

28. *Our Fireside Journal*, May 13, 1876, 15.

29. Lee, *Twenty-Five Years in the Mail Order Business*, 56–57.

30. M. Young to Allen, May 21, 1884, E. C. Allen Co. Incoming Letters, 1884, box XC-1, ECA; Home Manufacturing Company to Allen, November 13, 1885, and Allen to HMC, November 14, 1885, December 2 and 30, 1885, and April 3, 1886, all in LA-10, pp. 26–28, ECA.

31. Chicago Specialty Company to Allen, November 16, 1885, LA-10, pp. 348–49, ECA.

32. G. L. Erwin & Co. to Allen, October 30, 1886, LA-10, p. 96, ECA; Stokes & Co. to Allen, October 22, 1886, LA-10, p. 148, ECA.

33. Allen to Barnum & Co., November 13, 1885, February 18, 1886, March 13, 1886, and May 27, 1886, LA-10, pp. 416–17, ECA.

34. Fireside Publishing Co. to Allen, November 5, 1885, and response, November 13, 1885, LA-10, pp. 98–99; Phoenix Burner Co. to Allen, January 2 and 7, 1886, and Allen to Phoenix Burner Co., January 5, 1887, LA-10, p. 290, ECA.

35. B. F. Johnson & Co. to Allen, November 5, 1885, LA-10, p. 51, ECA.

36. Lovell Machine Co. to Allen, May 31 [1886], LA-10, p. 465, ECA; S. H. Moore & Co. to Allen, November 9, 1885, LA-10, p. 137, ECA.

37. A. B. Gehman to Allen, September 20, 1886, LA-10, p. 108, ECA.

38. Gay & Co. to Allen, April 22, 1886, LA-10, p. 61; Taylor Bros. & Co. to Allen, February 23, 1886, and Allen to Taylor Bros., March 6, 1886, LA-10, pp. 352–54, ECA.

39. W. C. Rogers to Allen, March 12, 1889, and March 21, 1889, E. C. Allen Co. Incoming Letters, 1889, box XC-1, ECA.

40. Allen to Industrial Art Exchange, LA-10, p. 182.

41. Allen to Globe Bible Publishing Co., March 22, 1886, LA-10, p. 170, ECA; Allen to D. L. Moody's, March 1, 1886, LA-10, 75, ECA.

42. Allen to Jay Bronson, November 18, 1885, LA-10, pp. 305–6, ECA; J. Hampton Johnston to Allen, December 3, 1886, LA-10, p. 266, ECA.

43. P. H. Woodward, *Guarding the Mails; or, The Secret Service of the Post Office Department* (Hartford, CT: Dustin, Gilman, 1876), 419, 422–31. On scams, see Balleisen, *Fraud*; Timothy J. Gilfoyle, *A Pickpocket's Tale: The Underworld of Nineteenth-Century New York* (New York: Norton, 2007); Amy Reading, *The Mark Inside: A Perfect Swindle, a Cunning Revenge, and a Small History of the Big Con* (New York: Knopf, 2012).

44. See correspondence between Standard Silverware Co. and Allen, October 25, 26, 27, and 28, 1885, November 3, 4, 13, 19, and 28, 1885, December 2, 18, and 31, 1885, January 5 and 7, 1886, June 27, 1886, November 11 and 12, 1886, December 13, 1886. All in LA-10, pp. 2–5, 479–80, ECA.

45. "Standard Silverware Co.," Massachusetts, vol. 88, p. 27, RGD.

46. Allen to Eugene Pearl, March 25, 1886, LA-10, p. 361, ECA; J. T. Smith to Allen, February 23, 1886, and response, March 1, 1886, LA-10, p. 237, ECA; Samuel Sawyer, *Secrets of the Mail-Order Trade: A Practical Manual for Those Embarking in the Business of Advertising and Selling Goods by Mail* (New York: Sawyer, 1900), 36, 104–13. On information flows, see JoAnne Yates, *Control Through Communication: The Rise of System in American Management* (Baltimore: Johns Hopkins University Press, 1989).

47. Allen to William Small, March 23, 1886, LA-10, 71, ECA; Allen to Brohard & Co., October 22, 1886, LA-10, 116–17; Western Lace Manufacturing Co. to Allen, March 27, 1886, LA-10, 174, ECA; Standard Silverware Co. to Allen, January 29, 1886, LA-10, 476, ECA.

48. Stuart Banner, *American Property: A History of How, Why, and What We Own* (Cambridge, MA: Harvard University Press, 2011), 130–61; Sarah E. Igo, *The Known Citizen: A History of Privacy in Modern America* (Cambridge, MA: Harvard University Press, 2018), 24–44.

49. Buckley v. Geraty, No. 22082, 145 La. 935, 83 So. 197, 1919 La. LEXIS 1811 (Supreme Court of Louisiana, November 3, 1919); Madson v. Clark, Gen. No. 15,924, 165 Ill. App. 228, 1911 Ill. App. LEXIS 161 (Court of Appeals of Illinois, Chicago, First District, October 25, 1911); "Taken as Mail List Thieves," *Chicago Daily Tribune*, December 28, 1913, 6.

50. "Names Obtained by Fraud," *New York Times*, November 4 1888, 9; "Demorest Fashion and Sewing Machine Company," advertisement, *American Magazine Advertiser*, December 1887, 52; "G. S. & F. M. Scofield," *American Advertiser Review*, November 5, 1988, box U-3, ECA.

51. "Taken as Mail List Thieves," 6.

52. "Clipped & Condensed," *Agricultural Advertising*, May 1905, 450.

53. On data ownership in the twentieth century, see Sarah Igo, "Me and My Data," *Historical Studies in the Natural Sciences* 48, no. 5 (2018): 616–26.

54. Lauer, *Creditworthy*; Bouk, *How Our Days Became Numbered*; Bouk, "History and Political Economy of Personal Data," 89–98.

55. Clifford Geertz, "Suq: The Bazaar Economy in Sefrou," in *Meaning and Order in Moroccan Society: Three Essays in Cultural Analysis* by Clifford Geertz, Hildred Geertz, and Lawrence Rosen (Cambridge: Cambridge University Press, 1979), 229, 125.

Chapter 3

1. Pinkerton's National Detective Agency, *General Principles* (Chicago: Geo. H. Fergus, 1867), 1, 6, Hagley Digital Archives, http://digital.hagley.org/08031912_pinkertons.

2. For recent histories of the Pinkertons and the growth of the private detective industry in the late nineteenth-century United States, see S. Paul O'Hara, *Inventing the Pinkertons; or, Spies, Sleuths, Mercenaries, and Thugs: Being a History of the Nation's Most Famous (and Infamous) Detective Agency* (Baltimore: Johns Hopkins University Press, 2016); John Walton, *The Legendary Detective: The Private Eye in Fact and Fiction* (Chicago: University of Chicago Press, 2015).

3. JoAnne Yates, *Control Through Communication: The Rise of System in American Management* (Baltimore: Johns Hopkins University Press, 1989).

4. Lisa Gitelman, *Paper Knowledge: Toward a Media History of Documents* (Durham, NC: Duke University Press, 2014), 1, 5, quotation on 1. On paperwork, see Max Weber, "Bureaucracy," in *Economy and Society: An Outline of Interpretive Sociology*, ed. Guenter Roth

and Claus Wittich (Berkeley: University of California Press, 1978), 956–1005; Yates, *Control Through Communication*; Thomas Augst, *The Clerk's Tale: Young Men and Moral Life in Nineteenth-Century America* (Chicago: University of Chicago Press, 2003); Ben Kafka, "Paperwork: The State of the Discipline," *Book History* 12 (2009): 340–53; Craig Robertson, *The Passport in America: The History of a Document* (New York: Oxford University Press, 2010); Ben Kafka, *The Demon of Writing: Powers and Failures of Paperwork* (New York: Zone Books, 2012); Michael Zakim, *Accounting for Capitalism: The World the Clerk Made* (Chicago: University of Chicago Press, 2018); Carla Bittel, Elaine Leong, and Christine von Oertzen, eds., *Working with Paper: Gendered Practices in the History of Knowledge* (Pittsburgh: University of Pittsburgh Press, 2019).

5. Seth Rockman, introduction, "Forum: The Paper Technologies of Capitalism," *Technology and Culture* 58, no. 2 (2017): 487–505.

6. On the relevance of actor-network theory to the history of capitalism, see Bruce E. Baker and Barbara Hahn, *The Cotton Kings: Capitalism and Corruption in Turn-of-the-Century New York* (New York: Oxford University Press, 2016), 154. See also Bruno Latour, *Reassembling the Social: An Introduction to Actor-Network Theory* (New York: Oxford University Press, 2005).

7. Kenneth Lipartito, "The Economy of Surveillance," February 10, 2010, available online at SSRN, http://dx.doi.org/10.2139/ssrn.1582218. On economies of commercial surveillance, see Sarah E. Igo, *The Known Citizen: A History of Privacy in Modern America* (Cambridge, MA: Harvard University Press, 2018); Josh Lauer, *Creditworthy: A History of Consumer Surveillance and Financial Identity in America* (New York: Columbia University Press, 2017).

8. Frank Morn, *"The Eye That Never Sleeps": A History of the Pinkerton Detective Agency* (Bloomington: Indiana University Press, 1982), x.

9. Morris Friedman, *The Pinkerton Labor Spy* (New York: Wilshire Book Co., 1907), 4–5, HathiTrust Digital Library, https://catalog.hathitrust.org/Record/010822778; Weber, "Bureaucracy," 956. By 1907, Pinkerton's had twenty offices across the country, in Boston, New York, Philadelphia, Chicago, St. Louis, Kansas City, St. Paul, Denver, Portland (Oregon), Seattle, San Francisco, Buffalo, Pittsburgh, Cincinnati, Cleveland, Minneapolis, Omaha, Spokane, Los Angeles, as well as Montreal.

10. Friedman, *Pinkerton Labor Spy*, 4–5.

11. Walton, *Legendary Detective*, 81–82. On the genre of operatives' reports in the contexts of railroad spotting, labor spying, and criminal investigations, see Stephen Robertson, "The Pinkertons and the Paperwork of Surveillance: Reporting Private Investigation in the United States, 1865–1940," in *Private Security and the Modern State: Historical and Comparative Perspectives*, ed. David Churchill, Dolores Janiewski, and Pieter Leloup (New York: Routledge, 2020), 117–34.

12. Friedman, *Pinkerton Labor Spy*, 16, 24–28.

13. Ibid., 27–28.

14. F. J. Sullivan to R. N. Swanson, June 18, 1904, folder 7, box 42, Pinkerton's National Detective Agency Records, Library of Congress (hereafter PNDA Records).

15. The Pinkerton Protective Patrol, a division created in Chicago in 1858 to provide businesses with night watchmen, occupied the niche between "the independents" (private police forces) and the public police. It existed only in Chicago until branching out to New York in 1881 and other cities thereafter. Morn, *"The Eye That Never Sleeps,"* 29–30, 98. On the centrality of Pinkerton's National Detective Agency to the rise of undercover investigation and

private surveillance in the United States, see Jennifer Fronc, *New York Undercover: Private Surveillance in the Progressive Era* (Chicago: University of Chicago Press, 2009), 11.

16. Wm. A. Pinkerton to William J. Chalmers, February 19, 1918, MSS Alpha Pinkerton, William, Manuscripts Collection, Chicago History Museum Research Center.

17. Wm. A. Pinkerton to Robert A. Pinkerton, May 26, 1904; Wm. A. Pinkerton to J. T. Jansen, May 25, 1904, both in folder 8, box 42, PNDA Records.

18. Wm. A. Pinkerton to William J. Chalmers, February 19, 1918, MSS Alpha Pinkerton, William, Manuscripts Collection, Chicago History Museum Research Center. For a similar account of the Pinkerton & Coe agency, see A. T. Andreas, *History of Chicago*, vol. 3 (Chicago: A. T. Andreas, 1886), 11, Google Books, https://books.google.com/books?id=THd5AAAAMAAJ.

19. Andreas, *History of Chicago*, 3:119.

20. Pinkerton National Detective Agency, circular, July 23, 1904, folder 7, box 42; Robt. A. Pinkerton, report, July 16, 1904, p. 2, folder 3, box 43; Copy of Bill of Complaint, Robert A. Pinkerton et al. v. Pinkerton's United States Detective Agency, United States Circuit Court, Eastern District of Wisconsin, June 30, 1904, pp. 8, 4, folder 9, box 42, all in PNDA Records.

21. Wm. to R. A. Pinkerton, June 1, 1904, folder 8, box 42; Wm. to Robt. Pinkerton, June 2, 1904, folder 8, box 42; Wm. Pinkerton to Wm. Inman, folder 1, box 43, all in PNDA Records.

22. Pinkerton's National Detective Agency, circular, December 12, 1904, folder 8, box 42, PNDA Records.

23. Copy of Bill of Complaint, Robert A. Pinkerton et al. v. Pinkerton's United States Detective Agency, United States Circuit Court, Eastern District of Wisconsin, June 30, 1904, p. 7, folder 9, box 42, PNDA Records.

24. Pinkerton's United States Detective Agency, "Application for Membership," undated form, folder 7, box 42, PNDA Records.

25. An important exception is the existence of Black-owned detective agencies in northern cities, such as Sheridan A. Bruseaux's Keystone National Detective Agency in Detroit. On Bruseaux and Black detectives more broadly, see Walton, *Legendary Detective*, 51–52.

26. "Pinkerton's Training by Mail," advertisement, *International Detective Review* 2, no. 6 (June 1904): 8, folder 8, box 42, PNDA Records.

27. United States Detective Agency, *Brief Explanatory Notes to Prospective Operatives*, folder 7, box 42, PNDA Records.

28. Other detective agency circulars sometimes offered similarly long lists of services. See, for example, Patterson's Detective Agency (Toronto), circular, November 10, 1893; Hawkeye Detective Agency (Sioux City, Iowa), circular, n.d., both in Records of the Pinkerton National Detective Agency, Pinkerton Administrative Subject Files: Detective Agency Advertisements, folder 102595-018-0937, ProQuest History Vault, https://congressional.proquest.com/histvault.

29. Gitelman, *Paper Knowledge*, 5.

30. United States Detective Agency, *Brief Explanatory Notes*.

31. F. J. Sullivan, *The Detective Adviser, Containing Valuable Information, Instructions, and Advice for the Government and Guidance of Private Detectives*, 2nd ed. (Milwaukee, WI: International Detective Agency, 1902), folder 9, box 42, PNDA Records; *International Detective Review* 2, no. 6 (June 1904): 8, folder 8, box 42, PNDA Records.

32. H. W. Minster to Edw. S. Gaylor, June 28, 1904, folder 7, box 42, PNDA Records.

33. Statement by J. T. Janssen, chief of police, April 20, 1902, folder 7, box 42, PNDA Records.

34. H. J. Biderman to H. W. Bearce, July 13, 1904, folder 3, box 43, PNDA Records.

35. John F. Winchell to Robert Pinkerton, July 9, 1904, folder 7, box 42, PNDA Records.

36. John H. Smith to Pinkerton Detective Agency, September 3, 1905, folder 7, box 42, PNDA Records.

37. Allan Pinkerton to William A. Pinkerton and Robert A. Pinkerton, July 6, 1904, folder 7, box 42, PNDA Records.

38. Allan Pinkerton to R. A. and W. A. Pinkerton, June 4, 1904, folder 8, box 42, PNDA Records.

39. Robert A. Pinkerton to William A. Pinkerton, July 1, 1904, folder 7, box 42, PNDA Records; William A. Pinkerton to Robert A. Pinkerton, June 3, 1904, folder 8, box 42, PNDA Records.

40. Samuel B. Diehl to Charles R. Wright, July 2, 1904, folder 7, box 42, PNDA Records.

41. Copy of Order for Preliminary Injunction, Robert A. Pinkerton and William A. Pinkerton v. Pinkerton's United States Detective Agency, United States District Court, Eastern District of Wisconsin, July 12, 1904, folder 8, box 42, PNDA Records.

42. Copy of Bill of Complaint, Robert A. Pinkerton et al. v. Pinkerton's United States Detective Agency, United States Circuit Court, Eastern District of Wisconsin, June 30, 1904, pp. 8, 9, folder 9, box 42, PNDA Records; "Pinkerton Gets Injunction," *Inter Ocean*, July 12, 1904, box 3, folder 43, PNDA Records.

43. Pinkerton's National Detective Agency, circular, July 23, 1904, folder 7, box 42, PNDA Records.

44. Edw. S. Gaylor to Geo. D. Bangs, August 1, 1904; J. C. Fraser to James McParland, August 1, 1904; F. H. Tillotson to E. S. Gaylor, August 1, 1904; O. O. Rindal to Edw. S. Gaylor, August 1, 1904; H. W. Minster to Edw. S. Gaylor, August 1, 1904; B. F. Kemble to Jas. McParland, August 2, 1904; H. J. Biderman to H. W. Bearce, July 29, 1904; F. J. Heine to J. H. Schumacher, August 1, 1904; M. F. Donahae to James Nevins, August 3, 1904; Geo. Bird to Samuel B. Diehl, July 30, 1904, all in folder 2, box 43, PNDA Records.

45. M. F. Donahae to Geo. D. Bangs, August 5, 1904, folder 2, box 43, PNDA Records.

46. Robt. A. Pinkerton to Wm. A. Pinkerton, July 14, 1904, folder 3, box 43, PNDA Records.

47. William A. Pinkerton to Robert A. Pinkerton, May 25, 1904, folder 8, box 42, PNDA Records.

48. James McParland to B. F. Kemble, May 29, 1904, folder 8, box 42, PNDA Records.

49. Robert A. Pinkerton to Wm. A. Pinkerton, May 30, 1904, folder 8, box 42, PNDA Records.

50. "Tin Stars Are Thick," *Los Angeles Times*, July 26, 1904, folder 9, box 42, PNDA Records.

51. W. G. Baldwin to Robert A. Pinkerton, July 26, 1904, and enclosure; Elijah Carter to Baldwin's Detectives, July 18, 1904; W. G. Baldwin to Elijah Carter, July 26, 1904, all in folder 9, box 42, PNDA Records.

52. United States Detective Agency, undated circular, folder 7, box 42, PNDA Records.

53. Wm. A. Pinkerton to R. A. Pinkerton, July 16, 1904, folder 3, box 43, PNDA Records.

54. Robt. A. Pinkerton, report, July 16, 1904, p. 4, folder 3, box 43, PNDA Records.

55. Ibid.

56. Wm. A. Pinkerton to J. T. Janssen, July 29, 1904, folder 2, box 43; "Postal Officers Hold Detective Agency's Mail," *Milwaukee Free Press*, June 9, 1904, in folder 1, box 43; Wm. A. Pinkerton to Robt. A. Pinkerton, June 11, 1904, folder 1, box 43, all in PNDA Records.

57. Wm. A. Pinkerton to Messrs. Hoyt, Doe, Umbreit, and Olwell, July 30, 1904, folder 2, box 43, PNDA Records.

58. Joseph B. Doe to Wm. A. Pinkerton, August 1, 1904, folder 2, box 43, PNDA Records.

59. Robt. A. Pinkerton, report, July 16, 1904, p. 3, folder 3, box 43, PNDA Records.

60. John T. Janssen to W. A. Pinkerton, June 21, 1904, folder 1, box 43; P. K. Ahern to James Nevins, August 23, 1904, folder 2, box 43, both in PNDA Records.

61. Geo. Bangs to Wm. A. and Robt. A. Pinkerton, August 2, 1904, folder 2, box 43, PNDA Records. For newspaper clippings and transcripts of advertisements, see folder 2, box 43, PNDA Records.

62. "Detectives—Every Locality," advertisement, *Syracuse Sunday Herald*, August 7, 1904, newspaper clipping, folder 2, box 43, PNDA Records. On the simultaneous exclusion of and selective reliance on women in the detective industry, see Walton, *Legendary Detective*, 48–50.

63. "Detectives—Men Everywhere," advertisement, *Philadelphia North American*, August 7, 1904, newspaper clipping, folder 2, box 43, PNDA Records.

64. H. M. Bearce to John Cornish, August 3, 1904; Geo. F. Leith to John Cornish, July 31, 1904; James Nevins to James McParland, August 1, 1904; H. D. Bailey to B. F. Kemble, August 1, 1904, all in folder 2, box 43, PNDA Records.

65. P. K. Ahern to James Nevins, August 9, 1904, folder 2, box 43, PNDA Records.

66. Edw. S. Gaylor to Geo D. Bangs, August 10, 1904; O. O. Rindal to Edw. S. Gaylor, August 17, 1904, both in folder 2, box 43, PNDA Records.

67. Edw. S. Gaylor to Geo. D. Bangs, August 18, 1904, folder 2, box 43, PNDA Records.

68. Robt. A. Pinkerton, report, July 16, 1904, folder 3, box 43, PNDA Records.

69. D. C. Thornhill to E. E. Haskins, January 10, 1905, folder 1, box 43, PNDA Records.

70. See folder 2, box 43, PNDA Records.

71. M. F. Donahae to James Nevins, August 23, 1904; Allan Pinkerton to James McParland, August 30, 1904, both in folder 2, box 43, PNDA Records.

72. "Paid $3 for the Badges," *St. Louis Republic*, August 3, 1904, folder 2, box 43; Robt. A. Pinkerton, report, July 16, 1904, p. 3, folder 3, box 43; Wm. A. Pinkerton to Joseph B. Doe, July 12, 1904, folder 3, box 43; Wm. A. Pinkerton to Robt. A. Pinkerton, July 12, 1904, folder 3, box 43; Wm. A. Pinkerton to Robt. A. Pinkerton, July 14, 1904, folder 3, box 43, all in PNDA Records.

73. Robert A. Pinkerton, report, July 18, 1904, pp. 3–4; Wm. A. Pinkerton to P. C. Holland, July 22, 1904, both in folder 3, box 43, PNDA Records.

74. J. H. Schumacher to Edw. S. Gaylor, December 6, 1904, folder 8, box 42, PNDA Records.

75. Edw. S. Gaylor to Geo. D. Bangs, December 12, 1904, folder 8, box 42, PNDA Records.

76. Joseph B. Doe to Pinkerton's National Detective Agency, December 13, 1904, folder 8, box 42, PNDA Records.

77. Edw. S. Gaylor to Geo. D. Bangs, October 6, 1904; Geo. D. Bangs to Edw. S. Gaylor, October 8, 1904, both in folder 3, box 43, PNDA Records.

78. J. J. Goodwin to S. B. Diehl, October 10, 1904, folder 3, box 43, PNDA Records.

79. Geo. D. Bangs to Edw. S. Gaylor, October 17, 1904, folder 3, box 43, PNDA Records.

80. E. S. Gaylor to J. H. Schumacher, October 24, 1904; Allan Pinkerton to Edw. S. Gaylor, October 19, 1904, both in folder 3, box 43, PNDA Records.

81. Edw. S. Gaylor to Geo. D. Bangs, October 11, 1904; Edw. S. Gaylor to Geo. D. Bangs, October 14, 1904, both in folder 3, box 43, PNDA Records.

82. "Use of Mails Denied to Pinkerton & Co. U.S. Detective Agency," *Bulletin of the Commercial Law League of America* 20, no. 4 (April 1915): 172. On the "blacklist" of delinquent debtors as "the archetypal credit report," see Lauer, *Creditworthy*, 57–58.

83. For a brief mention of the *Pinkerton v. Pinkerton* case (mentioning only Matt W. Pinkerton), see Katherine Unterman, *Uncle Sam's Policemen: The Pursuit of Fugitives Across Borders* (Cambridge, MA: Harvard University Press, 2015), 66.

84. "To Whom It May Concern," *Los Angeles Herald*, June 17, 1912, p. 2, California Digital Newspaper Collection, https://cdnc.ucr.edu/cgi-bin/cdnc?a=d&d=LAH19120617.2.36.2. The Pinkerton's National Detective Agency archives contain advertisements from other detective/collection agencies. See, for example, Timothy Whitney and W. W. Lee, Whitney and Lee Law, Collection, and Detective Agency circular, August 8, 1900, Records of the Pinkerton National Detective Agency, Pinkerton Administrative Subject Files: Detective Agency Advertisements, folder 102595-018-0937, ProQuest History Vault, https://congressional.proquest.com/histvault.

85. John Cornish to J. J. Goodwin, September 26, 1904, folder 3, box 43, PNDA Records.

86. "Pinkerton Men Protest Against Report," *Daily Missoulan*, September 11, 1914, Library of Congress *Chronicling America*, http://chroniclingamerica.loc.gov/lccn/sn83025316/1914-09-11/ed-1/seq-10/.

87. "Fake Detective Firm Denied Mails," *Retail Grocers' Advocate* 20, no. 14 (April 2, 1915): 13.

88. "Use of Mails Denied to Pinkerton & Co. U.S. Detective Agency," *Bulletin of the Commercial Law League of America* 20, no. 4 (April 1915): 172.

89. William Townsend, "The Detective's Place in Business," *Rand McNally Bankers' Monthly* 31, no. 5 (May 1914): 41.

90. "Use of Mails Denied," 172.

91. On Homestead as a "hinge" on which public opinion turned against the Pinkertons, see O'Hara, *Inventing the Pinkertons*, chap. 6, quotation at p. 2.

92. Pinkerton's National Detective Agency, circular, August 12, 1913, author's personal collection.

93. "Rival Pinkertons at War," *New York Times*, December 22, 1913; "Fraud Order Issued Against Pinkerton & Co. U.S. Detective Agency," *Bulletin of the National Association of Credit Men* 15, no. 4 (April 1915): 260.

94. "Fake Detective Firm Denied Mails," *Retail Grocers' Advocate* 20, no. 14 (April 2, 1915): 13. On the increasing power and reach of postal fraud orders in the Progressive Era, see Daniel P. Carpenter, *The Forging of Bureaucratic Autonomy: Reputations, Networks, and Policy Innovation in Executive Agencies, 1862–1928* (Princeton, NJ: Princeton University Press, 2001), 148; Edward J. Balleisen, *Fraud: An American History from Barnum to Madoff* (Princeton, NJ: Princeton University Press, 2017), 128–39; Dorothy Ganfield Fowler, *Unmailable: Congress and the Post Office* (Athens: University of Georgia Press, 1977), 59, 92–108.

95. Pinkerton's National Detective Agency, undated circular, enclosure in Wm. A. Pinkerton to William J. Chalmers, February 19, 1918, MSS Alpha Pinkerton, William, Manuscripts Collection, Chicago History Museum Research Center.

96. "Use of Mails Denied," 172.

97. J. W. Hoodwin Co. v. Pinkerton, 204 Ill. App. 298, March 12, 1917, in *Reports of Cases Determined in the Appellate Courts of Illinois*, Google Books, https://books.google.com /books?id=JUVIAQAAMAAJ.

98. Balleisen, *Fraud*; Michael Pettit, *The Science of Deception: Psychology and Commerce in America* (Chicago: University of Chicago Press, 2013); David Roth Singerman, "Science, Commodities, and Corruption in the Gilded Age," *Journal of the Gilded Age and Progressive Era* 15 (July 2016): 278–93.

Chapter 4

1. "Address of Mr. W. G. McAdoo, President, to the Train Employees of the Hudson & Manhattan Railroad Company, at Hoboken Station, New Jersey, February 21, 1908," 4, box 12, vol. 1, McAdoo Papers, Huntington Library, San Marino, California (hereafter McAdoo Papers).

2. "Opening of the Hudson and Manhattan Railroad's Tunnels," *Wall Street Journal*, February 18, 1908, box 12, vol. 1, McAdoo Papers; Ray Morris, *Railroad Administration* (New York: D. Appleton, 1910), 222; John A. Wyeth, "Wants Competition: Thinks It Is Time to Look to Mr. McAdoo for Subways," *New York Times*, December 11, 1910, 16.

3. "Vanderbilt in the West: The Railroad Millionaire Expresses Himself Freely," *Chicago Daily Tribune*, October 9, 1882, 8; "'The Public Be Damned,'" *International Railway Journal*, April 1922, 12; "Address of Mr. W. G. McAdoo," McAdoo Papers. McAdoo's first recorded use of the phrase "public be pleased" occurred five months after his February 1908 speech, in July 1908, when McAdoo opened his second tunnel; see McAdoo, *Crowded Years: The Reminiscences of William G. McAdoo* (New York: Houghton Mifflin, 1931), 105.

4. Paul E. Johnson, *A Shopkeeper's Millennium: Society and Revivals in Rochester, New York, 1815–1837* (New York: Hill and Wang, 1978), 38–60; William Cordes, "Keep in Touch with John and Jim," in *Handling Men: Selecting and Hiring; How to Hold Your Men; Breaking In and Developing Men; Putting More Than Money in Pay Envelopes*, ed. John Wanamaker, Frank Disston, Edward B. Butler, and James A. Farrell (Chicago: A. W. Shaw, 1917), 108–11.

5. William G. McAdoo, *The Relations Between Public Service Corporations and the Public* (New York: Alexander Hamilton Institute, [1910]), 19, 21.

6. "Penalty of Submitting to Traction Monopoly," *New York American*, February 26, 1908, box 12, vol. 1, McAdoo Papers; "One Subway Best, Mayor's Board Finds," *New York Times*, December 29, 1910, 4.

7. N. C. Kingsbury, "Publicity: A Paper Presented May 7, 1912, Before the Philadelphia Telephone Society," folder: Publicity, box 1, record group 6 (Publications, 1893–1912), collection 6, AT&T Corp., AT&T Archives and History Center, San Antonio, Texas (hereafter AT&T-TX).

8. John M. Mulvihill, "Popularizing Utility Companies," *Public Service*, December 1908, 171; Samuel M. Kennedy, *Winning the Public*, 2nd ed. (New York: McGraw-Hill, 1921), 106; P. H. Gadsden, "The Committee Chairman's Viewpoint," *National Electric Light Association Proceedings* (hereafter *NELA Proceedings*), vol. 81 (1924): 152–55; Richard E. Smith, "The Fellow in the Street," *Edison Current Topics* 8, no. 8 (August 1919): 91, box 308, folder 7, Southern California Edison Records, Huntington Library, San Marino, California (hereafter SCE Records); Paul C. Rawson, "Prize-Winning Article in Forbes Contest," *NELA Proceedings* 81

(1924): 178; G. C. Staley and F. C. Jordan, "The Utility Customer," *Journal of the American Water Works Association* 16, no. 5 (November 1926): 645; W. P. Graef, "The Electrical Salesman," *Edison Current Topics*, May 1912, 19–21, box 308, folder 1, SCE Records.

9. "Training for Better Public Contact—Its Necessity and Importance," *NELA Proceedings*, Public Relations National Section, June 5, 1928, 281.

10. Arlie Russell Hochschild, *The Managed Heart: Commercialization of Human Feeling* (Berkeley: University of California Press, 1983), 5–7.

11. Samuel M. Kennedy, "Transforming Public Opinion: An Address by Mr. Samuel M. Kennedy, Vice-President Southern California Edison Co., Los Angeles, California, Before the Convention of Managers and Executives of the Management Division of Stone & Webster Inc., Held in Boston, October 10–18, 1921," pp. 24–25, 29–30, box 389, folder 26, SCE Records.

12. Ibid., 44; David B. Sicilia, "Selling Power: Marketing and Monopoly at Boston Edison, 1886–1929" (Ph.D. diss., Brandeis University, 1991), 526; "Errors Checked, Manner Improved," *Peoples Gas Light & Coke Company Year Book, 1926*, p. 21, folder 54-13, Samuel Insull Papers, Loyola University Chicago Archives.

13. Wm. A. Durgin, "Appendix C (Continued): Public-Contact Training and Measurement of Results by Service Sampling," in *Public-Contact-Training Methods and Principles: Experiences of Member Companies Presented and Discussed at the Chicago Conference, September, 1929; A Report of the Industrial Relations Committee, Public Relations National Section* (1929), 18. This obscure source was bound together with other publications as *Special Publications, 1929* of the National Electric Light Association and filed in the University of California, Berkeley, library catalog under call no.: TK 1 N 24, 1929:3.

14. Ibid., 15, 18–19.

15. Sanford M. Jacoby, "Employee Attitude Testing at Sears, Roebuck and Company, 1938–1960," *Business History Review* 60, no. 4 (Winter 1986): 605–6.

16. J. David Houser, J. David Houser & Associates, "Employee-Customer Relations," *American Gas Association, Twelfth Annual Convention, October 13–17, 1930* (New York: American Gas Association), 736.

17. Ibid., 736–37; "Report of Bell System Commercial Operations, 1930, Compiled by the Commercial Engineer, American Telephone and Telegraph Company," in *Operating Papers Conference—Absecon, New Jersey, Year 1931*, p. 15, file: Conference, 1926, 1931, box 10 (Company Leaders, Presidential Office Files, Complaints of Service—Northern California Conferences), record group 5 (Pacific Telephone & Telegraph), collection 3, AT&T-TX.

18. "Criticism—Good and Bad," *Southern Telephone News*, March 1921, p. 1, AT&T-TX; Edward H. Mulligan, "Courteous Service," *Edison Current Topics* 4, no. 7 (July 1915): 127, box 308, folder 4, SCE Records; Kennedy, "Transforming Public Opinion," 25–27; *Pacific Electric Magazine*, August 10, 1916; Margaret Lindley, "Training," in *Fifth Annual Chief Operators Conference, Los Angeles, February 15th, 1929*, p. 39, box 10, record group 5, collection 3, AT&T-TX.

19. Michel Foucault, "Part Four: The Deployment of Sexuality," in *The History of Sexuality*, vol. 1, trans. Robert Hurley (New York: Vintage Books, 1990), 75–132; W. J. O'Connor, "The Why and How of Personnel Work in the Bell System," in *Conference of Personnel Group, Bell System, April 18–25, 1922*, p. 3, box 88, record group 4, collection 6, AT&T-TX; Verne Ray, "Public Relations Committees and the Pink Ticket Plan," in *Conference of Personnel Group, Bell System, April 18–25, 1922*, pp. 4, 7.

20. "New Edison Building Beautiful and Modern," *Edison Current Topics* 8, no. 1 (January 1919): 4, box 308, folder 7, SCE Records; Kennedy, "Transforming Public Opinion," 18.

21. Charles Heston Peirson, "Service," *Edison Current Topics* 3, no. 3 (March 1914): 460, box 308, folder 3, SCE Records; Kennedy, "Transforming Public Opinion," 17–18.

22. "Organization Diagram," October 1913, box 470, folder 6, SCE Records; "Stock Salesmen Meeting, October 8, 1921," pp. 3, 8, box 114, folder 8, SCE Records; G. Haven Bishop, *Pomona Local Office—Interior*, 1923, Southern California Edison Photographs; Bishop, *Local Offices A–Z*, Pomona, California, district office in 1923, 02-08845, Southern California Edison Photographs and Negatives, Huntington Library, San Marino, California; Kennedy, "Transforming Public Opinion," 17–18; *Commerce Journal* 4, no. 1 (August 1923): 5–8, box 470, folder 6, SCE Records; "El Centro Has New Business Office," *Pacific Telephone Magazine*, August 1929, 9, AT&T-TX; photograph 13706, folder: "Pacific Bell—California Prints—by exchange—Oakland—Buildings and Facilities—3545 E. 14th St. Business Office, 1927-1930," box 88, record group 4, collection 6, AT&T-TX.

23. "Spokane's Newly Completed Business Office," *Pacific Telephone Magazine*, January 1927, 30, AT&T-TX; Kennedy, "Transforming Public Opinion," 17; Robt. E. Power, "Business Office Management," in *Meeting of Managers* (San Francisco: Pacific Telephone and Telegraph Company, March 30, 1926), 1, 8, Pacific Bell Company Leaders Executive Office Files, Conference, 1925, 2 of 8, box 10, record group 5, AT&T-TX; Michel Foucault, *Discipline and Punish: The Birth of the Prison*, trans. Alan Sheridan (New York: Vintage, 1979).

24. D. C. Thomas, "New Type Business Office Has No Counters," *Southern Telephone News*, January 1929, 9, AT&T-TX; "The Work of the Commercial Department," part 1, "A Reading Assignment," in *Employees' General Training Course: The Pacific Telephone and Telegraph Company, 1927*, 9–10, Public Relations and Publicity, box 3, record group 5, collection 3, AT&T-TX; Stephen H. Norwood, *Labor's Flaming Youth: Telephone Operators and Worker Militancy, 1878-1923* (Urbana: University of Illinois Press, 1990), 37; "Report of Bell System Commercial Operations, 1930."

25. Clark Davis, *Company Men: White-Collar Life and Corporate Culture in Los Angeles, 1892-1941* (Baltimore: Johns Hopkins University Press, 2000), 225–27; Oliver Zunz, *Making America Corporate, 1870-1920* (Chicago: University of Chicago Press, 1990), 202; J. P. Ingle, "Seeing Ourselves as Others See Us," *American Gas Association Monthly*, March 1922, 153.

26. David F. Noble, *Forces of Production: A Social History of Industrial Automation* (New York: Oxford University Press, 1986); Michael Burawoy, *Manufacturing Consent: Changes in the Labor Process Under Monopoly Capitalism* (Chicago: University of Chicago Press, 1979), 81–82; Kempster B. Miller, *Modern Telephone Engineering*, lecture delivered before the New York Electrical Society, February 14, 1901 (New York: New York Electrical Society, 1901), 4; John E. Kingsbury, *The Telephone and Telephone Exchanges: Their Invention and Development* (London: Longmans, Green, 1915), 212, 365; Venus Green, *Race on the Line: Gender, Labor, and Technology in the Bell System, 1880-1980* (Durham, NC: Duke University Press, 2001), 26, 34, 43–45; Kenneth Lipartito, "When Women Were Switches: Technology, Work and Gender in the Telephone Industry, 1890–1920," *American Historical Review*, October 1994, 1082, 1096–97.

27. Miller, *Modern Telephone Engineering*, 9; Arthur Vaughan Abbott, *Telephoney: A Manual of Design, Construction, and Operation of Telephone Exchanges* (New York: McGraw, 1903), 26; Miller, "Modern Telephone Engineering," 2; F. Barrows Colton, "The Miracle of

Talking by Telephone, *National Geographic Magazine*, October 1937, 407, box 485, folder 1, SCE Records.

28. "The Reality—A Typical Exchange," *Pacific Telephone Magazine*, October 1914, 14, AT&T-TX; "The Work of the Traffic Department," part 1, "Organization, Employment & Training, Operator's Quarters, Local Operating, and Toll Operating: Reading Assignment," *Employees' General Training Course: The Pacific Telephone and Telegraph Company, 1928*, p. 4, Publications—Non-Periodic, 1928, box 6, record group 5, collection 3, AT&T-TX.

29. R. T. Barrett, "The Changing Years as Seen from the Switchboard," *Bell Telephone Quarterly*, April 1935, 113; Colton, "Miracle of Talking," 410; "General Operating Department, Western Union Telegraph Building, New York," photograph, 1875, Library of Congress; "'Switch' General Operating Department, Western Union Telegraph Building, New York," photograph, 1875, Library of Congress; Green, *Race on the Line*, 29; "Barclay Telegraph Instruments, Showing Instruments on Stand with Women Operators; One Handling the Receiving Tape," Cincinnati, Ohio, photograph, 1908, Library of Congress; *Bell Telephone Quarterly*, July 1925, 211; Kingsbury, *Telephone and Telephone Exchanges*, 232–33.

30. F. A. Pickernell, "Some General Remarks on Telephone Exchange Construction and Equipment," in *Twelfth Meeting of the National Telephone Exchange Association . . . September 9th and 10th, 1890* (Brooklyn, NY: Eagle, 1890), 67–68; this statement was partly self-plagiarized by Pickernell from a paper he gave the year before; see A. S. Hibbard, J. J. Carty, and F. A. Pickernell, "The New Era in Telephony," in *Eleventh Meeting of the National Telephone Exchange Association . . . September 10th and 11th, 1889* (Brooklyn, NY: Eagle, 1889), 34–43; see also Green, *Race on the Line*, 57, 29, 45; Miller, "Modern Telephone Engineering," 2–3.

31. Kingsbury, *Telephone and Telephone Exchanges*, 385–86; Barrett, "Changing Years as Seen from the Switchboard," 117; M. D. Fagen, ed., *A History of Engineering and Science in the Bell System*, vol. 1, *The Early Years, 1875–1925* (New York: Bell Telephone Laboratories, 1975), 501–2; Norwood, *Labor's Flaming Youth*, 34, 37; Green, *Race on the Line*, 45; Lipartito, "When Women Were Switches," 1096–97; AT&T, *Her Right Place*, 1929 recruiting film, http://techchannel.att.com/play-video.cfm/2013/7/1/AT&T-Archives-Her-Right-Place.

32. R. S. Masters, R. C. Smith, and W. E. Winter, *An Historical Review of the San Francisco Exchange* (San Francisco: Pacific Telephone and Telegraph Company, 1927), 62; Colton, "Miracle of Talking," 407; "The Speech-Weaver's School," *Pacific Telephone Magazine*, December 1916, 11, AT&T-TX; Studs Terkel, *Working: People Talk About What They Do All Day and How They Feel About What They Do* (New York: New Press, 1974), 34.

33. Power, "Business Office Management," 5–6; "The Speech-Weaver's School," 10.

34. Douglas B. Craig, *Progressives at War: William G. McAdoo and Newton D. Baker, 1863–1941* (Baltimore, MD: Johns Hopkins University Press, 2013), 342–45; McAdoo, *Crowded Years*; Charles A. Willis, 2908 S. St., Sacramento, California to Hon. Wm. McAdoo, Secretary of the Treasury, Washington, DC, September 14, 1918, file "Complaints—Misc, 1914–1918," box 9, record group 5, collection 3, AT&T-TX; Richard R. John, *Network Nation: Inventing American Telecommunications* (Cambridge, MA: Belknap Press of Harvard University Press, 2010), 403, 401.

Chapter 5

1. "Way of Transgressor," *Hotel World* 92, no. 7 (February 12, 1921): 23–24.

2. Molly W. Berger, *Hotel Dreams: Luxury, Technology, and Urban Ambition in America, 1829–1929* (Baltimore: Johns Hopkins University Press, 2011), 180.

3. Timothy D. Spears, *100 Years on the Road: The Traveling Salesman in American Culture* (New Haven, CT: Yale University Press, 1995).

4. E. M. Statler "Satisfying the Guest Is Hotel's Most Effective Advertising," *Hotel World* 105, no. 21 (November 19, 1927): 8.

5. Lucius M. Boomer, *Hotel Management: Principles and Practice* (New York: Harper & Brothers, 1925), 279.

6. A. K. Sandoval-Strausz. *Hotel: An American History* (New Haven, CT: Yale University Press, 2007), 204.

7. Jefferson Williamson, *The American Hotel: An Anecdotal History* (New York: Knopf, 1930), 105.

8. Josh Lauer, *Creditworthy: A History of Consumer Surveillance and Financial Identity in America* (New York: Columbia University Press, 2017), 103–12.

9. Ibid.

10. Clyde B. Douthat, "Tactful Handling of Undesirable Guests," *American Greeter* 25, no. 4 (February 1933): 12.

11. Thomas J. Sugrue, *Sweet Land of Liberty: The Forgotten Struggle for Civil Rights in the North* (New York: Random House, 2009), 133–34.

12. Lucius M. Boomer, *Hotel Management: Principles and Practice,* 3rd rev. ed. (New York: Harper & Brothers, 1938), 279.

13. Victor H. Green, ed., *The Negro Motorist Green Book* (New York: Victor H. Green, 1948).

14. Douthat, "Tactful Handling of Undesirable Guests," 12.

15. Ibid.

16. Hugh Ryan, *When Brooklyn Was Queer* (New York: St. Martin's Press, 2019), 294.

17. See George Chauncey, *Gay New York: Gender, Urban Culture, and the Makings of the Gay Male World, 1890–1940* (New York: Basic Books, 1994), for more on attempts to prevent gay socializing in New York bars and hotels.

18. "Catch a Bad One," *Hotel Bulletin* 41, no. 3 (September 1928): 213–14.

19. Louise S. May, "Manager Explains How He Keeps Down Bad Check Losses," *Hotel World* 105, no. 1 (July 2, 1927): 30–32.

20. [Report of Protective Committee, AHA], *Hotel Bulletin* 41, no. 4 (October 1928): 299–301.

21. Helen Christene Hoerle and Florence B. Saltzberg, *The Girl and the Job* (New York: Henry Holt, 1919), 40. Although the majority of front desk clerks were male, there were enough women in the field that the authors of this guide to women's employment felt comfortable including it in their work.

22. Douthat, "Tactful Handling of Undesirable Guests."

23. "Commits Suicide in Waldorf," *New York Sun*, December 22, 1927, Waldorf Astoria Collection Scrapbooks, vol. 3, New York Public Library Special Collections, New York.

24. "Cornell University to Add Psychology to Summer Hotel Curriculum," *Hotel Monthly* 37, no. 431 (March 1929): 52–53.

25. "Guest Likes to Be Recognized," *Hotel Bulletin* 41, no. 4 (October 1928): 274.

26. William J. Stuart, "Tips from a Former Hotel Crook," *Hotel Management*, July 1933, 19.

27. Boomer, *Hotel Management* (1925), 282.

28. Boomer, *Hotel Management*, 282.

29. J. G. Hilliard, "Editorial Page: Essaying the Role of Banker," *Western Hotel Reporter* 59, no. 9 (September 1935): 20.

30. "Way of Transgressor," *Hotel World*, February 12, 1921.

31. Ibid.

32. "List Hotel Deadbeats," *Hotel Bulletin* 36, no. 9 (September 1926): 244.

33. "Catch a Bad One," *Hotel Bulletin*.

34. Joseph G. Buch, "The A.H.A Protective Committee Reports Progress Being Made," *Hotel World* 106, no. 22 (June 2, 1928): 8.

35. "Action by Southern Hotels to Halt Hotel Crooks Is Started," *Hotel World* 102 (February 27, 1926): 9.

36. "New York Police Department Assigns Special Detail to Protect N.Y. Hotels," *Hotel World* 104, no. 11 (March 12, 1927): 28.

37. "The Register of Trends and Tendencies," *Hotel Management* 22, no. 3 (September 1932): 138.

38. Lewis, "As I View It."

39. "Way of Transgressor," *Hotel World* 88, no. 2 (January 11, 1919): 13.

40. Ernest H. Piper, "How Michigan Hotel Men Are Combating the 'Rubber Check' and the 'Skipper,'" *Hotel World* 107, no. 12 (September 22, 1928): 16–17.

41. [Report of Protective Committee, AHA], *Hotel Bulletin*.

42. Piper, "How Michigan Hotel Men."

43. Sandoval-Strausz, *Hotel*, 211.

44. Chic Sale, "There Was a Mystery About Hotels in Those Days," *Hotel World-Review Pictorial* 113, no. 1 (July 1931): 15.

45. Henry J. Bohn, "Editorial," *Hotel World* 92, no. 5 (January 29, 1921): 1.

46. Sandoval-Strausz, *Hotel*, 211.

47. B. D. Gibson, "Makes Accusations Against Hotels," *Hotel World* 94, no. 1 (January 7, 1922): 58.

48. Edwin R. Young, "Replying to B.D.G's Ridiculous Charges," *Hotel World* 94, no. 3 (January 21, 1922): 13.

49. "Interesting Legal Decisions," *Hotel Bulletin* 34, no. 3 (March 1925): 180.

50. Henry J. Bohn, "Editorial Comment," *Hotel World* 100, no. 10 (March 7, 1925): 9.

51. "Guest Likes to Be Recognized," *Hotel Bulletin*.

52. Ralph Hitz, *Standard Practice Manuals for Hotel Operation: Miscellaneous Departments*, vol. 5 (New York: Harper & Brothers, 1936).

53. Elizabeth Johnson, "What Is Unconscious Bias?," April 4, 2019, American Hotel and Lodging Educational Institute, accessed April 4, 2020, https://www.ahlei.org/what-is-unconscious-bias/.

Chapter 6

1. "Drastic Police Curb Put on Night Clubs: Many Face Closing," *New York Times*, July 21, 1931, 1. George Chauncey, *Gay New York: Gender, Urban Culture, and the Making of the Gay Male World, 1890–1940* (New York: Basic Books, 1994), details the 1920s rise in visibility of gay men and some lesbians in "clubs, streets, newspapers, novels, and films," and the backlash in New York City by 1931.

2. A beer baron and a local crime boss ended an altercation with knives, and an associate added the gunshots. See Emanuel H. Lavine, *Secrets of the Metropolitan Police* (Garden City, NY: Garden City Publishing Co., 1937), 212. Chauncey recounts these events and subsequent actions in *Gay New York*, 331–32.

3. "Clubs Raided," *New York Herald Tribune*, January 29, 1931, 4; "Different Causes Are Given for Club Abbey Mix-Up by Bad Men," *Variety*, January 28, 1931, 63; "1 A.M. Curfew Would Be Final Washup on B'way Clubs; 'Pansy' Stuff Dying," *Variety*, February 4, 1931, 84.

4. Elizabeth Alice Clement discusses how commercial sex practices changed in the 1930s in *Love for Sale: Courting, Treating, and Prostitution in New York City, 1900–1945* (Chapel Hill: University of North Carolina, 2006), 178. For earlier context, see also Christine Stansell, *City of Women: Sex and Class in New York, 1789–1860* (New York: Knopf, 1986); Ruth Rosen, *The Lost Sisterhood: Prostitution in America, 1900–1918* (Baltimore: Johns Hopkins University Press, 1982). Note about nomenclature: scholars have debated the use of "prostitution" or "sex work," terms used interchangeably in this work. The particular loose categorization of what counted as "prostitution," much as with "deviance," early in the twentieth century is colloquial and time-bound. For some, "sex work" better represents the empowering opportunities to profit from their sexuality, while "prostitution" suggests subjugation and lack of opportunity. Using both represents both realities in the context portrayed.

5. Thomas C. Mackey recounts the role of the Committee of Fourteen in prostitution reform in the 1920s, especially their failed attempts to prosecute male customers through "the customer amendment." See Thomas C. Mackey, *Pursuing Johns: Criminal Law Reform, Defending Character, and New York City's Committee of Fourteen, 1920–1930* (Columbus: Ohio State University, 2005). Today, similar objections are raised about the 2018 billed passed in Congress and signed by President Trump, FOSTA/SESTA. Advocates of decriminalized sex work argue that the bill fails to recognize or protect voluntary sex workers and fails to assess the role of the customer. See, for example, Heidi Tripp, "All Sex Workers Deserve Protection: How FOSTA/SESTA Overlooks Consensual Sex Workers in an Attempt to Protect Sex Trafficking Victims," *Penn State Law Review* 124, no. 1 (2019): 219.

6. Many studies of queer communities in the 1950s and 1960s are location specific, but the role of gay-friendly bars is commonly central to early gay rights organizing. See Nan Alamilla Boyd, *Wide-Open Town: A History of Queer San Francisco to 1965* (Berkeley: University of California Press, 2005); Timothy Stewart-Winter, *Queer Clout: Chicago and the Rise of Gay Politics* (Philadelphia: University of Pennsylvania Press, 2016). David Carter's New York City–based book on the topic, *Stonewall: The Riots that Sparked the Gay Revolution* (New York: St. Martin's Press, 2010), focuses on the most famous gay bar of the time.

7. For a comprehensive history of slumming in New York and Chicago in the decades surrounding the turn of the century, see Chad Heap, *Slumming: Sexual and Racial Encounters in American Nightlife, 1885–1940* (Chicago: University of Chicago Press, 2000). Police targeted Harlem clubs for reasons other than violence in the 1930s. See, for example, "New York Cops Hit Vulgar Dance in Cafes; New York Police Launch Drive on Harlem Cafes," *Chicago Defender*, March 17, 1934, 5.

8. Burton W. Peretti, *Nightclub City: Politics and Amusement in Manhattan* (Philadelphia: University of Pennsylvania Press, 2011), 167.

9. The Committee of Fourteen used prostitution to refer to female prostitution. Male sex, for money or not, was listed as "perversion." See Mackey, *Pursuing Johns*. Oral sex was often specifically referred to as a "French perversion." See Heap, *Slumming*, 136.

10. Several historians note the indeterminacy of pre–World War II terminology regarding sexuality, sexual activities, and gender identity; see, for example, Chauncey, *Gay New York*; and Margot Canaday, *The Straight State: Sexuality and Citizenship in Twentieth-Century America* (Princeton, NJ: Princeton University Press, 2009), 10–12, 15.

11. The word "queer" has evolved from general meaning, to derogatory sexual connotation, to positive reclamation by members of the LGBTQIA+ communities. See Siobhan B. Somerville, "Queer," in *Keywords for American Cultural Studies*, ed. Bruce Burgett and Glenn Hendler, 2nd ed. (New York: New York University Press, 2014), 203–7.

12. Lewis A. Erenberg, "From New York to Middletown: Repeal and the Legitimization of Nightlife in the Great Depression," *American Quarterly* 38, no. 5 (1986): 761–78.

13. In this same way, the subthemes of popular burlesque entertainment early in the twentieth century as belittling of attractive women's intellect can be compared to the "fairy" stereotyping that made pansy shows popular for many well-to-do mainstream audiences, a reminder that representation alone does not signify acceptance.

14. William N. Eskridge, *Gaylaw: Challenging the Apartheid of the Closet* (Cambridge, MA: Harvard University Press, 2009), 13, 27.

15. Scholarly sources abound on the history of the Hays Code. See, for example, Gregory D. Black, *Hollywood Censored: Morality Codes, Catholics, and the Movies* (Cambridge: Cambridge University Press, 1994); Thomas Doherty, *Hollywood's Censor: Joseph I. Breen and the Production Code Administration* (New York: Columbia University Press, 2009). For more on lesbian and gay themes in film under the Hollywood code, see David M. Lugowski, "Queering the (New) Deal: Lesbian and Gay Representation and the Depression-Era Cultural Politics of Hollywood's Production Code," *Cinema Journal* 38, no. 2 (1999): 3–35; and for more on the code's specifications of dress as they intersected with race, see Ellen Scott, "More Than a 'Passing' Sophistication: Dress, Film Regulation, and the Color Line in 1930s American Films," *Women's Studies Quarterly* 41, nos. 1–2 (Spring–Summer 2013): 61–86.

16. I adapt the suggestion of "nightly" from Shane Vogel's application of "everynight life," in turn borrowed from Celeste Fraser Delgado and José Esteban Muñoz. See Shane Vogel, *The Scene of Harlem Cabaret: Race, Sexuality, Performance* (Chicago: University of Chicago Press, 2009), 17; Celeste Fraser Delgado and José Esteban Muñoz, eds., *Everynight Life: Culture and Dance in Latin/o America* (Durham, NC: Duke University Press, 1997).

17. Scholarly assessment of rising criminological ideas of the time as related to municipal regulations is sparse. Passing references suggest their importance in Peretti, *Nightclub City*, 146–47. For more on the history of crime prevention in the 1930s, see Claire Bond Potter, *War on Crime: Bandits, G-Men, and the Politics of Mass Culture* (New Brunswick, NJ: Rutgers University Press, 1998).

18. Clement, *Love for Sale*. 9–10. Timothy Gilfoyle offers the foundational assessment of New York City and sex exchange in *City of Eros: New York City, Prostitution, and the Commercialization of Sex, 1790–1920* (New York: W. W. Norton, 1992); Chad Heap discusses the ways in which such encounters crossed class boundaries in *Slumming*.

19. "N.Y. Police Ban 'Pansies' in Nite Clubs," *Afro-American*, July 25, 1931, 17; "The Strange Theatre: Female Impersonators Taboo Here, Are All the Rage in China," *Afro-American*, August 29, 1931, 9.

20. See "A Local Law to Regulate Dance Halls and Cabarets and Providing for Licensing the Same," *Proceedings of the Board of Aldermen* (New York, 1926), 138–40. Paul Chevigny,

Gigs: Jazz and the Cabaret Laws in New York City (London: Routledge, 1991), details the effects of the 1926 Cabaret Law, especially on jazz musicians.

21. For more on the history and effects of zoning and licensing changes in New York City in the period, see, for example, S. J. Makielski, Jr., *The Politics of Zoning: The New York Experience* (New York: Columbia University Press, 1966), 40–44. See also Department of Licenses of the City of New York, annual report, 1927, 8–9, cited in Peretti, *Nightclub City*, 65.

22. Peretti, *Nightclub City*, 156–67.

23. Scholars have conducted extensive explorations of the successes and failures of Prohibition. Michael Lerner recounts the massive lobbying efforts in New York in *Dry Manhattan: Prohibition New York City* (Cambridge, MA: Harvard University Press, 2009), 48; Lisa McGirr, *The War on Alcohol: Prohibition and the Rise of the American State* (New York: W.W. Norton, 2015), gives an account of how Prohibition served to massively expand the federal government's regulatory power.

24. Peretti, *Nightclub City*, 6. See also numerous newspaper reports on the local effects of federal raids; for example, "More Cabarets Face Padlocks: Clean-Up on Night Clubs on Broadway Continues," *Los Angeles Times*, August 3, 1928, 3.

25. Lerner, *Dry Manhattan*, 3, 53, 115; see also Ralph G. Giordano, *Satan in the Dance Hall: Rev. John Roach Straton, Social Dancing, and Morality in 1920s New York City* (Lanham, MD: Scarecrow Press, 2008), 13–14; Giordano discusses the way in which Prohibition was used to close the dance halls that moral reformers also viewed as evils of the times.

26. Clement, *Love for Sale*, 107–10.

27. Mackey, *Pursuing Johns*, recounts the role of the Committee of Fourteen in prostitution reform in the 1920s, especially the committee's failed attempts to prosecute male customers through "the customer amendment."

28. Ibid., 42–43.

29. Clement, *Love for Sale*, 108–10; Peretti, *Nightclub City*, 30. For more on the changes in prostitution surrounding World War I, see also Timothy J. Gilfoyle, "Prostitutes in History: From Parables of Pornography to Metaphors of Modernity," *American Historical Review* 104, no. 1 (1999): 117–41; and Rosen, *The Lost Sisterhood*.

30. Clement notes that these broader trends created a racial inequality in sex work that persists today, as most burlesques and taxi dance halls would only hire white women. These at least quasi-legal forms of sex work drove prostitution even further into the margins and exposed nonwhite women to greater risk of violence and arrest and less remuneration. Clement, *Love for Sale*, 9, 178.

31. For a personal account of the development of high-end, domestically housed sex work, see Polly Adler, *A House Is Not a Home* (New York: Rinehart, 1953). Adler was a madam to the wealthy, and she was especially elusive to authorities.

32. See Peretti, *Nightclub City*, esp. chap. 2, "The Hostess Evil."

33. Case 1302, Trial Transcript Project, John Jay College of Criminal Justice, New York City, quoted in Clement, *Love for Sale*, 110.

34. Kathy Peiss notes working-class women's preference for fashion tones more associated with prostitutes than the upper class as early as the turn of the twentieth century in *Cheap Amusements: Working Women and Leisure in Turn-of-the-Century New York* (Philadelphia: Temple University Press, 1986), esp. chap. 3, "Putting on Style."

35. For more on the role of fashion in New York City, see Cheryl Buckley and Hazel Clark, *Fashion and Everyday Life: London and New York* (London: Bloomsbury, 2017). For a

discussion of the meaning of flapper dress and discourse, see, for example, Kenneth Yellis, "Prosperity's Child: Some Thoughts on the Flapper," *American Quarterly* 21, no. 1 (1969): 44–64.

36. Personal Description Cards, 1927–32, box 50, Committee of Fourteen records, New York Public Library.

37. "In Our Pages: 100, 75 and 50 Years Ago; 1930: Police Linked to Graft," *International Herald Tribune* (Paris), November 28, 2005, 2. See also Mackey, *Pursuing Johns*, 31–34.

38. These findings are summarized in Kevin Mumford, *Interzones: Black/White Sex Districts in Chicago and New York in the Early Twentieth Century* (New York: Columbia University Press, 1997), 82; and supported other studies, including John D'Emilio and Estelle B. Freedman, *Intimate Matters: A History of Sexuality in America* (New York: Harper & Row, 1988).

39. Chauncey, *Gay New York*, esp. introduction and chap. 4.

40. Local reports frequently recounted "the nightclub mayor's" outfits. See, for example, "Mr. Walker's Gay Togs Had Early Rivals," *New York Times*, October 2, 1927, sect. 8, p. 22; and "Talk of the Town," *New Yorker*, June 2, 1928, 20–21. For more on Mayor Jimmy Walker, see Gene Fowler, *Beau James: The Life and Times of Jimmy Walker* (New York: Viking, 1949).

41. Peretti, *Nightclub City*, 167.

42. Emory S. Bogardus, "Exploring for the Causes of Crime," *Journal of Social Forces* 3, no. 3 (1925): 464–66; C. E. Gehlke, "Crime," *American Journal of Sociology* 34, no. 1 (1928): 157–71; Harry M. Shulman, "Crime Prevention and the Public Schools," *Journal of Educational Sociology* 4, no. 2 (1930): 69–81; Peretti, *Nightclub City*, 46–47; see also Potter, *War on Crime*.

43. Anti-homosexual media aimed at young boys included television commercials, such as *Boys Beware* (Sid Davis Productions, produced with the cooperation of the Inglewood Police Department and the Inglewood Unified School District, 1961), Prelinger Archives, online video clip, accessed April 29, 2020, https://archive.org/details/boys_beware. The PSA warns boys of the undue interest from and corrupting influence of older gay men.

44. George Chauncey details Malin's career, including his brief and confusing-to-many marriage the same month as the Club Abbey violence. Malin died in a car accident on August 10, 1933. See Chauncey, *Gay New York*, esp. chap. 11, "'Pansies on Parade': Prohibition and the Spectacle of the Pansy."

45. Vogel, *The Scene of Harlem Cabaret*, 12–19.

46. Langston Hughes, *The Big Sea: An Autobiography* (New York: Farrar, Straus and Giroux, 2015), 273; Vogel, *The Scene of Harlem Cabaret*, 19. See also Mumford, *Interzones*; and Eric Garber, "A Spectacle in Color: The Lesbian and Gay Subculture of Jazz Age Harlem," in *Hidden from History: Reclaiming the Gay and Lesbian Past*, ed. Martin B. Duberman, Martha Vicinus, and George Chauncey, Jr. (New York: New American Library, 1989), 318–31.

47. "Drastic Police Curb Put on Night Clubs: Many Face Closing," *New York Times*, July 21, 1931, 1.

48. U.S. Congress, House Committee on Interstate and Foreign Commerce, *Motion-Picture Films: Hearing Before a Subcommittee . . . on Bills to Prohibit and to Prevent the Trade Practices Known as "Compulsory Block-Booking" and "Blind Selling" in the Leasing of Motion Picture Films in Interstate and Foreign Commerce*, 74th Cong., 2nd sess. (Washington, DC: Government Printing Office, 1936), 21.

49. For an account of the rise and decline of burlesque, see Robert Allen, *Horrible Prettiness: Burlesque and American Culture* (Chapel Hill: University of North Carolina Press, 1991). For a broader account of striptease, see Rachel Shteir, *Striptease: The Untold History of the Girlie Show* (New York: Oxford University Press, 2004); see also Peretti, *Nightclub City*, 117–19.

50. Allen, *Horrible Prettiness*, 255–58; "Burlesque Again Purified," Topics of the Times, *New York Times*, May 17, 1933, 16. For more on the motives for shuttering burlesques, see also Daniel Makagon, *Where the Ball Drops: Days and Nights in Times Square* (Minneapolis: University of Minnesota Press, 2004), 59–64.

51. H. I. Brock, "Now Our Night Life Glows Anew," *New York Times*, February 11, 1934, SM10; see also a later article reiterating the slightly checked fun, but also pointing out the persistence of a Prohibition-era "influence that has not yet been completely dislodged," Bosley Crowther, "New York's Night Life Burgeons Again," *New York Times*, February 24, 1935, SM9.

52. Eskridge, *Gaylaw*, 27; 1845 N.Y. Laws ch. 3, §6, amended by 1876 N.Y. Laws ch. 1 (codified at 1881 N.Y. Code Crim. Proc. §887[7]). According to Eskridge, the practice of allowing police permission follows European standards. See Angus McLaren, *The Trials of Masculinity: Policing Sexual Boundaries, 1870–1930* (Chicago: University of Chicago Press, 1997), 16–17.

53. Emilia Müller, "Fashion and Fancy in New York: Costume Balls of the Gilded Age," *Critical Studies in Fashion & Beauty* 3, no. 1 (2012): 17–38.

54. Eskridge, *Gaylaw*, 27–28.

55. Peretti, *Nighclub City*, 167. Chauncey recounts the various groups involved, especially right before the 1939 New York World's Fair, including army officers. See Chauncey, *Gay New York*, 339–54.

56. Stanley Walker, *The Night Club Era* (New York: Frederick A. Stokes, 1933), 205; Peretti, *Nightclub City*, 116.

57. For more on stage censorship of non-gender-conforming dress, see Laura Horak, *Girls Will Be Boys: Cross-Dressed Women, Lesbians, and American Cinema, 1908–1934* (New Brunswick, NJ: Rutgers University Press, 2016).

58. Black, *Hollywood Censored*; Doherty, *Hollywood's Censor*.

59. For more on the 1933 film *So This Is Africa* as an illuminating code example, see Francis G. Couvares, "So This Is Censorship: Race, Sex, and Censorship in Movies of the 1920s and 1930s," *Journal of American Studies* 45, no. 3 (2011): 581–97. On lesbian and gay themes in film under the Hollywood code, see Lugowski, "Queering the (New) Deal"; and on the code's specifications of dress as they intersected with race, see Scott, "More Than a 'Passing' Sophistication."

60. For more on the economic motives of the Hays Code, see Doherty, *Hollywood's Censor*, 78–80.

61. "Text of Mulrooney's Review of Year of Liquor," *New York Times*, December 5, 1934, 15.

62. "Liquor Fees Here Total $6,519,485," *New York Times*, October 6, 1934, 17.

63. "New York Police Ban 'Pansies' in Nite Clubs."

64. "Drastic Police Curb Put on Night Clubs"; for more on Adler's legally elusive sex work services, see Peretti, *Nightclub City*, 41–45, 139–42, 159–60.

65. Peretti, *Nightclub City*, 41–43, 68.

66. Histories of the evolution of the role of bouncer in this period remain anecdotal, as do tales about the role of nightclub owners in resisting anti-homosexual laws. See Dick

Hobbs, Philip Hadfield, Stuart Lister, and Simon Winlow, *Bouncers: Violence and Governance in the Night-Time Economy* (Oxford: Oxford University Press, 2003). For more comprehensive details about how the mafia in New York City and Chicago operated to protect clubs allowing gay nightlife, see Phillip Crawford, *The Mafia and the Gays* ([Middletown, DE]: CreateSpace Independent Publishing Platform, 2015); C. Alexander Hortis and James B. Jacobs, *The Mob and the City: The Hidden History of How the Mafia Captured New York* (Amherst, NY: Prometheus Books, 2014); Carter, *Stonewall*; Peretti, *Nightclub City*, 178.

67. Edward P. Mulrooney, "As the Police See It: New York Police Commissioner, in an Address to the Bond Club," *New York Times*, April 3, 1932, XX2.

68. For material descriptions of speakeasies, see Committee of Fourteen, June 25, 1924, meeting minutes, box 35, C14, Committee of Fourteen record, New York Public Library; Herbert Asbury, *The Great Illusion: An Informal History of Prohibition* (1953; repr. New York: Greenwood, 1968), 228; Peretti, *Nightclub City*, 11.

69. Mulrooney, "As the Police See It"; "Temperance Chief Goal; Mulrooney Also Aims to End Bootlegging and Speakeasies; Drinking at Tables Only," *New York Times*, November 10, 1933, 1.

70. "Temperance Chief Goal," 1; Peretti, *Nightclub City*, 95–96.

71. Peretti details the material changes in clubs, as well as the linguistic shift. See Peretti, *Nightclub City*, 174–76.

72. Reported in *New York Times*, July 4, 1926, 3. Quoted in Peretti, *Nightclub City*, ix.

73. For details on the late 1930s crackdown on bars tolerant of homosexuals, see Chauncey, *Gay New York*, 331–54.

74. Lerner, *Dry Manhattan*, 2.

75. Peretti, *Nightclub City*, 65.

Chapter 7

Epigraphs: William Huston, security chief, Boise Cascade; Loren Siegel, ACLU attorney; George H. W. Bush; from "Quotelines," *USA Today*, April 19, 1990.

1. Kevin Brass, "Firms Hire Detectives to Stem Drug Abuse," *Los Angeles Times*, September 8, 1987, in Vertical File–Drugs, 1980s, Walter P. Reuther Library of Labor and Urban Affairs, Detroit, Michigan (hereafter RVF-D80s).

2. See Michelle Alexander, *The New Jim Crow: Mass Incarceration in the Age of Colorblindness* (New York: New Press, 2012); Kathleen Frydl, *The Drug Wars in America, 1940–1973* (Cambridge: Cambridge University Press, 2013); Julilly Kohler-Hausmann, "'The Attila the Hun Law': New York's Rockefeller Drug Laws and the Making of a Punitive State," *Journal of Social History* 44, no. 1 (2010): 71–95; Heather Ann Thompson, "Why Mass Incarceration Matters: Rethinking Crisis, Decline, and Transformation in Postwar American History," *Journal of American History* 97, no. 3 (2010): 703–34; Donna Murch, "Crack in Los Angeles: Crisis, Militarization, and Black Response to the Late Twentieth-Century War on Drugs," *Journal of American History* 102, no. 1 (2015): 162–73.

3. Executive Order 12564 of September 15, 1986, Drug-Free Federal Workplace, https://www.archives.gov/federal-register/codification/executive-order/12564.html.

4. Harry Levine and Craig Reinarman, "What's Behind 'Jar Wars,'" *Nation*, March 28, 1987, 388–90.

5. William Hoffer, "Business' War on Drugs," *Nation's Business*, October 1986, 19.

6. Ibid., 22.

7. Stuart D. Brandes, *American Welfare Capitalism, 1880–1940* (Chicago: University of Chicago Press, 1976), 98–102; Margaret Crawford, *Building the Workingman's Paradise: The Design of American Company Towns* (New York: Verso, 1995); Niki Mandell, *The Corporation as Family: The Gendering of Corporate Welfare, 1890–1930* (Chapel Hill: University of North Carolina Press, 2002), 115–30; Daniel M. G. Raff, "Ford Welfare Capitalism in Its Economic Context," in *Masters to Managers: Historical and Comparative Perspectives on American Employers*, ed. Sanford Jacoby (New York: Columbia University Press, 1991), 90–110.

8. Elizabeth A. Brown, "The Fitbit Fault Line: Two Proposals to Protect Health and Fitness Data at Work," *Yale Journal of Health Policy, Law, & Ethics* 16, no.1 (Winter 2016): 1–49.

9. Ifeoma Ajunwa, Kate Crawford, and Jason Schultz, "Limitless Worker Surveillance," *California Law Review* 105 (2017): 735–76; Scott D'Urso, "Who's Watching Us at Work? Toward a Structural-Perceptual Model of Electronic Monitoring and Surveillance in Organizations," *Communication Theory* 16, no. 3 (2006): 281–303; John Gilliom, *Surveillance, Privacy, and the Law* (Ann Arbor: University of Michigan Press, 1994); Steven L. Nock, *The Costs of Privacy: Surveillance and Reputation in America* (New York: Walter de Gruyter, 1993); Graham Sewell, "Organizations, Employees, and Surveillance," in *Routledge Handbook of Surveillance Studies*, ed. Kirstie Ball, Kevin D. Haggerty, and David Lyon (London: Routledge, 2012), 303–12.

10. Kirstie Ball, "The Labours of Surveillance," *Surveillance Studies* 1, no. 2 (2003): 125–37; and Ball, "Workplace Surveillance: An Overview," *Labor History* 51, no. 1 (2010): 87–106; Karen Levy, "The Contexts of Control: Information, Power, and Truck-Driving Work," *Information Society* 31, no. 2 (2015): 160–74; Shoshana Zuboff, *In the Age of the Smart Machine* (New York: Basic Books, 1988).

11. Shoshana Zuboff, *The Age of Surveillance Capitalism: The Fight for a Human Future at the New Frontier of Power* (New York: PublicAffairs, 2019), 157–58.

12. Agis Salpukas, "Workers' Use of Drugs Widespread in Nation," *New York Times*, June 21, 1971; on the creation of fears about the return home of heroin-addicted Vietnam veterans, see Jeremy Kuzmarov, *The Myth of the Addicted Army: Vietnam and the Modern War on Drugs* (Amherst: University of Massachusetts Press, 2009).

13. "R. Brinkley Smithers: Gave Millions for Alcoholism Research," *Los Angeles Times*, January 15, 1994. Smithers reportedly resigned from his position at IBM because it "interfered with his . . . drinking."

14. Leo Perlis, "The Broad Brush, Employee Assistance, Troubled Employee Programs—or What Happened to Alcoholism?," box 33, file 14, UAW Women's Department Collection, Reuther Library.

15. Harrison Trice and Paul Roman, *Spirits and Demons at Work: Alcohol and Other Drugs on the Job* (Ithaca, NY: New York State School of Industrial Relations, 1978), 36–37.

16. "General Motors Employe Alcoholism Recovery Program," box 123, file 4, UAW Region 1 Collection, Reuther Library.

17. William White, *Slaying the Dragon: The History of Addiction Treatment and Recovery in America* (Granite City, IL: Chestnut Health Systems, 1998), 282–83.

18. Salpukas, "Workers' Use of Drugs."

19. *Drug Use Among Workers: Developing Policies and Guidelines* ([Albany]: New York State Drug Abuse Control Commission and Provide Addict Care Today, 1975), pp. 9–10, in

box 42.1, file 61, Harrison Trice Additional Papers, Kheel Center for Labor-Management Documentation and Archives, Cornell University, Ithaca, New York.

20. Ibid., 30–31

21. Ibid., 33.

22. Kenneth D. Tunnell, *Pissing on Demand: Workplace Drug Testing and the Rise of the Detox Industry* (New York: New York University Press, 2004), 15; Robert Reinhold, "Congressman Says Most Killed in Nimitz Crash Showed Traces of Drugs," *New York Times*, June 17, 1981; Irvin Molotsky, "Tests Indicate a Decline in Drug Use in Navy," *New York Times*, September 19, 1982.

23. For an authoritative contemporary critique of these studies, see Craig Reinarman, Dan Waldorf, and Sheigla B. Murphy, "Scapegoating and Social Control in the Social Construction of a Public Problem," *Research in Law, Deviance, and Social Control* 9 (1987): 37–62.

24. Hoffer, "Business' War on Drugs," 19, 22.

25. Ibid., 26.

26. Courtland Milloy, "The Need for Drug Testing," *Washington Post*, January 6, 1987.

27. Howard Kurtz, "Employer Drug 'Surveillance' Urged," *Washington Post*, October 31, 1986.

28. Tunnell, *Pissing on Demand*, 2.

29. Reinarman, Waldorf, and Murphy, "Scapegoating and Social Control," 51. Quayle's quote originally appeared in *American Psychologist*.

30. Milt Freudenheim, "Workers' Substance Abuse Is Increasing, Survey Says," *New York Times*, December 12, 1988.

31. Helaine Olen, "Drug Users Seeking Jobs Turning to Small Firms," *Los Angeles Times*, May 2, 1991.

32. J. Thomas Menaker, "Drug Screening: Protecting the Employer and the Employee," *Cornell ILR Report*, Spring 1986, box 42.1, file 65, Harrison Trice Additional Papers, Kheel Center, p. 20.

33. Henry Weinstein, "Drug Tests: Privacy vs. Job Rights," *Los Angeles Times*, October 26, 1986, RVF-D80s.

34. DuPont quoted in Elizabeth Symonds, "Round 2: The Case Against Drug Testing," *Washington Post*, April 30, 1989, RVF-D80s. DuPont, a former senior government drug adviser, also called for warehousing those with several drug test positives. In 2018, he advised Attorney General Jeff Sessions, sparking complaints that he stands to benefit financially from any expansion of the drug testing he continues to advocate. See Chloe Aiello, "Advisor to Jeff Sessions Calls for Mandatory Drug Testing Amid Increasing Marijuana Legalization," CNBC, January 3, 2018, https://www.cnbc.com/2018/01/03/sessions-advisor-calls-for-mandatory-drug-testing-as-states-legalize.html.

35. Letter from Tom Delaney to the *Albany Times Union*, July 6, 1989, box 3, Harrison Trice Additional Papers, Kheel Center.

36. Luc Boltanski and Eve Chiapello, *The New Spirit of Capitalism*, 2nd English ed. (London: Verso Books, 2018); Steven L. Nock, *The Costs of Privacy: Surveillance and Reputation in America* (Berlin: Walter de Gruyter, 1993).

37. Ulrich Beck, *Risk Society: Towards A New Modernity* (London: Sage, 1992); Anthony Giddens, "Risk and Responsibility," *Modern Law Review* 62, no. 1 (1999): 1–10; John Sherry, "The Management of Blue Collar Alcoholism: An Ethnography of an Industrial Containment System" (Ph.D. diss., University of Notre Dame, 1983).

38. U.S. Congress, Senate, Committee on the Judiciary, *Drug Testing in the Workplace: Hearings*, 100th Cong., 1st sess. (Washington, DC: Government Printing Office, 1989), 48–49.

39. Ibid., 51.

40. Luc Boltanski and Eve Chiapello, *The New Spirit of Capitalism*, 2nd English ed. (London: Verso Books, 2018).

41. Menaker, "Drug Screening," 18: "the growing legal risks of 'unjust dismissal,' and the need for hard evidence before imposing strong discipline. Depending upon a variety of circumstances, scientific drug screening may help provide the employer with such hard evidence and relieve the managers' frustration. It may also serve to clear certain employees of unwarranted suspicion."

42. "Four Million Tests," *Washington Post*, November 16, 1988, RFV-D.

43. Philip Weiss, "Watch Out," *Harper's*, June 1986, 57.

44. U.S. Congress, Senate, Committee on the Judiciary, *Drug Testing in the Workplace*, 179.

45. Elizabeth Kolbert, "Test of Teachers for Use of Drugs Is Ruled Illegal," *New York Times*, June 10, 1987, RVF-D80s.

46. U.S. Congress, Senate, Committee on the Judiciary, *Drug Testing in the Workplace*, 156.

47. Michael Abramowitz and Martha H. Hamilton, "Drug Testing on Rise," *Washington Post*, September 21, 1986, D4.

48. "Researcher Resigns U.S. Post After Performing Fake Tests," *New York Times*, June 13, 1987.

49. Thomas H. Maugh II, "Soaring Demand Erodes Drug-Test Labs Efficiency," *Los Angeles Times*, October 28, 1986, RVF-D80s.

50. Tunnell, *Pissing on Demand*, 20.

51. Chris Spolar, "When Privacy and Company Prerogatives Clash," *Washington Post*, December 5, 1988, RVF-D80s.

52. Brass, "Firms Hire Detectives."

53. Tracy Kaplan and Phil Sneiderman, "Companies Cracking Down on Drugs Turn to Undercover Spies," *Los Angeles Times*, April 13, 1990, Vertical File–Drugs, 1990s, Walter P. Reuther Library of Labor and Urban Affairs, Detroit, Michigan (hereafter RVF-D90s).

54. Bureau of National Affairs, *Alcohol and Drugs in the Workplace: Costs, Controls, and Controversies* (Washington, DC: BNA, 1986), 88, box 42.1, file 66, Harrison Trice Additional Papers, Kheel Center.

55. Greg Johnson, "New Twist on Testing Job Impairment," *Philadelphia Inquirer*, undated, RVF-D90s.

56. Bureau of National Affairs, *Alcohol and Drugs in the Workplace*, 129.

57. Jon Lowell, "No Quick Fix: Prohibition Hits the Auto Industry," *Ward's Auto World*, June 1988, 34; Gilliom, *Surveillance, Privacy, and the Law*, 77–82.

58. Gilliom, *Surveillance, Privacy, and the Law*, 85–130; Tunnell, *Pissing on Demand*, 10–12.

59. Tunnell, *Pissing on Demand*, 10–12.

60. Joseph B. Treaster, "For Transit Union, A Change of Heart on Drug Testing," *New York Times*, August 30, 1991, RVF-D90s.

61. Speech by Victoria L. Frankovich, "1987: A Year to Celebrate Freedom or the Arrival of the Dreaded 'Big Brother' Society?," box 42.1, file 54, Harrison Trice Additional Papers, Kheel Center.

62. Tunnell, *Pissing on Demand*, 24.

63. Chris Spolar, "An Off-Duty User's Fate," *Washington Post*, December 4, 1988. Kelley used marijuana off the job but was still fired.

64. Lowell, "No Quick Fix," 35.

65. BCC Research, "Drug Testing Industry Sees Steady Expansion," *Globe Newswire*, June 15, 2017, https://globenewswire.com/news-release/2017/06/15/1024596/0/en/Drug-Testing-Industry-Sees-Steady-Expansion.html.

66. Abbie Hoffman, *Steal This Urine Test* (New York: Penguin Books, 1987), 159.

67. Nock, *Costs of Privacy*, vii.

68. This dovetails with Ball's argument regarding employer's motivations in "Workplace Surveillance."

69. Bureau of National Affairs, *Alcohol and Drugs in the Workplace*, 44.

70. Ibid., 129.

71. Paul M. Roman, "Fighting the War on Drugs," *Employee Assistance* 1, no. 3 (October 1988): 33, in box 32, file 16, Irving Bluestone Papers, Reuther Library.

72. On this shift, see White, *Slaying the Dragon*, 285. White argues that, in addition to a "financial backlash," EAPs were challenged by "an era of federal drug control policy that dramatically shifted the public emphasis from treatment and research to law enforcement. It was in this broader de-valuation of treatment, 'zero tolerance' of drug users, and re-criminalization of addiction that more specific attacks of the conceptual foundation of treatment occurred."

73. Brown, "The Fitbit Fault Line," 5.

Chapter 8

1. Stephanie Strom, "Billboard Owners Switching, Not Fighting," *New York Times*, April 4, 1990, B1, B4.

2. Ibid.

3. Joel Dreyfuss, "Harlem's Ardent Voice" *New York Times*, January 20, 1991. Indeed, billboard advertising was an issue across the urban United States. In 1990, a Baltimore survey found where 76 percent of billboards in black communities featured tobacco products, white neighborhoods had both fewer billboards and fewer tobacco advertisements, sitting at 20 percent. See Michael Quinn, "Don't Aim That Pack at Us," *Time*, January 29, 1990, 60. Similar actions took place across the United States throughout the early 1990s, including on Chicago's South Side, where Henry McNeil Brown, Jr., a court reporter, worked under the alias "Mandrake," whitewashing billboards advertising tobacco and alcohol as well. "Fighting Ads in the Inner City: A Grass-Roots Battle Against 'Minority Marketing,'" *Newsweek*, February 8, 1990, 18; Kenan Heise, "Henry McNeil Brown, 61, Activist," *Chicago Tribune*, September 28, 1996.

4. In framing marketing as a kind of race work, I am drawing on the work of historians of race and political economy such as Thomas Holt and Barbara and Karen Fields, who in tracing the reproduction of racial ideology across epochal economic shifts, point us toward an essential question: what "work" does race do for/in different formations of capitalism? See

Thomas C. Holt, *The Problem of Race in the 21st Century* (Cambridge, MA: Harvard University Press, 2000); Karen Fields and Barbara Fields, *Racecraft: The Soul of Inequality* (New York: Verso, 2014).

5. "MRD Research Proposal (MRD#88-41106): Project Delta Exploratory Focus Groups and In-Depth Interviews," September 19, 1989, RJ Reynolds Records, Industry Documents Library, University of California, San Francisco, accessed January 28, 2018, https://www.industrydocumentslibrary.ucsf.edu/tobacco/docs/tzck0081.

6. Vance Packard, *The Naked Society* (New York: David McKay, 1964); "If You've Got a Name and an Address, You're on Somebody's List," *News Front*, January 1970, J. Walter Thompson, Chicago Information Center Flash, February 13, 1970, J. Walter Thompson Collection, Rubinstein Library, Duke University. On consumer surveillance in the 1980s, see Josh Lauer, *Creditworthy: A History of Consumer Surveillance and Financial Identity in America* (New York: Columbia University Press, 2017), 242–68; on direct mail marketing and consumer data collection, see Andrew N. Case, "'The Solid Gold Mailbox': Direct Mail and the Changing Nature of Buying and Selling in the Postwar United States," *History of Retailing and Consumption* 1, no. 1 (2015): 28–46.

7. V. J. Dallaire, "U.S. Negro Growing Market Growing Target for Advertisers," *Printers Ink* 252 (1955): 52–62.

8. Elspeth H. Brown, "Black Models and the Invention of the U.S. 'Negro Market,' 1945–1960," in *Inside Marketing*, ed. Detlev Zwick and Julien Cayla (New York: Oxford University Press, 2011), 185–211; Jason Chambers, *Madison Avenue and the Color Line: African Americans in the Advertising Industry* (Philadelphia: University of Pennsylvania Press, 2008).

9. Gehrmann Holland, "A Study of Ethnic Markets," September 1969, Joe Camel Collection, Industry Documents Library, accessed February 15, 2019, https://www.industrydocuments.ucsf.edu/docs/rnvv0095.

10. Ibid.

11. Ibid.

12. Ibid.

13. Ibid.; emphasis in original.

14. The Last Drag," *Newsweek*, January 4, 1971, 65. "For good measure," reported *Newsweek*, Congress had decided "to permit traditional, heavy cigarette sponsorship of the bowl games." In a recognition of the end of an advertising tradition, Philip Morris pushed "hard to score last-minute points," buying "fifteen and a half minutes of bowl-game time (at up to $135,000 a minute); pre-midnight minutes of network commercial time on all three late night talk shows (at $5,000 to $18,000 per), and a minute on the CBS movie." With the end of what was then a "$215 million in annual ad revenues" relationship between the three major broadcast networks and tobacco corporations, *Newsweek* surmised that nonbroadcast media would "absorb 40 to 50 per cent of the TV advertising dollar; newspapers can look forward to doubling or quadrupling their $16 million dollar share of the action, while cigarette advertising on billboards may leap from $2 million to as much as $40 million."

15. Ibid.

16. Ibid.

17. Thomas Whiteside, *Selling Death* (New York: Liveright, 1971).

18. Thomas Whiteside, "Selling Death," *New Republic*, March 27, 1971, 15–17.

19. John H. Johnson, "Why Negroes Buy Cadillacs," *Ebony*, September 1946; John H. Johnson, "Does Your Sales Force Know How to Sell the Negro Trade? Some Dos and Don'ts,"

Advertising Age, March 17, 1952, 73–75; Joseph T. Johnson, *The Potential Negro Market* (New York: Pageant Press, 1952); *Ebony and Jet Magazines Present the Urban Negro Market for Liquors, Wines and Beers*, studies 1 and 2 (Chicago: Johnson Publications, 1953–54). For sales films, see Chambers, *Madison Avenue and the Color Line*, 43. On visual strategy, see Brenna Greer, *Represented: The Black Imagemakers Who Reimagined African American Citizenship* (Philadelphia: University of Pennsylvania Press, 2019).

20. R. Cooper and B. E. Simmons, "Cigarette Smoking and Ill Health Among Black Americans," *New York State Journal of Medicine* 85 (1985): 344–49.

21. Judann Dagnoli, "Reynolds Smolders; Saatchi Dismissal Prompts Look at All Agencies," *Advertising Age*, April 11, 1988, 1.

22. Ibid.

23. "1988 Constituent Organization Annual Report," January 5, 1989, Philip Morris Records, Industry Documents Library, accessed January 25, 2018, https://www.industrydocuments.ucsf.edu/docs/zymj0045; G. L. Smith, "September Report," October 11, 1990, Philip Morris Records, accessed January 25, 2018, https://www.industrydocumentslibrary.ucsf.edu/tobacco/docs/sxbw0124.

24. Richard C. Nordine, "Summary of Black/Hispanic Research," Marketing Development Department, R. J. Reynolds Tobacco Company, December 20, 1985, Joe Camel Collection, accessed January 25, 2018, https://www.industrydocumentslibrary.ucsf.edu/tobacco/docs/tmpg0097.

25. John T. Winebrenner, "Special Efforts for Special Markets," July 21, 1988, RJ Reynolds Records, accessed January 25, 2018, https://www.industrydocumentslibrary.ucsf.edu/tobacco/docs/jtvl0094.

26. Ibid.

27. Ibid.

28. Ibid.

29. Nordine, "Summary of Black/Hispanic Research."

30. Ibid.

31. Addendum Proposal: "Inner City Black Tracker," 1989, RJ Reynolds Records, accessed January 25, 2018, https://www.industrydocuments.ucsf.edu/docs/kthk0023.

32. Gloria Eskridge and Tammie Greene, "Project Delta—Suggestions," September 14, 1988, RJ Reynolds Records, accessed January 25, 2018, https://www.industrydocuments.ucsf.edu/docs/rrkg0087.

33. Ibid.

34. "MRD Research Proposal."

35. "Project Delta" notes, 1989, RJ Reynolds Records, accessed January 23, 2018, https://www.industrydocuments.ucsf.edu/docs/xppg0087.

36. Ibid.

37. Ibid.

38. J. T. Winebrenner to L. J. Breininger, "RE: Project Delta," March 2, 1989, RJ Reynolds Records, accessed January 23, 2018, https://www.industrydocuments.ucsf.edu/docs/zxm10092.

39. Kelvin Wall, "Black Young Adult Smoker Profile," November 28, 1988, RJ Reynolds Records, accessed January 25, 2018, https://www.industrydocuments.ucsf.edu/docs/gyyl0092.

40. Ibid.

41. Ibid.

42. Leber Katz, "Project UT Photography Pre-Production," June 7, 1989, RJ Reynolds Records, accessed February 15, 2018, https://www.industrydocuments.ucsf.edu/docs/gpyl0092.

43. Ibid.

44. "Government Relations/PR Plan Project UT," 1989, RJ Reynolds Records, accessed January 13, 2018, https://www.industrydocuments.ucsf.edu/docs/kfck0084.

45. Ibid.

46. Ibid.

47. Ibid.

48. Judann Dagnoli, "RJR's New Smokes Look Uptown," *Advertising Age,* June 6, 1990, 6.

49. No title, *Philadelphia New Observer,* 1990, cited in Sutton, "The Coalition Against Uptown Cigarettes: Marketing Practices and Community Mobilization," November 29, 1993. Reprinted at *Daily Kos,* August 26, 2013, accessed January 23, 2018, https://www.dailykos.com/stories/2013/8/26/1233917/-Musings-From-My-Mom-The-Coalition-Against-Uptown-Cigarettes.

50. For example, not a half-mile from City Hall, Philadelphia's Ridge Avenue was saturated with Newport billboards standing between and in front of buildings, while storefronts were plastered with the brand's paraphernalia and other product lines. "In Philadelphia, R. J. Reynolds Made All the Wrong Moves," *Adweek,* January 25, 1990, 8.

51. Cited in Charyn Sutton, "The Coalition Against Uptown Cigarettes: Marketing Practices and Community Mobilization," November 29, 1993.

52. Ibid.

53. Ibid.

54. Quoted in Anthony Ramirez, "A Cigarette Campaign Under Fire," *New York Times,* January 12, 1990, D1.

55. Dan Blake, "Uptown: Downtown, They Want No Part of It," *Philadelphia Tribune,* January 26, 1990, 7A; "Philadelphians Want Tobacco Company to Avoid Other Cities," *Chicago Defender,* January 27, 1990, 8.

56. Anthony Ramirez, "A Cigarette Campaign Under Fire," *New York Times,* January 12, 1990, D1.

57. Ibid.

58. Sutton, "The Coalition Against Uptown Cigarettes."

59. "Dr. Sullivan's Unfiltered Anger," *New York Times,* January 21, 1990; Philip J. Hilts, "Health Chief Assails a Tobacco Producer for Aiming at Blacks," *New York Times,* January 19, 1990; Rick Christie, "RJR Unit Blasted for New Cigarette Aimed at Blacks," *Wall Street Journal,* January 19, 1990; Marlene Cimons, "New Cigarette Condemned by Health Secretary Marketing: Louis Sullivan Says the Promotion Campaign for a New R. J. Reynolds Brand Targeted to Blacks Is 'Slick and Sinister' and Promotes a 'Culture of Cancer,'" *Los Angeles Times,* January 19, 1990.

60. Referenced in Richard Pollay, Jung Sook Lee, and David Carter-Whitney, "Separate, But Not Equal: Racial Segmentation in Cigarette Advertising," *Journal of Advertising* 16 (1992): 45–57.

61. James R. Schiffman, "After Uptown, Are Some Niches Out?," *Wall Street Journal,* January 22, 1990, 3.

62. Steven Colford, "Ad-Bashing Is Back in Style," *Adweek*, April 30, 1990.

63. Howard Schlossberg, "Segmenting Becomes Constitutional Issue," *Marketing News*, April 16, 1990, 1.

64. Ibid.

65. Ibid.

66. "Anatomy of a Failure—Uptown Cigarettes," no date, Philip Morris Records, accessed January 25, 2018, https://www.industrydocumentslibrary.ucsf.edu/tobacco/docs /npjh0124.

67. Ibid.

68. Ibid.

69. Debra Goldman, "Census Data Poses Ethical Questions," *Adweek—Southwest Edition*, April 8, 1991, 1, 4.

70. Randall Rothenberg, "Blacks Are Found to Be Still Scarce in Advertisements in Major Magazines," *New York Times*, July 23, 1991, A18.

71. Ibid.

72. Caroline Jones, "Targeted Marketing, or Why Did Uptown Go Down in Flames?," undated, Caroline Jones Papers, series 2, subseries A, box 3, folder 30, Archives Center, National Museum of American History, Smithsonian Institution, Washington, DC.

73. Ibid.

74. Caroline Jones, "Daily News Opinions Column Draft," May 10, 1990, Caroline Jones Papers, series 2, box 4, folder 7.

75. Cigarettes editorial for *New York Daily News*, October 5, 1990, Caroline Jones Papers, series 2, subseries B, box 4, folder 7. Jones's claims were backed up by indexing data that suggested black consumers outstripped white buyers for Pan American Airlines, Busch Gardens, Beech-Nut infant cereal, and Florida Gold grapefruit juice. Advertising for each of these products had failed to feature black consumers.

76. National Association of African Americans for Positive Imagery, "African American Activists Seek End to Menthol Cigarettes in Civil Rights Lawsuit Against Tobacco Companies," news release, October 21, 1998.

77. Summary of MIP/RIP proposal, 1994, RJ Reynolds Records, accessed January 26, 2018, https://www.industrydocuments.ucsf.edu/docs/krdv0087.

78. Safiya Noble, *Algorithms of Oppression: How Search Engines Reinforce Racism* (New York: New York University Press, 2018); Ruha Benjamin, *Race After Technology: Abolitionist Tools for the New Jim Crow* (Cambridge: Polity, 2019).

Chapter 9

1. Shoshana Zuboff, *The Age of Surveillance Capitalism: The Fight for a Human Future at the New Frontier of Power* (New York: PublicAffairs, 2019).

2. Lisa Gitelman, ed., *"Raw Data" Is an Oxymoron* (Cambridge, MA: MIT Press, 2013).

3. Josh Lauer, "Surveillance History and the History of New Media: An Evidential Paradigm," *New Media & Society* 14, no. 4 (2012): 566–82, here 568.

4. Zuboff, *Age of Surveillance Capitalism*, 68 (quoting Kenneth Cukier, "New Rules for Big Data: Regulators are having to Rethink Their Brief," *Economist*, February 27, 2010, https:// www.economist.com/special-report/2010/02/27/new-rules-for-big-data).

5. Tim Wu, "How Capitalism Betrayed Privacy," *New York Times*, April 19, 2019, https://www.nytimes.com/2019/04/10/opinion/sunday/privacy-capitalism.html.

6. Tim Wu, *The Attention Merchants: The Epic Scramble to Get Inside Our Heads* (New York: Vintage, 2017).

7. Joseph Turow, *The Daily You: How the New Advertising Industry Is Defining Your Identity and Your Worth* (New Haven, CT: Yale University Press, 2012).

8. Julie Cohen, *Between Truth and Power: The Legal Constructions of Informational Capitalism* (New York: Oxford University Press, 2019).

9. Nick Couldry and Ulises A. Mejias, *The Costs of Connection: How Data Is Colonizing Human Life and Appropriating It for Capitalism* (Stanford, CA: Stanford University Press, 2019).

10. Paul Starr, *The Creation of the Media: Political Origins of Modern Communications* (New York: Basic Books, 2004), 5.

11. Ibid.

12. Launched in 1994.

13. One of the first businesses building commercial websites, cofounded in 1993 with Jonathan Nelson, Cliff Skolnick, and Matthew Nelson. "Everyone had a side hustle in those days." Brian Behlendorf, in discussion with the author, September 18, 2019.

14. Brian Behlendorf, "Session Tracking," www-talk electronic mailing list, April 17, 1995, https://lists.w3.org/Archives/Public/www-talk/1995MarApr/0456.html.

15. Ibid.

16. Lou Montulli, "Re: Session Tracking.," www-talk electronic mailing list, April 18, 1995, https://lists.w3.org/Archives/Public/www-talk/1995MarApr/0462.html.

17. Lou Montulli, "The Reasoning Behind Web Cookies," *The Irregular Musings of Lou Montulli*, May 14, 2013, https://montulli.blogspot.com/2013/05/the-reasoning-behind-web-cookies.html; John Schwartz, "Giving Web a Memory Cost Its Users Privacy," *New York Times*, September 4, 2001, https://www.nytimes.com/2001/09/04/business/giving-web-a-memory-cost-its-users-privacy.html.

18. Valerie Quercia and Tim O'Reilly, *X Window System User's Guide* (Sebastopol, CA: O'Reilly, 1988), appendix A, "System Management."

19. Brian Behlendorf, "Re: Session Tracking," www-talk electronic mailing list, April 18, 1995, https://lists.w3.org/Archives/Public/www-talk/1995MarApr/0468.html.

20. Quercia and O'Reilly, *X Window System User's Guide*.

21. Dave Kristol and Lou Montulli, "HTTP State Management Mechanism (RFC 2109)," Internet Engineering Task Force, February 1997, https://tools.ietf.org/html/rfc2109.

22. Marc Hedlund, "Re: Session-ID Redux," www-talk electronic mailing list, July 26, 1995, https://lists.w3.org/Archives/Public/www-talk/1995JulAug/0215.html.

23. Koen Holtman, "Session-ID and Privacy Mechanisms," www-talk electronic mailing list, July 22, 1995, http://1997.webhistory.org/www.lists/www-talk.1995q3/0158.html.

24. Koen Holtman, in discussion with author, August 12, 2019.

25. Robert Robbins, "Re: Session-ID and Privacy Mechanisms," www-talk electronic mailing list, July 22, 1995, http://1997.webhistory.org/www.lists/www-talk.1995q3/0157.html, July 26, 1995, http://1997.webhistory.org/www.lists/www-talk.1995q3/0207.html.

26. Brian Behlendorf, "Session-ID Redux," www-talk electronic mailing list, July 25, 1995, https://lists.w3.org/Archives/Public/www-talk/1995JulAug/0192.html.

27. Kevin O'Connor, interview by Brian McCullough, *Internet History Podcast*, June 23, 2014, http://www.internethistorypodcast.com/2014/06/co-founder-of-doubleclick-kevin-oconnor/.

28. Ibid.

29. Ibid.

30. Keith J. Kelly, "Millard Heading for Internet: Publishing Exec Hired by DoubleClick to Boost Brand," *Advertising Age*, August 19, 1996, 32.

31. Abbey Klaassen, "Fewer Than Six Degrees of Wenda Harris Millard," *Advertising Age*, April 27, 2008, 10.

32. Lisa Napoli, "DoubleClick Buys NetGravity," *New York Times*, July 14, 1999, https://archive.nytimes.com/www.nytimes.com/library/tech/99/07/cyber/articles/14advertising.html.

33. Others include Match Logic (bought and shuttered by Excite), 24/7 Media (merged with Real Media), AdForce and AdKnowledge (bought by CMGI), Avenue A, Burst Media (bought UK ad network OTP Media and sold to Blinkx, now RhythmOne), DoubleClick (bought by Google), and Engage (bought by CMGI).

34. Merged with 24/7 Media to become 24/7 Real Media in 2001 and was acquired by the British advertising firm WPP in 2007.

35. The Pennsylvania Newspaper Association and the Mid-Atlantic Newspaper Services, Inc.

36. Engage became a subsidiary of CMGI (which in the 1980s sold mailing lists of university faculty and librarians to educational and professional publishers) and together the companies acquired AdKnowledge, Flycast, and AdForce to complement CMGI's growing internet portfolio and incubator projects.

37. Julia Angwin, *Dragnet Nation: A Quest for Privacy, Security, and Freedom in a World of Relentless Surveillance* (New York: Times Books, 2014), 174–75.

38. Gil Beyda, in discussion with author, September 24, 2019.

39. Martin Nisenholtz, "How to Market on the 'Net: Simple Rules of the Road Will Help Advertisers Think Before They Leap," *Advertising Age*, July 11, 1994, 28.

40. Andrew N. Case, "The Solid Gold Mailbox: Direct Mail and the Changing Nature of Buying and Selling in the Postwar United States," *History of Retailing and Consumption* 1, no. 1 (2015): 28–46; "Address and List Management, Data Processing and Software, and Document Management," *Smithsonian National Postal Museum*, https://postalmuseum.si.edu/exhibition/america's-mailing-industry-industry-segments/address-and-list-management-data-processing.

41. Michael W. Miller, "Firms Peddle Information from Driver's Licenses," *Wall Street Journal*, November 25, 1991, B1.

42. John Markoff, "More Threats to Privacy Seen as Computer Links Broaden," *New York Times*, June 1, 1988, A1.

43. Caroline Jack, "Circulating Database Marketing in the 1990s U.S. Business Press" (2019, under review, on file with author); Laura J. Gurak, *Persuasion and Privacy in Cyberspace: The Online Protests over Lotus MarketPlace and the Clipper Chip* (New Haven, CT: Yale University Press, 1999).

44. Evan I. Schwartz, "Advertising Webonomics 101," *Wired*, February 1, 1996, https://www.wired.com/1996/02/webonomics-2/.

45. Peter H. Lewis, "An Ad (Gasp!) in Cyberspace," *New York Times*, April 19, 1994, D1.

46. Behlendorf, "Session Tracking," www-talk electronic mailing list, April 17, 1995.

47. Nisenholtz, "How to Market on the 'Net."

48. Ibid.

49. Privacy policies on the web still have an unclear origin, as do terms of service. Although copyright policies are found on many sites preserved from the 1990s, the oldest privacy policy, as we think of them today, I found by digging in the Internet Archive was on the Warner Bros. website between April 6 and April 15, 1997. Between those dates a "Legal/Privacy Information About This Site" was added to the site. The privacy portion states, "As a general policy, no personal information is automatically collected from visitors to its sites nor is so-called 'cookie' technology used by the sites created by WB Online." Warner Bros., "Terms of Use," April 15, 1997, https://web.archive.org/web/19970415184347/warnerbros.com /terms.html. AOL's first privacy policy appears between fall 1997 and April 25, 1998. Netscape and Wired post privacy policy between spring and December 1998, and Yahoo! between spring and June 1998.

50. Tim Jackson, "This Bug in Your PC Is a Smart Cookie," *Financial Times*, February 12, 1996, 15.

51. Ibid.

52. Lou Montulli, "Re: Session Tracking," www-talk electronic mailing list, April 20, 1995, https://lists.w3.org/Archives/Public/www-talk/1995MarApr/0503.html.

53. Dave Kristol, "HTTP Cookies: Standards, Privacy, and Politics," *ACM Transactions on Internet Technology* 1, no. 2 (November 2001): 151–98.

54. Dave Kristol and Lou Montulli, "Proposed HTTP State Management Mechanism (Internet Draft)," Internet Engineering Task Force, February 16, 1996, https://web.archive.org /web/19990429122709/http://portal.research.bell-labs.com/~dmk/cookie-2.3.txt.

55. Ibid., February 19, 1996, https://web.archive.org/web/19990203222345/http://portal .research.bell-labs.com/~dmk/cookie-2.4.txt.

56. Ted Hardie, "Re: Unverifiable Transactions / Cookie Draft," www-talk electronic mailing list, March 18, 1997, https://lists.w3.org/Archives/Public/ietf-http-wg-old/1997JanApr /0472.html.

57. EPIC was founded by Marc Rotenberg in 1994 after establishing and directing the Computer Professionals for Social Responsibility in Washington, DC.

58. Dwight Merriman, "Unverifiable Transactions / Cookie Draft," www-talk electronic mailing list, March 13, 1997, https://lists.w3.org/Archives/Public/ietf-http-wg-old/1997JanApr /0416.html.

59. EPIC, "Net Users Urge Standards Group to Protect Privacy," EPIC press release, April 7, 1997, https://epic.org/privacy/internet/cookies/ietf_letter.html.

60. Ibid.

61. Rick Bruner, "Interactive: 'Cookie' Proposal Could Hinder Online Advertising; Privacy Backers Push for More Data Controls," *Advertising Age*, March 31, 1997, http://adage .com/article/news/interactive-cookie-proposal-hinder-online-advertising-privacy-backers -push-data-controls/68730/.

62. Ibid.

63. Kristol, "HTTP Cookies."

64. Keith Moore and Ned Freed, "Use of HTTP State Management (RFC 2964)," Internet Engineering Task Force, October 2000.

65. Montulli, "Reasoning Behind Web Cookies."

66. Bruner, "Interactive: 'Cookie' Proposal."

67. Lynette Millett, Batya Friedman, and Edward Felten, "Cookies and Web Browser Design: Toward Realizing Informed Consent Online," *Proceedings of the SIGCHI Conference on Human Factors in Computing Systems* (2001): 46–52.

68. Montulli, "Reasoning Behind Web Cookies."

69. Ibid.

70. Margaret O'Mara, *The Code: Silicon Valley and the Remaking of America* (New York: Penguin Press, 2019).

71. Meghan Grosse, "Laying the Foundations for a Commercial Internet: International Internet Governance in the 1990s" (2019, under review, on file with author).

72. Starr, *Creation of the Media*, 5.

73. The same year that the U.S. Post Office became a government corporation called the U.S. Postal Service, after 180 years of congressional ratemaking, "arguably the most fundamental restructuring of a major federal agency in American history." Richard B. Kielbowicz, "Origins of the Junk-Mail Controversy: A Media Battle over Advertising and Postal Policy," *Journal of Policy History* 5, no. 2 (1993): 248–72.

74. U.S. Congress, Senate, *Data Protection, Computers, and Changing Information Practices: Hearing Before the Government Information, Justice, and Agriculture Subcommittee*, 101st Cong., 2nd sess., May 16, 1990 (Washington, DC: Government Printing Office, 1990), 44.

75. U.S. Congress, House, *Mailing Lists: Hearing Before the Committee on Post Office and Civil Service*, 91st Cong., 2nd sess., July 22, 1970 (Washington, DC: Government Printing Office, 1970), 4.

76. Ibid., 57.

77. "Statement of the Direct Mail Advertising Association, Inc.," April 28, 1971, in *U.S. Congress, House, Treasury, Post Office, and General Government Appropriations for 1972: Hearings Before a Subcommittee of the Committee on Appropriations*, 92nd Cong., 1st sess., part 2, *Postal Service* (Washington, DC: GPO, 1971), 772.

78. U.S. Department of Health, Education, and Welfare, *Records, Computers and the Rights of Citizens*, Report of the Secretary's Advisory Committee on Automated Personal Data Systems, July 1973, 41; the five principles included in the report are referred to as fair information practices (FIPs) and read:

- There must be no personal data record keeping systems whose very existence is secret.
- There must be a way for an individual to find out what information about him is in a record and how it is used.
- There must be a way for an individual to prevent information about him that was obtained for one purpose from being used or made available for other purposes without his consent.
- There must be a way for an individual to correct or amend a record of identifiable information about him.
- Any organization creating, maintaining, using, or disseminating records of identifiable personal data must assure the reliability of the data for their intended use and must take precautions to prevent misuse of the data.

79. Ibid., 294–96.

80. Ibid., 295 (Daniel H. Lufkin, "Appendix H: Mailing Lists").

81. Ibid.

82. Privacy Protection Study Commission, *Public Hearing Regarding the Study of Mailing Lists*, Washington, D.C., November 12, 1975, 2.

83. Privacy Protection Study Commission, *Personal Privacy in an Information Society* (Washington, DC: U.S. Government Printing Office, 1977), 125–54.

84. Ibid., 143–45.

85. Ibid., 151–53.

86. National Telecommunications and Information Administration (NTIA), "Elements of Effective Self-Regulation for Protection of Privacy" (discussion draft), January 27, 1998.

87. Federal Trade Commission, *Privacy Online: A Report to Congress*, June 1998, 7, https:// www.ftc.gov/sites/default/files/documents/reports/privacy-online-report-congress/priv-23a .pdf.

88. Ibid., 9.

89. U.S. Department of Energy, Computer Incident Advisory Capability (CIAC), "Internet Cookies," information bulletin I-034, March 12, 1998.

90. Andrea Petersen, "DoubleClick and Abacus Direct Are Set to Merge in $1 Billion Stock Deal," *Wall Street Journal*, June 14, 1999, B10.

91. Federal Trade Commission, "Re: DoubleClick, Inc." (letter explaining that the investigation concluded after finding no personally identifiable information other than for those purposes stated in the privacy policy was disclosed), January 22, 2001, https://www.ftc.gov /sites/default/files/documents/closing_letters/doubleclick-inc./doubleclick.pdf.

92. Founding members were 24/7 Media, AdForce, AdKnowledge, Avenue A, Burst! Media, DouleClick, Engage, and MatchLogic.

93. Marc Rotenberg (founder of EPIC), in discussion with the author, August, 29, 2019; Jules Polonetsky (DoubleClick first chief privacy officer), in discussion with the author, May 14, 2019.

94. Network Advertising Initiative (NAI), "History," n.d., https://www.networkadvertising .org/about-nai/history/.

95. Federal Trade Commission, "Federal Trade Commission Issues Report on Online Profiling," July 27, 2000, https://www.ftc.gov/news-events/press-releases/2000/07/federal -trade-commission-issues-report-online-profiling. The NAI was one of a handful of organizational efforts that popped up to promote self-regulation, and the FTC was not the only government entity supporting self-regulation. In fact, two years earlier the Better Business Bureau announced a more rigorous self-regulatory program that involved verification and dispute resolution services. Bob Gellman and Pam Dixon, "Many Failures: A Brief History of Privacy Self-Regulation in the United States," *World Privacy Forum Report*, October 14, 2011, http://www.worldprivacyforum.org/wp-content/uploads/2011/10/WPFselfregulationhistory .pdf.

96. "DoubleClick Loses Its Cookies," *Wired*, August, 26, 2002, https://www.wired.com /2002/08/doubleclick-loses-its-cookies/.

97. Polonetsky, in discussion with the author, May 14, 2019; Jerry Ceresale (DMA senior vice president of government affairs from 1995 to 2013), in discussion with the author, September 23, 2019.

98. Jason Freeman, "The Most Feared Man in Silicon Valley," *Forbes*, July 6, 2000, https://www.forbes.com/2000/07/06/freeman_0706.html#45d97c6a2fcb; Jeffrey Toobin, "The Man Chasing Enron," *New Yorker*, September 9, 2002, 86.

99. Patrick Dillon and Carl Cannon, *Circle of Greed: The Spectacular Rise and Fall of the Lawyer Who Brought Corporate America to Its Knees* (New York: Broadway Books, 2010).

100. In re Doubleclick Inc. Privacy Litigation, 154 F. Supp.2d 497 (S.D.N.Y., March 28, 2001).

101. In re DoubleClick, Inc. Privacy Litigation, Objection by Settlement Class Members Case No. 00-CIV-0641 (S.D.N.Y., 2001).

102. Matthew Crain, "The Limits of Transparency: Data Brokers and Commodification," *New Media & Society* 20, no. 1 (2018): 88–104.

103. "Shoshanna Zuboff on Surveillance Capitalism," interview by Russ Roberts, *Econ-Talk*, July 29, 2019, https://www.econtalk.org/shoshana-zuboff-on-surveillance-capitalism/.

104. Zuboff, *Age of Surveillance Capitalism*, 11–13.

CONTRIBUTORS

Cameron Black is a doctoral candidate in history at the University of California, Berkeley, who studies labor and cultural history. He is writing a dissertation on the labor history of college student athletes in the United States.

Megan J. Elias is director of the Gastronomy Program at Boston University and an associate professor of the practice. She earned her Ph.D. in history from the City University of New York and is the author of five books about food history in the United States. Her current research is about the modern hospitality industry.

Dan Guadagnolo is an assistant professor, teaching stream, at the Institute of Communication, Culture, Information, and Technology and a research associate in American studies at the University of Toronto. His research on the history of consumer marketing and market segmentation in the United States has appeared in *American Studies* and *Modern American History*.

Sarah E. Igo is the Andrew Jackson Professor of History and director of American Studies at Vanderbilt University. She is the author of *The Known Citizen: A History of Privacy in Modern America* (2018) and *The Averaged American: Surveys, Citizens, and the Making of a Mass Public* (2007).

Meg Leta Jones is an associate professor in the Communication, Culture, and Technology program, affiliate faculty in the Institute for Technology Law and Policy, and core faculty in the Science, Technology, and International Affairs program at Georgetown University. Her first book, *Ctrl+Z: The Right to Be Forgotten* (2016), analyzes the social, legal, and technical aspects of digital oblivion. Her forthcoming book *Cookies* tells the transatlantic history of computer privacy through the lens of a familiar technical object.

Josh Lauer is an associate professor of media studies at the University of New Hampshire. He is the author of *Creditworthy: A History of Consumer Surveillance and Financial Identity in America* (2017). His articles on the history of surveillance, communication technology, and financial culture have appeared in *Big Data & Society*, *New Media & Society*, and *Technology and Culture*.

Jennifer Le Zotte is an assistant professor of U.S. history and material culture at the University of North Carolina Wilmington. She researches and teaches about capitalism and dress, especially as they intersect with race and gender in the twentieth century. Her first book, *From Goodwill to Grunge: A History of Secondhand Styles and Alternative Economies* (2017), traces the cultural and economic roles of pre-owned clothing as secondhand style went from a signifier of poverty to a declaration of rebellion.

Kenneth Lipartito is a professor of history at Florida International University and past president of the Business History Conference. His most recent book, *Capitalism's Hidden Worlds* (coedited with Lisa Jacobson), appeared in 2020. His 2012 book *Corporate Responsibility: The American Experience* received the 2014 Best Book Award from the Social Issues in Management Division, Academy of Management. He is currently writing a history of surveillance and capitalism.

Jeremy Milloy is a historian of work, substance use, recovery, violence, and capitalism. He is currently writing a history of addiction and recovery in the American workplace over the last fifty years, under contract with the University of Michigan Press.

Jamie L. Pietruska is an associate professor of history at Rutgers University, New Brunswick. She is the author of *Looking Forward: Prediction and Uncertainty in Modern America* (2017), and her articles on the history of forecasting have appeared in the *Journal of American History*, *Journal of the Gilded Age and Progressive Era*, and *Environment and History*. Her current research focuses on paperwork, bureaucracy, and investigation in the late nineteenth- and early twentieth-century United States.

Richard K. Popp is an associate professor of history at the University of Wisconsin–Milwaukee. He is the author of *The Holiday Makers: Magazines,*

Advertising, and Mass Tourism in Postwar America (2012), and his articles have appeared in the *Journal of American History, Technology and Culture,* and *Enterprise & Society.* He is currently writing a book about Time-Life and the transformation of American media culture in the 1960s and 1970s.

Daniel Robert received his Ph.D. in history from the University of California, Berkeley, in 2016. He then lectured at Berkeley in American history, business history, and history of science and technology. His contribution to this collection was drawn from his book, *Courteous Capitalism: Public Relations and the Monopoly Problem, 1900–1930,* which is forthcoming from the Johns Hopkins University Press.

Caitlin Rosenthal is an associate professor of history at the University of California, Berkeley, where her research and teaching focus on the evolution of data practices, information technologies, and labor management. Her first book, *Accounting for Slavery: Masters and Management* (2018), explores the business history of plantation slavery in the U.S. South, Jamaica, and Barbados.

INDEX

Adair, James M., 34–35

Allen, Robert, 131

American hotels' guest surveillance in the interwar period: and the American Hotel Association Protective Committee, 105; 111–113; and bigger hotels, 98–99, 100; and compared to earlier inns/innkeepers, 98–99, 108–109, 113; and customer service, 98–99, 100; and development of credit checking and "credit cards," 105–106, 112–113; and gendered roles of desk clerks, 104–107, 234n21; and monitoring to prevent [bill] "skipping," [check] "bouncing," and using rooms for illicit and "immoral purposes," 97, 100–102, 104–105, 107–109, 111–113; and imperson-ation of salesmen, 109–110; and profes-sionalization of "hotel men" 99–101; as purveyor of modern convenience, 99–100, 116–117; and racial discrimination, 102–104; and reports on suspicious guests from industry journal *Hotel World*, 97–98, 110; and traveling salesmen/sample rooms, 98–99; and wedlock and sexuality, 104–105

Ball, Kirstie, 142

Beck, Ulrich, 150

Beckford, William, and *Descriptive Account of the Island of Jamaica*, 33

Bell Telephone: and employee self-monitoring, 90; and maximization of employee surveillance through design of telephone operating rooms, 93–95; and visits to employee homes, 95–96. *See also* surveillance in public service/utilities monopolies

Bentham, Jeremy, 8, 92

Berger, Molly, 98

Bertillon, Alphonse, and the biometric rogue's gallery, 9, 67

Bohn, Henry, J. (*Hotel World* editor), 113–114, 115. *See* American hotels' guest surveillance in the interwar period

Boltanski, Luc, and Eve Chiapello, *The New Spirit of Capitalism*, 150

Boomer, Lucius (hotelier), 100, 107–108. *See* American hotels' guest surveillance in the interwar period

Bouk, Dan, 10

Brenton, Myron, and *The Privacy Invaders*, 6

Brinkley Smithers, R., 144

British West Indies plantation system: and control of information systems in, 29, 44–45; and countersurveillance in the *Watchman*, 28–29, 38–44, 45; and enslaved watchmen, 22–23, 27–29; and Jamaican Maroons, 35, 40; and orga-nizational structure of, 27–29; and Parnassus Plantation (Jamaica 1779), 29–30; and suspected insurrection (1807), 36–38. *See also* enslaved watchmen; The *Watchman*

Brown, Elizabeth A., 141, 158

Brown, Jesse W., Jr., Reverend, 180–181. *See* RJR Nabisco's target marketing strategies of Uptown Cigarettes

Browne, Randy, 37

Browne, Simone, and "dark sousveillance," 28, 42

business's war on drugs: and difference between drug testing and earlier employee surveillance, 141; and Employee Assistance Programs (EAP), 142, 144–145, 158, 248n72; and government bureaucrats

surveillance in public service (continued)
capitalism," 85–87, 89–90; and use of the
Bible, 90; and use as a strategy against
antimonopoly sentiment, 84, 89, 96
Sutton, Charyn (an organizer and
spokesperson for the Uptown Coalition),
172. *See* RJR Nabisco's target marketing
strategies of Uptown Cigarettes

Taylor, Frederick W., and *The Principles of
Scientific Management*, 6; and the
Taylorization of labor, 13
Thompson, E.P., 6
Tunnell, Kenneth D., and *Pissing on
Demand: Workplace Drug Testing and the
Rise of the Detox Industry*, 147, 153,
155–156
Turow, Joseph, 184

Wall, Kelvin (African American market
researcher), 168–169. *See* RJR Nabisco's
target marketing strategies of Uptown
Cigarettes
Walton, John, 67–68
The *Watchman* (abolitionist Jamaican
newspaper, 1829): and coverage of the

Christmas Rebellion/Baptist War
(1831–32), 39–42; as a form of counter-
survelliance, 28–29, 38–44, 45. *See also*
British West Indies plantation system;
enslaved watchmen
Ware, Willis, 198. *See* cookies and digital
surveillance capitalism
Weber, Max, 3
White, Richard, 52
Whyte, William H., 6
Williamson, Adam, 36–38
Williamson, John, Dr., and *Medical and
Miscellaneous Observations Relative to
the West Indies*, 36–37
Winebrenner, John T. (R. J. Reynold's senior
vice president for marketing), 167. *See* RJR
Nabisco's target marketing strategies of
Uptown Cigarettes
Wu, Tim, and *The Attention Merchants*, 184

Yates, JoAnne, 65

Zuboff, Shoshana, and *The Age of Surveillance Capitalism*, 1–2, 14–15, 19, 183–184,
196, 202; and *The Age of the Smart
Machine*, 142–143

ACKNOWLEDGMENTS

We would like to thank Roger Horowitz and the Hagley Museum & Library, which hosted the conference where many of the papers in this volume were first presented. Roger and our editor at the University of Pennsylvania Press, Robert Lockhart, also flawlessly shepherded this volume through review, editing, and production. For that we are most grateful. Kenneth Lipartito also acknowledges the support of CIFAR's Program in Innovation, Equity, & the Future of Prosperity, CIFAR, Toronto, Canada.

Lightning Source UK Ltd.
Milton Keynes UK
UKHW011252080921
390216UK00001B/24